The Real Cyber War

THE HISTORY OF COMMUNICATION

Robert W. McChesney
and John C. Nerone, editors

A list of books in the series appears at the end of this book.

The Real Cyber War

The Political Economy of Internet Freedom

SHAWN M. POWERS
AND MICHAEL JABLONSKI

UNIVERSITY OF ILLINOIS PRESS

Urbana, Chicago, and Springfield

Library of Congress Cataloging-in-Publication Data
Powers, Shawn M., 1981–
The real cyber war : the political economy of Internet freedom /
Shawn M. Powers and Michael Jablonski.
pages   cm. — (History of communication)
Includes bibliographical references and index.
ISBN 978-0-252-03912-6 (hardback) — ISBN 978-0-252-08070-8
(paperback) — ISBN 978-0-252-09710-2 (e-book)
1. Internet—Political aspects. 2. Internet and international
relations. 3. Internet governance. 4. Internet—Government
policy—United States. I. Jablonski, Michael. II. Title.
HM851.P6878   2015
303.48'33—dc23   2014036202

Contents

Preface

The genesis of *The Real Cyber War* was a series of discussions we had trying to make sense of developments in global communications since the end of the Cold War. The evolution of a global communication order resulted in a system characterized not only by shifting relationships between states but by the emergence of other actors wielding sufficient power to change the conversation. More than anything, we came to believe, the evolving system would be dynamic rather than static. Using Dan Schiller's description of information as both a commodity and a resource as an initial hypothesis,[1] we began to investigate the political economy of the emerging global power struggle for control of information as a valuable resource.

This investigation included: twelve Freedom of Information Act (FOIA) requests resulting in our acquisition of more than three thousand official documents from the Department of Commerce, Department of State, Federal Communications Commission, Federal Trade Commission, and the National Security Agency; archival work conducted at UNESCO in Paris, France, and at the ITU in Geneva, Switzerland; and sixty-two in-person interviews with practitioners, industry experts, and civil-society leaders from Azerbaijan, Brazil, Canada, China, Egypt, France, Germany, Hungary, India, Italy, Israel, the Netherlands, Nigeria, Qatar, Russia, South Africa, Spain, Switzerland, Turkey, Tunisia, the United Arab Emirates, the United Kingdom, the United States, and Ukraine.

Over the course of the research process we consistently found significant political assumptions being embedded within the regulatory schemes derived from ideas like "information freedom," "free flow of information," "sovereignty," and "multistakeholderism." These terms, and others, disguise endeavors to control resources by stripping away their underlying political and economic values. Each embodies a particular myth perpetuated to cloak the strategies employed to effect a disproportionate division of resources. The political economy approach employed in *The Real Cyber War* situates the power struggle over information as a resource in history, in practice, and in geopolitics.

Our main intent in writing the book has been to engage scholars and practitioners in communication, economics, law, political science, public policy, and international relations. We believe that it can be useful, and accessible, to technologists interested in understanding the forces that constrain what they can do within the emerging information regime or regimes. The book offers scholars in science and technology studies context for the study of the interrelationship between information technology and social, political, and cultural values inherent in governance. It also speaks directly to policymakers and internet activists operating in the spheres of internet governance and human rights online. Just as information technologies foster dynamic realignment of power relations in a given society, we hope that *The Real Cyber War* creates porosity in boundaries separating disciplines to further a sustained and academically diverse conversation about the intersections of technology, science, and geopolitics.

Successful collaborations always necessitate a division of labor. Shawn Powers conducted the interviews, performed the archival work, and reviewed the FOIA documents that formed much of the primary research drawn upon herein. He was also primarily responsible for the introduction and chapters 2, 3, 4, 5, 7, and the conclusion. Michael Jablonski led the effort to track the history of American information policy, was primarily responsible for chapter 1, and provided research assistance for the introduction. Chapter 6 was co-produced by both authors.

This book came together with the help of many colleagues and friends. Monroe Price, whose thinking has continuously pushed our work in the area of global media, inspired its focus. Amelia Arsenault played an invaluable role in refining many of the book's core arguments and in improving the clarity of the text. Richard Hill offered insightful suggestions and questions that helped improve the book from start to finish. Research was made possible due to generous support from Georgia State University and in particular from David Cheshier, Carol Winkler, and James A. Weyhenmeyer. Central European University's Institute for Advanced Study and Center for Media, Data, and Society offered crucial space and support to finalize this project, for which we are incredibly grateful. Jason Jarvis, Jillian Martin, Ryan Mixon, and Kyle Wrather each provided helpful research assistance at various points throughout the project. John Krige, Ellen Witte Zegura, and Mike Best provided guidance on understanding various technologies. Emily Kofoed's diligent attention to detail was extraordinarily helpful in finalizing the text and index. Last but not least, Tom Corcoran, Betty Hanson, Sarah Meyers, Vincent Mosco, Ben O'Loughlin, Dan Schiller, Ben Wagner, and Janet Wasko provided valuable feedback about earlier drafts of the manuscript. We are extraordinarily grateful to each of them for their interest in and support of this project.

Abbreviations and Acronyms

ARPA	Advanced Research Projects Agency
ARPANET	Advanced Research Projects Agency Network
ccTLD	Country-code Top-Level Domain
CFR	Council on Foreign Relations
CIA	Central Intelligence Agency
CYBERCOM	U.S. Cyber Command
DARPA	Defense Advanced Research Projects Agency
DHS	Department of Homeland Security
DeVenCI	Defense Venture Catalyst Initiative
DNS	Domain Name System
DOD	Department of Defense
DRCI	Defense Reinvestment and Conversion Initiative
DSB	Direct-Satellite-Broadcast
EU	European Union
ENTO	European Telecommunications Network Operators' Association
FCC	Federal Communications Commission
FDR	Franklin D. Roosevelt
FISA	Foreign Intelligence Surveillance Act
FOIA	Freedom of Information Act
GAC	General Advisory Council
GATT	General Agreement on Tariffs and Trade
GATS	General Agreement on Trade in Services
GCHQ	Government Communications Headquarters

GDP	Gross Domestic Product
GPS	Global Positioning System
GII	Global Information Infrastructure
gTLD	Generic Top-Level Domain
GWP	Gross World Product
HPCCI	High Performance Computing and Communications Initiative
IAB	Internet Architecture Board
IAHC	International Ad Hoc Committee
IANA	Internet Assigned Numbers Authority
IAOC	IETF Administrative Oversight Committee
IBM	International Business Machines
ICANN	Internet Corporation for Assigned Names and Numbers
ICEC	International Conference on Electrical Communications
ICT	Information and Communication Technology
IESG	Internet Engineering Steering Group
IETF	Internet Engineering Task Force
IGF	Internet Governance Forum
IP	Internet Protocol
ISI	Information Sciences Institute
ISOC	Internet Society
IT	Information Technology
ITIF	Information Technology and Innovation Foundation
ITR	International Telecommunications Regulation
ITU	International Telecommunications Union
JWICS	Joint Worldwide Intelligence Communications System
LEO	Low Earth Orbit
MGI	McKinsey Global Institute
MIC	Military-Industrial Complex
MSP	Multistakeholder Process
NAFTA	North American Free Trade Agreement
NICTBB	National Information and Communication Technology Broadband Backbone
NIPRNET	Nonsecure Internet Protocol Router Network
NNSA	National Nuclear Security Administration
NSA	National Security Agency
NSF	National Science Foundation
NSFNET	National Science Foundation Network
NSI	Network Solutions Incorporated

NTIA	National Telecommunications and Information Administration
NWICO	New World Information and Communication Order
OECD	Organization for Economic Co-operation and Development
PCAST	President's Council of Advisors on Science and Technology
PIR	Public Interest Registry
REA	Rural Electrification Administration
SIPRNET	Secret Internet Protocol Router Network
SSA	Social Security Act
TCP/IP	Transmission Control Protocol/Internet Protocol
TLP	Telecommunications Leadership Program
TRP	Technology Reinvestment Project
TVA	Tennessee Valley Authority
UDHR	Universal Declaration of Human Rights
UNESCO	United Nations Education, Scientific, and Cultural Organization
UPU	Universal Postal Union
URL	Universal Resource Locator
USC	University of Southern California
USIA	U.S. Information Agency
USTR	United States Trade Representative
USTTI	U.S. Telecommunications Training Institute
VC	Venture Capitalist
WCIT	World Conference on International Telecommunications
WGIG	Working Group on Internet Governance
WSIS	World Summit on the Information Society
WTO	World Trade Organization

Geopolitics and the Internet

States, terrorists, and those who would act as their proxies must know that the United States will protect our networks. Those who disrupt the free flow of information in our society or any other pose a threat to our economy, our government, and our civil society. Countries or individuals that engage in cyber attacks should face consequences and international condemnation. In an internet-connected world, an attack on one nation's networks can be an attack on all. And by reinforcing that message, we can create norms of behavior among states and encourage respect for the global networked commons.

—Secretary of State Hillary Rodham Clinton, "Remarks on Internet Freedom," The Newseum, Washington, D.C., January 21, 2010

I think it's going to be a bloody fight, and I think that countries that have different views than the United States on Internet Freedom are going to fight like heck to make networks in their countries closed and controllable. . . . [I]t's really going to be a 196-country chessboard.

—Alec Ross, Senior Advisor for Innovation, U.S. State Department, interview with Sarah Lai Stirland, March 2013

Contemporary discussion and academic inquiry surrounding the role of the internet in society are dominated by words such as internet freedom, surveillance, cybersecurity, Edward Snowden, and, most prolifically, cyber war. Since introducing the world to the term in 2001,[1] John Arquilla has become increasingly vocal that "cyberwar is here, and it is here to stay."[2] Arquilla's assertion is correct, but for the wrong reasons. For him and many others, the term refers to the extension of military strategy and conflict into the realm of electronic networks or, more simply, to the use of the internet for various forms of covert, forceful attack. Hackers, cybercriminals, and internet activists are the most visible soldiers in this conflict, but, from our perspective, they are secondary.

Behind the rhetoric of Arquilla's cyber war is an ongoing, state-centered battle for information resources. This *real* cyber war between states is not new; it is as old as the systematic transfer of information across borders. From the invention of the postal service to the laying of international telegraph and telephone wires, to the rise of international broadcasting, to the modern day roll out of internet and mobile infrastructure, states have been preoccupied with how to leverage information systems for political, economic, and social power.

We propose a broader perspective of cyber war, conceptualized as the utilization of digital networks for geopolitical purposes, including covert attacks against another state's electronic systems, but also, and more important, the variety of ways the internet is used to further a state's economic and military agendas. In addition to covert attacks, the internet and the rules that govern it shape political opinions, consumer habits, cultural mores, and societal values. Unlike revolutionary communication technologies before it, such as radio and telephone, the internet has the potential to be truly global, interoperable, and interactive, thus magnifying its significance.

In order to broaden the discourse about cyber war, this book outlines the historical genesis of the "internet freedom" movement, tracing its origins to modern day. Rather than rehashing debates about the democratic value of new and emerging media technologies, we focus on the political, economic, and geopolitical factors driving internet-freedom policies, with particular emphasis on the U.S. policy and the State Department's freedom-to-connect doctrine. The book takes a systematic approach, arguing that efforts to create a singular, universal internet built upon Western legal, political, and social preferences alongside the "freedom to connect" is driven primarily by economic and geopolitical motivations rather than the humanitarian and democratic ideals that typically accompany related policy discourse. This freedom-to-connect movement, led by the U.S. government with the support of many powerful private-sector actors, has rich historical roots and is deeply intertwined with broader efforts to structure global society in ways that favor American and Western cultures, economies, and governments. This investigation and analysis reveal how internet policies and governance have emerged as critical sites for geopolitical contest between major international actors, the results of which will shape twenty-first-century statecraft, diplomacy, and conflict.

The world's information technology infrastructure has, until recently, been a relatively contained area of contestation in international relations. Technologies capable of reaching mass global audiences were few (for example, shortwave radio, undersea cables, satellites, and the like); those available for person-to-person communication (such as the telephone) were limited, and a relatively small number of actors were involved in their development and governance.[3] This, of course, has changed with the advent of the personal computer, the proliferation of mobile and internet technologies, and the rise of the information age. The diversity, diffusion, sophistication, and reach of the technologies enabling global communications are drastically different from those available just twenty years ago. Whereas the second half of the twentieth century witnessed extensive debates about the costs and benefits of protecting a state's media system from floods of foreign cultural exports, today's states—fearful of losing all control over the flow of information within their sovereign borders—are acting quickly to build, secure, and control the infrastructures that enable information to flow from one nation to another.

In the West, these contests are typically framed in the context of freedom expression, protection of intellectual property rights, and national security. Foreign policies enacted in non-Western states to better monitor or control the flow of information are often characterized as efforts at state censorship, antidemocratic, and contrary to fundamental human rights codified in international law. Heavy-handed efforts by China, Iran, and Russia, for example, to create state-level information infrastructures are contrasted to "a freedom to connect," a phrase Secretary of State Clinton used to describe a proposed fundamental, universal human right. This framing is, of course, strategic. Portraying efforts to control the flow of information via crude policy mechanisms as censorship normalizes the status quo, portraying the existing communications infrastructures and policies as preserving the global citizen's freedom to connect.[4]

In reality, all states enact policies to preserve sovereignty, and the emergence of the information age and knowledge-based societies requires greater control of information to preserve government legitimation and power projection.[5] In the 1980s and 1990s, the United States, the birthplace of the internet, benefited from a first-mover advantage, establishing the Global Information Infrastructure, driving the Telecommunications Annex to the GATTs Agreement and, for a time, dominating the ascendance of a global, information and data-driven economy. As a result, the United States, often through its private sector, drove the information technology policy agenda at the global level. The debates surrounding the 2012 World Conference on

International Telecommunications (WCIT) and 2014 NETmundial meeting, both discussed throughout the book, reflect the growing significance and tensions around a foundational question in international communication: to what extent can states act to manage the flow of information within their sovereign territory?

The remainder of this chapter outlines the geopolitical approach to information policy and introduces the debates over internet freedom and information sovereignty, as well as the theoretical antecedents driving both perspectives. We then offer a brief review of the literature, explain how a political economy approach to internet freedom adds an important perspective to this field, and introduce the remainder of the book's chapters.

The Geopolitics of Information

In 1899 Swedish professor of political science Rudolf Kjellen coined the term geopolitics, referring to an approach to international politics that accounted for real-world strategic considerations of statesman while emphasizing the role of territory and resources in shaping competition between governments.[6] Subsequently, a cross-section of political scientists began to embrace the study of geopolitics in reaction to what many of them perceived to be an overly legalistic approach to studying conflict between states. Rather than focusing exclusively on the legal culpability of states involved in international conflict, a geopolitical approach proposes that the laws of international politics are based on the "facts" of the global physical space, including how states are split up and what tangible resources they have access to as a result.

Trained in the natural sciences, ethnographer Fredrick Ratzel argued that every state is necessarily geopolitical, and that its capacity to compete is conditioned by its natural environment.[7] Ratzel conceptualized the state as a super-organism, operating in a world of competition and uncertainty. In order to survive, it needs to acquire sufficient territory and resources to defend itself from other aggressive states, deter potential adversaries, and provide security for its citizenry. Thus, a geopolitical approach suggests that states necessarily seek resources, including land, air, sea, human, and intellectual, deemed essential for their survival. In short, geopolitics refers to the strategic action by states to preserve their own national interests in an anarchical world. On the cusp of the twentieth century, the study of geopolitics drew significant academic attention because it called for greater investigation into the politics of geographic space and the allocation of valuable resources, topics that had previously been poorly understood or theorized outside of government.

While geopolitics has remained a vibrant area of study, relatively few scholars have investigated the ways governments compete to influence the policies, technologies, and norms governing information usage for the purpose of furthering their national interests.[8] Much work has been done on the importance of the internet to our economy, civil society, and security, but few have tried to address the central questions regarding why states enact and frame their varied internet policies. For example, what resources does the United States aim to access when it proclaims the existence of a new, fundamental freedom to connect to the World Wide Web? Or what resources does China aim to protect or harvest when it argues for greater protection of its information sovereignty? What is the significance of these policies outside the operation of the internet itself? Too often, discussion of policies relating to internet governance and norms ends with consideration of their implications for the structure and uses of the internet. There is another layer as well: internet policies reflect strategic pursuit of tangible resources. The internet is not only the object of struggle but, in the information age, represents a critical infrastructure for pursuing larger geopolitical goals.

Today's debates over internet policies typically focus on the importance of freedom of expression online, as well as the risks of government censorship and surveillance. While these discussions are important, they all too often fall into a trap of reenacting well-known arguments regarding the proper role of regulation and control of information in society. Rather than normatively assessing the different internet policies enacted by states, arguing which is more in line with a particular set of values, this book approaches the topic from a different perspective. It examines the geopolitics of internet policies, identifying and analyzing why and how states compete to shape policies, technologies, and norms that structure the role of the internet in society.

Such a geopolitical approach aims to add some perspective and balance to ongoing debates over the future of the internet itself, cybersecurity, sovereignty, and human rights online. Specifically, it aims to facilitate a more pragmatic discussion that eschews the value-laden language of internet freedom, Orwellian surveillance, globalization, and censorship. This approach begins by acknowledging two simple yet often unstated facts: Every state regulates the flow of information within and across its borders to some degree; and every government surveils its citizenry through various mechanisms. The United States, for example, regulates content it deems harmful to society, such as child pornography and online gambling. It also regulates the sharing of copyrighted materials, aiming to ensure that control over the use of such content remains with the copyright holder. Other countries, like China, are more restrictive, focusing instead on political content as a threat to national order. While a legitimate debate regarding the efficacy or necessity of these restrictions can be engaged, it falls outside of the scope of this book.[9] Rather, we raise the comparison to make clear that it is a well-established legal and normative reality that every state regulates the flow of information within its borders to one extent or another. This book's central focus is not the legitimacy of such control mechanisms but rather how the pursuit of different controls, platforms, and norms online connect to broader competition for resources and power in the international system.

By examining the geopolitics of the internet, we aim to highlight the state-centered logic that drives internet policy and enable citizens, scholars, and practitioners alike to better engage and challenge the rationale and discourse guiding policy debates. This critical approach also provides a greater means of understanding and assessing future information policy and suggests a possible path for navigating the highly contentious, ideologically driven debate over defining and implementing internet rights around the world.

Geopolitics often comes veiled in ideological language, at least initially. The State Department's evolving doctrine of internet freedom, most clearly articulated by Secretary Clinton, is the realization of a broader strategy promoting a particular conception of networked communication that depends on American companies (for example, Amazon, AT&T, Facebook, Google, and Level 3), supports Western norms (such as copyright, advertising-based consumerism, and the like), and promotes Western products. There is certainly humanitarian value to these initiatives, as many in the mainstream media and government have suggested. But the underlying economic and political motivations driving these efforts deserve greater critical inquiry.

From Free Trade to Free Flow

On January 21, 2010, Secretary of State Clinton delivered a seminal speech, "Remarks on Internet Freedom," at The Newseum in Washington, D.C. The speech was touted as a major policy announcement, accompanied by viewing parties at U.S. embassies and consulates around the world. Clinton's remarks deployed historically charged, ideological language alongside contemporary anecdotes emphasizing the endless, collective possibilities of ubiquitous internet connectivity. Underlining the significance of the issue, Clinton called for a universal "freedom to connect." Referencing the foundations of the Universal Declaration of Human Rights (UDHR)[10] and Franklin Roosevelt's famous Four Freedoms Congressional address,[11] Clinton argued:

The final freedom, one that was probably inherent in what both President and Mrs. Roosevelt thought about and wrote about all those years ago, is one that flows from the four I've already mentioned: the freedom to connect—the idea that governments should not prevent people from connecting to the internet, to websites, or to each other. The freedom to connect is like the freedom of assembly, only in cyberspace. It allows individuals to get online, come together, and hopefully cooperate.[12]

Alongside the call for an expanded interpretation of the UDHR, Clinton announced the United States' steadfast support for internet freedom: "We stand for a single internet where all of humanity has equal access to knowledge and ideas." This declaration—arguing that internet connectivity be a fundamental, internationally recognized human right on par with freedom of speech, freedom of worship, freedom from want, and freedom from fear—represented the official launch of the State Department's internet-freedom doctrine.

The speech was not merely a diplomatic exercise. Clinton committed the State Department to a shift in policy that included "devoting the diplomatic, economic, and technological resources necessary to advance these freedoms." She provided several cues as to how this shift in resources would manifest in policy change, including support for and training of cyber dissidents in "internet censoring countries" and investment in technologies capable of circumventing government censorship and surveillance.

Clinton also highlighted the State Department's growing efforts to train and enable grassroots groups abroad to use connective technologies for social justice, nonviolence, and government accountability. These efforts—dubbed the Civil Society 2.0 Initiative[13]—include support for groups combatting drug and gang violence in Mexico, mobile banking in Afghanistan and Democratic Republic of the Congo, and nonviolence in Pakistan.

In a question-and-answer session with press the following day, State Department Senior Advisor for Innovation Alec Ross called attention to the large number of countries engaging in extreme censorship, affecting more than 31 percent of the world's citizenry. As a result, Ross declared, "we're elevating internet freedom as a matter of our foreign policy, we're going to be taking some immediate steps . . . to make sure that we're very aggressive in ensuring that there's a free and open internet."[14] Internet freedom quickly became a core element of the emerging twenty-first-century diplomacy initiative spearheaded by the Department of State.

The articulation of the internet-freedom doctrine was steeped in enlightenment and legal discourse that connected the proposed new freedom to a long history of individual rights. "The internet has become the public space of the twenty-first century—the world's town square, classroom, marketplace, coffeehouse, and nightclub," Secretary Clinton asserted in 2011. "We all shape and are shaped by what happens there."[15] This implicit reference to a Habermasian idealized public sphere, whereby rational arguments are on display for all to evaluate and engage, is not only symbolic of what the United States wants to see internet discourses look like, but it is also symbolic of the norms the State Department deems appropriate for how freedom of expression online should be regulated. Following American legal tradition, while speech is generally protected in town squares and classrooms, anonymous speech and privacy are not.[16]

In addition to this political narrative, the remarks also focused on the economic logic of allowing for greater transnational flows of information. Drawing from classic neoliberal economic theory, Clinton said, "The internet can serve as a great equalizer." "By providing people with access to knowledge and potential markets," she added, "networks can create opportunities where none exist." Clinton characterized government censorship as being antiquated, akin to trade barriers: "From an economic standpoint, there is no distinction between censoring political speech and commercial speech. If businesses in your nations are denied access to either type of information, it will inevitably impact on growth." Noting the importance of innovation in the modern global economy, Clinton went further: "Barring criticism of officials makes governments more susceptible to corruption, which create[s] economic distortions with long-term effects. Freedom of thought and the level playing field made possible by the rule of law are part of what fuels innovation economies."[17]

Combined, these political and economic narratives reflect what sociologist Vincent Mosco describes as the "neodevelopmentalist" perspective of international communication,[18] which grew out of modernization theory, an area of research that was highly influential in policy circles during the second half of the twentieth century. Pioneered by Daniel Lerner,[19] William Schramm,[20] Everett Rogers,[21] and Ithiel de Sola Pool,[22] modernization theory posits that the dissemination of media content and adoption of media systems and technologies are a crucial means to establishing robust, fast-growing, free-market economies in underdeveloped societies.

The neo-developmentalist perspective suggests that the dissemination and adoption of advanced communication technologies and skills, preferably through the private sector, is central to the integration of the global South into the modern, information-driven economy. It pairs this economic argument with the broader political narrative of the importance of freedom of expression and the free flow of information in a modern, democratic society. This combination of economic and political logic is compelling to many, as it reflects a coherent belief in individual freedom of choice and enterprise. It is also the underlying theory that has guided much of American information policy since World War II. Yet it is also implicitly geopolitical. According to communications scholars Kaarle Nordenstreng and Herbert Schiller, "Since World War II, the rhetoric of freedom has been the preferred usage of American corporate monopolies, press and other, to describe the mechanisms of the system that favors their operation."[23] According to this perspective, Clinton's articulation of the benefits of free and open communication on international peace, espousing the democratizing power of the internet and the economic benefits of being online—"A connection to global information networks is like an on-ramp to modernity"—obfuscates geopolitical motivations driving trends toward global connectivity.

Modernization theory grew out of a specific historical moment—the Cold War—and reflects Western anxiety about the possible spread of economic systems grounded in communist, nationalist, or socialist ideologies. According to Mosco, the U.S. government funded modernization research to provide intellectual and academic justification for the opening of markets around the world. Commissioned by the Department of Defense (DOD) and U.S. Information Agency (USIA), the data gathered to evaluate the significance of media in foreign contexts and to identify the impediments to development represented some of the most sophisticated research in the field at the time, inspiring numerous university communication programs and research centers. As an increasing number of researchers came from the developing world to the United States for training, the modernization program had a trickle-down effect, shaping research trajectories and curricula around the world for decades.[24]

Critiques of the modernization paradigm have been widespread. Researchers from the developing world eagerly pointed out how development programs propped up Western corporations and local political elite while rarely lifting the masses from poverty. Others pointed to the self-serving nature of modernization theory, normalizing a particular form of economic and social policy into international norms and laws. Despite this, the eventual collapse of the Soviet Union strengthened the modernization paradigm. Advocates argued that the end of the Cold War represented an unquestionable vindication of capitalism as the superior economic system, shunning countries unwilling to embrace the full force of Western economic institutions as turning away from the promise of "civilization."

Increased economic interdependence between nation-states intensified as a result of the success of the modernization paradigm. The World Trade Organization (WTO), as well as bilateral and regional agreements, substantially reduced trade barriers around the world, and today international trade drives the global economy. From 1980 to 1990, for example, trade constituted 40 percent of average GDP around the world through the entire decade. Starting in 1990, international trade grew; by 2012 it constituted 61 percent of average GDP.[25]

While countries around the world have embraced global economic institutions that facilitate a stable and productive international trading system, debate continues regarding what exactly falls within the boundaries of these institutions and what remains outside their purview. As more and more services can be provided online, trade itself becomes interlinked with the global internet. Concurrently, the data transfer that enables global electronic transactions and exchange may also facilitate the transmission of political or cultural content, information resources falling outside the realm of existing trade rules.

It is important to note that arguments in favor of treating information services as an aspect of international trade are a relatively recent phenomenon. According to Jonathan Aronson and Peter F. Cowhey, in 1988 "international communications were . . . still not considered to be trade."[26] Instead, telecommunications were considered jointly provided services, whereby a provider in country A connected with another provider in country B to connect customers from different countries. Treating information as a simple, tradable good or service becomes politically contentious as it decreases the legitimate right of governments to try and control the flow of information within their sovereign territory unless such controls are sanctioned by international trade law. For example, according to existing international trade law, while copyright concerns allow for the regulation of information, fears of a political revolution are not considered legitimate justifications for state intervention in the marketplace. By framing information as just another tradable good or service, the internet-freedom agenda would bring international data flows properly under the rubric of international trade law, a system of regulation that discourages protecting local industry or culture and favors well-established actors able to operate efficiently in a global marketplace. Thus, how the debate over internet freedom unfolds will have profound consequences for how governments react to information flows and what are considered to be legitimate state controls in the eyes of international law and domestic citizenries.

A central weakness of the modernization paradigm, as well as its neo-developmentalist progeny, is its inability to account for or explain competition for power among state actors. Modernization theorists are largely silent on the question of sovereignty in many cases; they assume that state concerns with information sovereignty are either minor or nonexistent. As a result, an emerging paradigm, with roots in theories of cultural and media imperialism, places the question of sovereignty front and center in debates over international information flows. The following section outlines the origins of this perspective, drawing from China's reaction to Secretary Clinton's internet-freedom agenda as a means of exploring what an information sovereignty perspective entails.

Information Sovereignty

Kaarle Nordenstreng and Herbert Schiller, in their collection *National Sovereignty and International Communication: A Reader*—one of the first academic volumes explicitly addressing the topic of international communication—predicted: "The concept of national sovereignty will increasingly emerge as a point of reflection for the most fundamental issues of international communication."[27] Discussing the research that laid the bedrock for the modernization paradigm, Nordenstreng and Schiller note, "The notion of national sovereignty is hardly visible in the conceptual-theoretical overview, or paradigm, of these studies."[28]

The modernization paradigm's failure to account for questions of nation-state sovereignty also meant that it couldn't adequately explain competition for power among state actors, a central element of the Cold War era. As a result, the question of sovereignty became integral to debates in the 1970s regarding the rights of governments to prevent the intrusion of information flows from foreign actors. If states have a right to control the types of people allowed into their territory (immigration), and how its money is exchanged with foreign banks, why don't they have a right to control information flows from foreign actors?

Building information infrastructure in underdeveloped countries created an opportunity for these countries to communicate with each other. An unintended consequence turned out to be that these countries had something powerful to say about inequitable distribution of global resources. More than just complaining about unfairness, the telecommunications systems empowered developing countries to share stories and organize resistance movements. The New World Information and Communication Order (NWICO) grew out of discussions within the United Nations Education, Scientific, and Cultural Organization (UNESCO) meetings of nonaligned countries in Algiers (1973), Tunis (1976), and New Delhi (1976). With the emergence of Direct-Satellite-Broadcast (DSB) technology, governments around the world expressed concern about the American's interest in using satellites to increase dissemination of its cultural products in foreign countries. Fears of neocolonialism via international media flows became widespread, fueling the NWICO movement.

In direct conflict with the modernization paradigm, NWICO advocates argued that Western attempts to open and modernize the developing world were in fact reestablishing neocolonial hierarchies by economic means. Researchers, primarily from developing countries, established a body of work called "dependency theory," hypothesizing: "Transnational businesses based in core countries, with the support of their respective states, exercise control over countries outside the core by setting the terms for market transactions over resources, production, and labor. By controlling the terms of exchange and the structure of markets, transnational capital establishes the conditions of economic activity in the hinterland, including the extent of development."[29]

Dependency theorists, along with the NWICO movement, called for a greater balance in the flows of global media, including the subsidization of media production and training in the developing world and for greater domestic protections from unwanted international broadcasts. The movement succeeded to a certain extent. The majority of the world's governments supported its principles in discussions at the United Nations and in the major UNESCO report, written by the MacBride Commission, largely echoing NWICO's principles. The MacBride Commission's report (1980) isolated structural problems in the global telecommunications system that disadvantaged smaller countries. Among the problems, the MacBride Commission identified concentration of media and unequal access to communications resources as critical challenges.

Despite its global appeal, NWICO failed to achieve much in the way of substantial policy change. In fact, UNESCO's MacBride report contributed to a decline in U.S.-UNESCO relations that eventually resulted in the United States' withdrawing from the organization altogether. International debates about the fairness of regulation of global information flows resurfaced by way of the World Summit on the Information Society (WSIS) meetings in Geneva (2003) and Tunis (2005), focusing on critiques of a digital divide continuing to plague access to information resources. The International Telecommunication Union (ITU), a UN organization, sponsored the WSIS meetings.[30]

While the arguments for and against particular theories of international information flows have not changed significantly since the initial assertions of media imperialism and dependency, the stakes of the debate have altered. Whereas the NWICO movement argued in favor of a more equitable balance of information flows, today's information sovereigns strike a different tone, emphasizing the universally utilized political right of governments to manage their borders. This rhetorical shift, emphasizing the common rights that provide the foundation for the modern international system, is gaining traction.

The significance of the shift is in part related to how one goes about substantiating each theory differently. Dependency calls for longitudinal economic analysis to show how emerging economies transferred substantial resources to Western economies to acquire access to technologies and expertise, and that the unequal flow of resources occurred both over the long term and across geographical space. Information sovereignty advocates, on the other hand, first and foremost point to the simple fact that every government in the world exerts control over information flows within its borders, based on the mutually agreed-upon rules of international law. They would also argue that the ability for states to intervene in the informational marketplace is much more robust in Western societies than freedom of expression ideology indicates. While they also use economic arguments to show why it is important for states to be able to protect their information sovereignty, the emphasis is primarily political.

Information sovereignty's emphasis on the political rights of governments to control information flows within their borders does not differentiate between developed and developing worlds, thus, leveraging two simple facts. First, the majority of the world's governments remain eager to protect and strengthen their sovereignty. Second, the majority of citizens support the nation-state system, holding on to nationalist views. It also shifts the conversation from one of blame to one of rights and responsibilities. "*I have the right and responsibility to control information flows, same as every government in the world*" is a very different argument from "*Your information industries are dominant and are overwhelming our culture!*"

Today, while references to NWICO are few, its intellectual successor— information sovereignty—is gaining traction, especially outside the West. Its most vocal advocate is China, which was quick to criticize Secretary Clinton's internet-freedom doctrine. Through a series of remarks and policy papers, China aggressively asserted the right of a legitimate government, without interference from others, to regulate the flow of information within its territory. A brief review of Chinese media coverage offers a clear range of critiques of Clinton's proposal and a de facto articulation of the information sovereignty paradigm.

On January 25, 2010, just days after Clinton delivered her remarks at The Newseum, the official Communist Party newspaper, *People's Daily*, declared, "In the Internet era, the sovereignty of nations has expanded to the 'information frontier.'"[31] Chinese media also espoused the government's rationale for its internet management techniques—most notably, each government's responsibility to regulate the flow of information within its borders. For example, the *Global Times* suggested, "The so-called 'network freedom' is just a 'selective freedom,' which is based on where the U.S.'s national interest lies. Managing the information flow is one of a country's sovereign rights. It is a country's own decision on how to control and when to open up the internet."[32] China's official Xinhua News Agency portrayed the prospect of unfettered foreign information interventions as a threat to the foundation of China's sovereignty and, therefore, security: "The emergence of information technology has posed a great challenge to the traditional concept of national sovereignty, as well as one's ability to safeguard sovereignty."[33]

Calling attention to American legal control over the internet's root server, Chinese media framed the internet-freedom movement as geopolitically driven. According to the *People's Daily*, "The United States, the birthplace of the Internet, who has the most advanced Internet application, has found the most favorable battlefield for itself. If the United States really wants to make 'an Internet without restrictions' part of its national brand, why does it still control terminal servers firmly in its own hands[?] . . . It is the United States' national interests that [are] behind all these frequently changing tactics."[34] The *Global Times* also challenged the universality of the application of internet freedom, noting, "The U.S. will definitely not allow its enemies, like Bin Laden, to enjoy Internet freedom."[35]

Further challenging the idea that the internet-freedom agenda is driven by human-rights concerns, Chinese media characterized Clinton's new policy as a type of "network warfare," a form of intervention into China's internal affairs. According to the *People's Daily*, "The United States is the world's first country who introduced the concept of network warfare, established and developed a new military branch, and even set up a network of hacker forces. U.S. intelligence agencies also comprehensively monitor, track, delete and even alter information on the Internet that is not conducive to U.S. national interests."[36]

Central to China's reactions to Clinton's remarks were accusations of how the internet is a tool of Western imperialism and influence. One article written in the *Global Times* put the internet-freedom agenda in historical and comparative context, arguing: "Twenty years ago, the U.S. was expanding its high-profile imperialism in the way of foreign exports, represented by McDonalds and Coca Cola. Today, it has changed to exporting thoughts, concepts and 'online soft power with noble virtues.' The U.S. has developed a new means of sanction other than military, economic and trade sanctions: information sanction."[37]

The intellectual paper *Guangming Daily* similarly emphasized the geostrategic aspects of the new policy: "The Internet has become a tool for the United States to attack and accuse other countries, for example, the United States used Twitter to support Iranian oppositionists before and after the Iranian election. . . . The United States' practice of interfering in other countries' internal affairs by using the Internet has already been universally condemned by the international community."[38] That same day, the *Global Times* argued that what Secretary Clinton "is really concerned about is promoting political changes and the globalization of 'American democracy' by using the Internet."[39] Another *Global Times* editorial went further, accusing the United States of "trying to use its advantages in manufacturing and disseminating information to promote its Internet hegemony, hoping that the whole world could be subservient in an information world centered around American ideology."[40]

Chinese newspapers also challenged the economic rationale of Clinton's internet-freedom initiative. In another article in the *Global Times*, readers were cautioned about following the ways of the

> so-called mainstream civilization, represented by the West. But looking at the former Soviet Union's historical lesson, China should be cautious when participating in a civilization that was formed without China's influence. China's rise is happening in a rapid way, without the West's recognition. Historically, if China followed the lead of Western discourse, China would not be rising but would have repeated the collapse of the former Soviet Union and Yugoslavia. Along with China's rise, the rearrangement of the international order has begun, in which China's role is crucial. Chinese intellectuals should no longer follow the lead of Western discourse, but adopt independent thinking and explore and construct China's own discourse and strategy in the "post-America era."[41]

By logical extension, coverage portrayed the internet-freedom agenda was an effort to institutionalize America's competitive advantage in the ICT sectors. According to the *Global Times*, "From the chip to the operating system, from root server to domain name management, the United States dominates every part of the industry. The U.S., with its leading position in the information industry, and English as the primary Internet language, has become a truly sovereign nation of information." The article continues: "American Internet capitalists have almost dominated the whole Chinese Internet industry . . . [which] means that the U.S. shares the majority of Chinese Internet companies' profits."[42]

China's fear of losing economic ground to the United States as a result of dependence on its ICT industries reaches far beyond the internet-freedom debate. According to U.S. Ambassador to China John Huntsman, "A number of historical, cultural and technological factors have coalesced to put China in a technologically-aggressive state-of-mind." Citing a 2004 incident in which Microsoft deactivated all unlicensed Windows operating systems operating in China, resulting in a countrywide computer failure, Huntsman notes:

> [The] example of U.S. technology effectively wielding power over China's personal computers helped spur China's aggressive campaign for source codes and its own technology. This, combined with growing Chinese pride, economic clout and influence, and the "weakened" position of the U.S. and its allies after the global economic downturn, [is] emboldening the Chinese to take ever more aggressive positions in advancing its innovative industries at the expense of foreign ones.[43]

While nearly all of the coverage was critical of Clinton's remarks and the related policy shift, there was one area of agreement: the speech's significance. The *Global Times* English edition described it as a "milestone," a clear sign that U.S. and Western political interests were "taking over every dimension" of cyberspace.[44] The official Communist Youth paper, *China Youth Daily*, declared: "The White House started the Internet War."[45]

For China, the most appropriate path toward establishing universal internet freedom is through international organizations, not through unilateral American policy. According to the *Global Times*, "If there is to be Internet freedom, the U.S. should hand their service terminals within the U.S. to a world-recognized international organization, like the UN, and not keep them in its own hands."[46] The choice of the UN is not merely incidental, either. As is discussed in detail in chapter 5, the UN's one-state, one-vote system is preferred by many non-Western governments as a means to protect their sovereignty from an onslaught of powerful nongovernmental and corporate actors.

Beyond the Hyperbolic

The unfolding, ongoing competition by governments to shape the narrative surrounding the appropriate norms governing internet access and usage leaves little middle ground for thinking through a compromise solution. If states do have a right to exercise information sovereignty, as China argues, then what is to stop governments from implementing robust regimes of censorship and surveillance? Similarly, if the internet-freedom movement is a façade for American economic imperialism, then shouldn't governments have a right to limit the intrusion of foreign actors in order to protect and nourish local industries until they are able to compete globally? The answers to these questions require analytic and policy tools that are currently not advanced enough to allow for the types of careful deliberations required for compromise and advancement.

Much scholarship on internet-freedom policy mirrors the debate between the United States and Chinese governments outlined above. One area of work focuses on the possibility of an emerging cyber war between major powers. This genre of research was popularized by a 2001 RAND Corporation study, authored by John Arquilla and David Ronfeldt, describing a mode of international conflict based on weaponizing information technology into a new form of contestation that they call netwars.[47] Their predictions gained traction with revelations about cyberattacks on Estonia (2007) and the offensive use of a computer virus (Stuxnet) to disrupt Iranian nuclear facilities (2006 to 2012). The allegedly emerging "cold war" between the United States and China over internet policy and cyber warfare adds further interest in research on the future of cyber war.

According to this cyber war perspective, sovereignty is merely a cover for states protecting enclaves of hackers responsible for cyberattacks. A 2013 Council on Foreign Relations (CFR) Task Force report argued that assertions of national sovereignty over information entering a country had created opportunities for proliferating attacks and cybercrime by limiting the reach of American law enforcement.[48] According to the report, the threat posed by these systems transcends nation-states and thus calls for a solution that requires each government to limit its claim to sovereignty for the purpose of preserving a shared, common good: a safe and secure global internet.

Closely related is the field of internet governance. Information science scholar Milton Mueller has led the way with his in-depth knowledge of the institutions vying for legitimacy in governing the Web.[49] Lee A. Bygrave and Jon Bing's edited volume, *Internet Governance: Infrastructure and Institutions*, is largely descriptive and helpful for navigating the complicated terrain of organizations, institutions, and actors competing for authority in this emerging and contested space. Cowhey and Aronson argue that emerging media and networking technologies offer tremendous economic potential, but that governments risk slowing our transition to a fully integrated digital economy by introducing externalities into the market, preventing exploitation of economies of scale, introducing unnatural pricing, and politicizing network performance.[50]

Jack Goldsmith and Tim Wu are also concerned by the development of networks tethered to specific nation-states through regulations, arguing the so-called "balkanization" of the internet could produce incompatibilities that result in a fracturing of global communications.[51] Tim Wu's exploration of historical antecedents to the internet demonstrates that, although each new communication medium began with a history of unregulated openness, both government and market forces gradually curtailed competition by offering new services that encouraged consumers to accept oligopolies or cartels. Wu also argues compellingly that the historical tendency toward cartelization in media industries poses a threat to the open internet.[52]

Collectively, this vast body of work argues (among other things) that the existence of a right to access information and the effective operation of a global internet will inevitably require limitations on the exercise of sovereignty.

A third area of research has emerged surrounding the debate over the potential for internet and mobile connective technologies to enhance democratic practices around the world, including work aiming to expose government and corporation policies that may inhibit the democratic promise of the World Wide Web. For example, Rebecca MacKinnon discusses how repressive regimes, in collaboration with Western technology companies, have automated the craft of spying by using techniques such as deep-packet inspection to identify data containing intelligence useful to governments.[53] Closely related is Harvard University's Berkman Center for Internet and Society, which supports a variety of projects like the Internet Monitor[54] and the Global Network Initiative[55] that aim to spotlight and challenge the various ways governments and corporations restrict freedom online. The trilogy of *Access Denied*, *Access Controlled*, and *Access Contested* offers an exhaustive and chilling account of how governments and corporate actors are limiting the liberatory capacity of connective technologies.[56] Richard Fontaine and Will Rogers's report, "Internet Freedom: A Foreign Policy Imperative in the Digital Age," similarly calls for governments to embrace the Web's democratic potential.[57] In their book *The New Digital Age: Reshaping the Future of People, Nations and Business*, Eric Schmidt and Jared Cohen predict what the Web will look like if each government regulates it without coordination, arguing for Google's approach to global connectivity.[58] Ronald Deibert's latest work, *Black Code: Inside the Battle for Cyberspace*, offers a timely and compelling critique of the rise in government-led surveillance, highlighting the scale, significance, and relative success of state efforts to conquer cyberspace.[59] Collectively, this body of work calls for greater vigilance by users to protect their rights online and is harshly critical of the idea of "information sovereignty."

Also in this category, though arguing the issue from the other side, is Evgeny Morozov, who suggests that cyber utopians have been duped into believing in the democratic potential of the internet and mobile ICTs.[60] In his view, authoritarian governments are adept at using technology in ways that undermine and pacify individuals who might support change, and the corporations responsible for operating the network of networks are perhaps an even greater risk to the fabric of society than the authoritarian governments most known for suppressing freedom of speech online.

This admittedly limited overview of internet policy research highlights contributions that result from different perspectives used to interrogate social and political responses to the developing communications system. Each contribution illuminates a facet: policy, politics, international relations, sociology (civil society), economics and globalization. The task remaining requires synthesis of each perspective into a broader understanding of possibilities and limitations of internet freedom. Particularly lacking is a clear understanding of why states pursue the policies they do, or a clear articulation of how sovereignty fits within the espoused models promoting a global freedom to connect online. This failure to account for the importance of state interests in shaping future policy ignores the different geopolitical interests at stake in debates over internet freedoms and governance, reinforcing the gap between theory and practice.

This book addresses this gap by examining the relationship between geopolitics and modern connective technologies through the lens of the debate over internet freedom and information sovereignty. It focuses centrally on understanding the numerous ways in which power and control are exerted in cyberspace. Because so much of the internet is operated in the private sector, corporations have tremendous influence over how the internet operates, the cost of connectivity, and the standards that users must agree to before accessing the World Wide Web. Governments, too, exert considerable influence, both through domestic regulations and through international multistakeholder and multilateral fora. In order to fully understand how internet freedom functions as a geopolitical tool, we examine government efforts to exert control via regulation, norm development, and technological innovation, as well how the private sector aims to benefit from the normalization of internet-freedom ideologies.

Theory and Outline of Chapters

This book does not try and resurrect any of the theoretical traditions outlined above. Rather, it is grounded in the framework of critical political economy and aims to outline the geopolitical stakes involved in ongoing debates over internet governance and global connectivity. In so doing, it places questions of power (as opposed to culture, or rights and norms) at the center of debates about international communication.

To go about this endeavor, the book borrows from Mosco's "general and ambitious" definition of political economy as the "study of control and survival in social life."[61] In this context control refers to the political processes through which a society organizes and governs. Survival refers to the economic processes that determine how actors reproduce the resources required for existence. In the context of international politics, political economy relates to how states and other political actors compete for and control resources deemed necessary for their existence. Historically, this included competition for natural resources, like oil and coal, but also for human resources, including maintaining a citizenry capable of producing the goods, services, and ideas required for the state's continued strength vis-à-vis other states. Increasingly, information is also considered a valuable resource. Patents, surveillance data, state secrets, and highly sophisticated algorithms are all examples of valuable information, the control over which shapes how international actors compete with each other, and which ones will thrive. Along these lines, a 2011 panel at the World Economic Forum declared data as "the new oil of the 21st century," a statement that is dealt with in more depth in chapter 3.[62]

Vincent Mosco proposes that a substantive theory of political economy begin by mapping three "entry processes" of any given phenomenon or controversy.[63] The first, commodification, refers to the process of how use value is transformed into exchange value. The use value of any particular communicative act is determined by how effective it is at achieving a clear, tangible goal, such as expressing one's thoughts on a proposed rule change or notifying another person of a problem. Exchange value refers to how these same acts are converted into something that can be assessed, bought, and sold in a marketplace. Put another way, how is raw information, such as our reactions to a new law or our interpersonal communications, converted into a valuable and exchangeable commodity?

The second process is spatialization, or the "process of overcoming the constraints in social life."[64] In the context of the internet, spatialization refers to how powerful actors use technology, laws, and norms to reinforce and/or eviscerate the geographic (in other words, oceans) and geopolitical boundaries (state borders) that structure the world. The United States, for example, is keen on decreasing the significance of geographic and geopolitical boundaries that split the world up, while China and many developing nations are increasingly vocal in their support for a renewed emphasis on and respect for sovereignty.

Finally, according to Mosco, there is structuration, or an emphasis on the fact that social action is necessarily constrained and facilitated by the structures within which action occurs. Karl Marx referred to this concept by noting, "People make their own history, but they do not make it as they please; they do not make it under self-selected circumstances, but under circumstances existing already, given and transmitted from the past."[65] Structuration aims to emphasize the significance of human agency in bringing about real-world change while accounting for the significant power wielded by the institutions, organizations, networks, and norms that constrain and enable human behavior. Structuration is a useful concept in thinking through how institutions shape the use of ICTs in different contexts. For example, in societies where electronic communication is heavily monitored and archived by authorities, in cooperation with the private sector, ICTs are much less likely to pursue (with any success) democratic endeavors than in a society where communications are legally protected as private and confidential. At the same time, structuration emphasizes the possibility for social action, possibly enabled by new technologies, to challenge the governing institutions to reform.

The following chapters explain how the processes are central to understanding the geopolitics of internet freedoms and governance. Though there is considerable overlap, broadly speaking, chapters 1, 2, and 3 deal with the norms, institutions, and actors whose focus is the commodification of digital information. The structuration of information through international institutions and norms is featured in chapters 4 and 5, and chapters 6 and 7 focus on the spatialization of information through various state apparatuses.

Chapter 1 outlines a history of U.S. information policy, focusing on three case studies of how the American government shaped international norms governing information technologies and flows for its own geopolitical gain. Far from a systematic history of American information policies, these thick descriptions aim to establish a trend of using telecommunications laws and information-technology (IT) related exports to promote U.S. political economic interests around the world. Central to each example is the view of information as something apolitical, culturally neutral, and able to be bought and sold as part of the global exchange of goods and services. By normalizing information as a commodity, the United States sought to expand markets for its products, including content, software, and hardware. By placing information into the realm of free trade and open markets, the United States was more able to export U.S.-centric media freedoms, regulations, technologies, programming, and infrastructure, enhancing its global influence.

While limited, the selection of case studies stretches across most of the twentieth century, demonstrating a consistent pattern of utilizing a narrative of the freedom of information to bypass state boundaries and sovereignty. In contrast to the dominant, modernization paradigm, whereby the history of information policy is described as being driven by mutually benefiting, market-based principles, we offer insight into how debates over international communication have always been deeply geopolitical, highlighting the various ways international institutions and partnerships are leveraged, selectively, to support American foreign-policy goals.

Also historical in focus, chapter 2 outlines the emergence of an information-industrial complex in the United States, tracking the rise of computer and information technology and the modern knowledge economy. We identify a number of policy mechanisms through which government actors—ranging from the executive and legislative branches to the intelligence community—subsidized, partnered, and otherwise cleared the way for rapid innovation and growth in the information sector. Focusing on sector expansion at all costs, policy mechanisms deviated from the traditional regulatory role, rarely monitoring the private sector to ensure compliance with public-interest laws. The growth in America's information-technology sector also created a codependent relationship, whereby government investment was critical to the industry's growth, and the industry's expertise was considered critical for the government's survival. This symbiotic relationship, conceptualized as a silicon triangle connecting government, Silicon Valley, and the broader U.S. economy, is similar in structure and scope to the military-industrial complex that emerged during World War II. This analogue is instructive, not merely to put the information-industrial complex in context but also to foreshadow the likely consequences of continued industry-government codependence: weakened oversight, accountability, and industry vitality and competitiveness.

Chapter 3 focuses on one of the most important industrial actors operating in the areas of connective technologies and internet freedom: Google. Examining Google's aims to dominate the global market for information services and data, we outline how its various endeavors aspire to control each facet of the data market: production, extraction, refinement, infrastructure, and demand. This analysis of Google's market dominance also offers a detailed assessment of the processes by which information becomes commodified in the modern internet economy. Building on the analogue to the historical significance of the oil industry, there is no equivalent company that has ever been capable of dominance in each facet of the oil economy to the extent that Google leads in the data economy. The chapter proposes a model, separating five distinct aspects of the data economy, which has relevance not only in analyzing Google but also in assessing other actors aiming to intervene and compete in the data economy. It may also facilitate thinking about the type of regulatory intervention required to prevent monopolization of the entre sector.

The chapter concludes with a discussion of Google's role in the internet-freedom movement. While the company routinely espouses the economic and political benefits of a free flow of information between people and countries, there is little evidence that this is the reason it pursues greater global connectivity. Numerous examples of Google's compliance with law enforcement agencies in both democratic and authoritarian countries suggest that its desire for freedom of expression is certainly not driving its global business strategy. Instead, a more compelling explanation for Google's interest in internet freedom and connectivity is the simple fact that its survival (in the political economy sense of the word) depends on getting more and more people online to use its complimentary services.

Connecting commodification and structuration, chapter 4 focuses on the economics of internet connectivity and the fight over which international institutions are responsible for the regulation of digital information flows. We suggest that, at a basic level, U.S. internet policy can be boiled down to getting as many people using the network of networks as possible, while protecting the status quo legal, institutional, and economic arrangements governing connectivity and exchanges online. From the global infrastructure facilitating exchanges of data to the creation of unique content and services online, American companies are dominant, extraordinarily profitable, and, in most cases, well ahead of foreign competition. Building on chapters 2 and

3, chapter 4 traces how economic logic continues to drive U.S. policy as well as U.S. negotiating strategy in the international arena. From this perspective the real cyber war is not over offensive capabilities or cybersecurity but rather about legitimizing existing institutions and norms governing internet industries in order to assure their continued market dominance and profitability.

By outlining the economic significance of the issue—how economies of scale favor established, dominant actors, and how the current deregulated system enables a handful of Western corporations to profit handsomely from expanded internet connectivity—we attempt to deviate from the modernization and information-sovereignty paradigms that too often dominate discussions of internet governance. While heavy-handed government controls over the internet should be resisted, so should a system whereby internet connectivity requires the systematic transfer of wealth from the developing world to the developed. By focusing on the uneven empirics of the internet's economic significance, combined with a discussion of positive economic externalities and the network effect, this chapter offers an alternative framing of an ongoing debate over internet governance—and hopefully a more reasonable path forward.

Chapter 5 explores how multistakeholder institutions reflect dominant political and/or economic interests, arguing that the discourse of multistakeholderism is used to legitimize arrangements benefiting powerful, established actors like the United States and its robust ICT private sector. By incentivizing inclusion and consensus, multistakeholder processes risk stifling legitimate dissent from external actors who have no interest in lending legitimacy to the façade of an apolitical negotiation. By linking legitimacy to the inclusion of all stakeholders, pressure is exerted on actors to get involved, leaving very little place to legitimately criticize the outcomes of negotiations. If groups participate and then criticize, they will be labeled as hypocrites who pander to constituent interests after the fact.

Chapter 5 also details how ICANN, ISOC, and the IETF provide legitimacy for a process that has allowed continued U.S. control over many aspects of the internet's root server and continued dominance by American and Western private sectors. The chapter concludes by arguing that the veil of legitimacy created through the existence of multistakeholder processes makes it harder for marginalized groups to speak out credibly, masking the deep and systematic economic and political agenda embedded in the existing power arrangements.

Chapters 6 and 7 focus primarily on the spatialization of information, or how state actors assert authority over the physical nature of transnational data flows in order to maintain domestic stability and expand influence abroad. Continuously challenged, states naturally seek means of legitimating their authority, a process that increasingly requires providing a citizenry with some level of freedom of expression. At the same time, technologies are evolving quickly and in transformative ways, changing the ways communities are formed and authority legitimized. Chapter 6 focuses on how states control the flow of information within their sovereign territories, exploring the relationship between sovereignty, the nation-state, and connective technologies. For many states, allowing too much freedom of expression risks a loss of legitimacy by another sword: political challengers more able to engage the masses and offer alternative visions for the future. It is within this continuum—with absolute freedom of expression on one end and total information control on the other—that we explore four case studies (China, Egypt, Iran, and the United States), whereby governments control access to a singular internet while developing more malleable *intranets* capable of creating a balance between freedom and control.

The results indicate that a state's capacity to adapt is crucial to its survival, but that information control is also in increasingly effective means of reasserting state sovereignty. Despite substantial variations in policy, China and the United States are developing culturally specific, incremental, and advanced strategies for controlling internet access. Both acknowledge citizen demands for some privacy and free speech protections, yet they argue for some necessary level of government control. Both countries also connect to compelling narratives that resonate in each culture. In China, 85 percent of citizens support government control and management of internet content.[66] In the United States too, a majority of Americans support penalties for downloading copyrighted music and movies.[67] While the level of control exerted is drastically different, the strategies are quite similar analytically. The chapter concludes by arguing that, despite any promises that governments would fail at taming the internet, they have achieved an impressive level of success thus far.

Chapter 7 explores the tension between the internet-freedom movement and cybersecurity policy. Central to this tension is the question of anonymity, or, whether or not it is possible to connect behaviors or material online to a particular person. On the one hand, anonymity is central to freedom online, and for online speech in particular. For example, anonymous browsing is critical for political dissidents to be able to express oppositional views and feel protected from government repression. On the other hand, anonymity enables criminal behavior online, ranging from intellectual property theft to whole-scale cyber warfare.

By tracing the specific vision of internet freedom proposed by Secretary Clinton to the revelations of an NSA-lead globally robust surveillance apparatus, we explore how the United States' proposal for a freedom to connect deviates from traditional protections for freedom of expression by not protecting anonymous speech. This deviation is not merely the result of the NSA's surveillance programs but also derives from the specific legal vision proposed by internet-freedom advocates. Chapter 7 reviews the different ways anonymous speech online is eviscerated in the current political, economic, and legal environment and offers a brief legal history regarding the centrality of anonymous speech to freedom-of-expression doctrine.

We conclude by exploring the practical consequences of a global communications infrastructure that lacks any guarantee of confidentiality of messages across borders, outlining the centrality of protecting the secrecy of correspondence to the foundations of modern-day international cooperation and governance. Connecting to arguments forwarded in each of the previous chapters, the concluding chapter aims to challenge the relentless "internet freedom" versus "information sovereignty" approach to navigating questions of rights and security online, offering an alternative, historically grounded, and globally aware framing of this ongoing debate.

1

Information Freedom and U.S. Foreign Policy: A History

We must shape our course of action by the maxims of justice and liberality and good will, think of the progress of mankind rather than of the progress of this or that investment, of the protection of American honor and the advancement of American ideal rather than always of American contracts, and lift our diplomacy to the levels of what the best minds have planned for mankind.

—Woodrow Wilson, "A Message to Democratic Rallies," November 2, 1912

During the Industrial Revolution the new American nation supplemented native inventiveness with imported information allowing development of industrial systems. Technological artifacts acquired by the United States were useless without acquisition of knowledge necessary to assemble or use machines. Britain protected its industrial hegemony by restricting the outflow of information to protect comparative economic advantages from technology that it invented or refined. The United States adopted an identical policy. The realization that the flow of information encouraged innovation forced policymakers to consider the implications of controlling that flow. The result was that a contradictory view of information became fundamental to U.S. thinking. On the one hand, information should be freely available to all; on the other, access to information should be restricted to reward inventors by reserving to them the economic benefits of their inventions.

This chapter looks at four illustrative case studies after discussing the linkage between information and commerce. The first examines the U.S. challenge to British communications hegemony in the nineteenth and twentieth centuries. Woodrow Wilson framed the challenge of promoting world peace in terms of a worldwide free access to information that, not incidentally, promoted American commercial interests. The second example explores the view that U.S.-backed ventures to build up underdeveloped countries constituted a policy of creating new markets for U.S. products. As a global information economy developed, U.S. economic policy increasingly required that the rest of the world be able to import and consume "soft" products such as media content. Development promoted U.S. interests, although the rhetoric surrounding it channeled the modernization paradigm, framing access issues in terms of freedom to communicate and the right to expression.

The third narrative discusses the use of international structures such as the ITU and UNESCO by developing countries to assert grievances arising from a misbalance of power in world communication structures. The assertion of independence and demand for recognition in forums such as WSIS and NWICO was countered by the United States employing trade mechanisms—such as GATT (General Agreement on Tariffs and Trade), and its successor, WTO (World Trade Organization)—to control the flow of information. The application of trade policy to international communication embodies the shift toward treating information as a commodity. Finally, we establish the formation of the Internet Corporation for Assigned Names and Numbers (ICANN) as a U.S. policy that created an appearance of international cooperation in governance of the internet while reserving to the United States ultimate authority. ICANN, established as a counter to proposals to internationalize control of the internet by groups like the multistakeholder Internet Ad Hoc Committee (IAHC),[1] extends the neoliberal theme of framing issues for the betterment of the world, but doing so in a way that privileges the United States.

Far from a systematic history of American information policies, these thick descriptions aim to establish a trend of using telecommunications laws and information- and technology-related exports to promote U.S. political economic interests globally. Central to each example is the view of information as something apolitical, culturally neutral, able to be bought and sold as part of the global exchange of goods and services. By normalizing information as a commodity, the United States sought to expand markets for its products, including content, software and hardware. By placing information into the realm of free trade and open markets, the United States was more able to export of U.S.-centric media freedoms, regulations, technologies, programming, and infrastructure, enhancing U.S. "soft power" around the world.[2]

Control of Commodified Information

The conflict over internet governance represents the latest manifestation of international contestation over information management. Effective control of information creates a market aberration rewarding actors that can effectively manipulate dissemination. At the beginning of the Industrial Revolution, information was increasingly viewed as a potent resource because of its ability to drive technological innovation. For example, Great Britain enjoyed a comparative advantage in the production of textiles as a result of tweaks that built upon prior innovation: John Kay increased the rate of cloth production by developing the flying shuttle in 1733. James Hargreaves's spinning jenny (1764) allowed simultaneous production of multiple threads. Richard Arkwright patented a water-powered system producing stronger yarn at a higher capacity with lower cost in 1769. Samuel Crompton created the spinning mule in 1779 by hybridizing Arkwright's water frame with Hargreaves's spinning jenny. Richard Roberts automated the mule.[3] The cascade of developments revolutionizing cloth production resulted, in large part, from the availability of information regarding prior developments.

The British envisioned a dual policy encouraging the import of information while discouraging export. Resulting technological changes, both open source and controlled, influenced the entire British economy. England transformed itself from a primarily agricultural economy into an industrial one in the eighty years following 1770. James Watt knew of the steam engine developed by Thomas Newcomen, eventually securing patents for improvements in 1768 and 1782. Boldrin and Levine show that the patent system retarded commercial development of steam engines. Watt's steam engines suffered, due to patent restrictions, from an inability to employ efficiency gains developed by Thomas Pickard. Watt could only employ Pickard's more efficient designs after the expiration of the patent in 1794. Watt and his business partner, Matthew Boulton, litigated alleged patent violations to prevent the commercial use of numerous improvements. When the patents expired, the efficiency of generally available engines crept up.[4]

Britain controlled the flow of information by granting monopolies to entrepreneurs importing innovative techniques from other countries, as well as to domestic inventors. It also sought to control the outflow of information by making it illegal to transport technical information about certain innovations out of the country. Having developed a comparative advantage in the manufacture of textiles and iron, Britain sought to preserve its advantage by disrupting information flow.[5]

Naturally, other countries circumvented the restrictions. Alexander Hamilton, as U.S. Secretary of the Treasury, recommended to Congress "that it is the interest of the United States to open every possible avenue to emigration from abroad . . . for the encouragement of manufactures."[6] Hamilton proposed to Congress a comprehensive policy for the promotion of domestic manufacturing by, in part, increasing the flow of information about manufacturing machinery to the United States. "To procure all such machines as are known in any part of Europe, can only require a proper provision and due pains. The knowledge of several of the most important of them is already possessed."[7] The importation of information through immigrants was widespread in America. The most famous case was that of Samuel Slater, who memorized the operation of a textile mill in Britain before coming to America after having declaring to British officials that he was a common agricultural laborer. Slater became one of the most prominent industrialists in the new nation.[8]

The maturation of global trade empires established by European powers established an international communications network, albeit one with extraordinarily low bandwidth. The organization of global trading companies such as the Dutch and the English East India Companies prospered by exploiting technological capabilities to transport rare commodities that were in high demand from across long distances. The relevant technologies were not just ships minimally sufficient to make the journeys but the ability to organize data relevant to a multitude of functions essential to the commerce, such as provisioning ships, knowledge of routes, understanding markets, organizing capital, marketing, and insurance, as well as countless other critical activities. The absence of technology capable of moving information over water at speeds greater than rates maintained by ships meant that vessels operated autonomously once dispatched. Interplanetary robotic spacecraft today operate on the same information principle since the distance over which a craft sends information and receives instruction incurs a time delay greater than the seconds in which an operation requires execution. The inability to communicate information in a timely manner necessarily required that both spacecraft and sailing vessel maneuver with high degrees of autonomy within broad bounds established by their programming (software in the spacecraft; orders and manifests in ships).

A significant difference today is that transaction costs attendant with transnational flows of information approach zero. Hackers probing systems for trade secrets serve a similar function in circumventing information policy that Samuel Slater did by memorizing the operation of textile machinery before physically traveling to the United States.

Information policy is broader than laws and regulations. Sandra Braman defines information policy as "laws, regulations, and doctrinal positions—and other decision making and practices with society-wide constitutive effects—involving information creation, processing flows, access, and use."[9] Government regulation comprises undisguised manifestations of policy, but its social effects are influenced by constitutive elements other than ones imposed by state officials. Lawrence Lessig, for example, identifies architecture, economics, and social norms, and acknowledges the existence of many others, as factors regulating behavior.[10] The confluence of all the factors affecting human behavior, not just laws, forms the operating mechanism for policy.

The regulation of information by laws establishing property rights to promote advanced technical enterprises was consistent with economic policy promoting rapid industrialization. Information freedom, except where restriction promoted U.S. goals, formed an unstated theme that still permeates policy today, based on two changes in the way that United States viewed information. Woodrow Wilson's administration issued the first clear expressions of a U.S. information policy when it sought to include provisions guaranteeing access to information by all peoples in the negotiation of terms ending World War I. A second inflection point appeared during the Clinton administration. Vice President Gore led an effort both to publish information about the government online and to migrate government services as much as possible to Web pages available to the public. These efforts reflected a general understanding that information constituted a resource that could be harnessed to achieve other policy goals, like the spread of democracy, which developed as the United States progressed from an agricultural to an industrial to an information economy.

The Clinton administration's approach to information was pervasive. Beginning in 1997, any official statement regarding the collection, storage, or use of information was deemed to constitute an "information policy instrument." A broad range of items became policy instruments. Statutes, regulations, guidelines formed the basic corpus of information policy instruments, but the Clinton doctrine expansively categorized presidential executive orders, Office of Management and Budget circulars, bulletins, and memos—including internal agency documents—as documents regulating the use of information.[11] The breadth of information available to citizens was substantially curtailed in the name of national security after the 9/11 attacks. The tension between making information available and restricting it forms the principle debate of information policy domestically and globally. (NWICO and WSIS proposals, discussed later in this chapter, positioned the desire of developing countries to control information against a U.S. policy of alleged openness.)

Two principles emerge when the history of U.S. information policy is examined. The first is persistent discourse suggesting that unfettered access to information promotes democracy and global peace. The second is an empirical understanding of how fettered access to information, such as occurs with copyright and patent restrictions, promotes U.S. business interests. Both shape U.S. policy. As we have argued, this duality governing information flows stems from practices that the United States adopted from England during industrialization. The oppositional nature of these core beliefs resulted in the United States at once encouraging the flow of information into the country while at the same time trying to block the outflow, at least where the United States enjoys competitive advantages or a protected trade status.

The United States coupled freedom of expression to the availability of technology and information in its foreign policy. President Obama spoke of a fundamental human right to freedom of expression using technology.[12] The National Security Strategy of the United States for 2010 dedicated the country to freedom of expression through technological means.[13] The statements reflect a policy position that formed during the Industrial Revolution but became primary as the world developed an information economy dominated by the United States.

U.S. Information Policy on a World Stage: Commerce and Free Flows

Information policy is a creature of the historical and political dimensions in which it developed. The quest for economic growth drove the United States to adopt a policy encouraging the importation of information regarding industrial processes while at the same time restricting exportation of similar material. In this, as we have seen, the United States was not alone. The policy mirrored that of other countries. We focused on Britain because the diffusion of information across the Atlantic set the stage for global conflict over the regulation of information infrastructure. As Winseck and Pike suggest, the global information struggle after 1860 and lasting until 1930 shares "many commonalities with, and being the closest predecessor of, our own times."[14]

The international diffusion of information experienced a tremendous boost with the refinement of submarine cables capable of reliably transporting messages between countries separated by oceans. Numerous cables laid beneath the surface of the Atlantic at the end of the nineteenth century suffered from problems of low bandwidth and short lifespan. The Atlantic Telegraph Company, a transatlantic cable project undertaken by Cyrus Field, took four years to construct a seven-wire link between County Cork, Ireland, and Trinity Bay, Newfoundland. Field was an American who moved to Britain to obtain financing for the project. Completed in 1858, the line never worked as expected. Queen Victoria's celebratory ninety-eight-word telegram congratulating President Buchanan upon completion of the project required sixteen hours to transmit. The cable went dead within a month.

President Buchanan's reply to the queen—characterizing the communication system as "an instrument destined by Divine Providence to diffuse religion, civilization, liberty, and law throughout the world"[15]—reflected the American belief that the flow of information would be globally transformative. Despite the problems, investors remained excited by the possibility of commodifying the speedy communication of information. Technology improved until, by 1866, Field's next enterprise, the Anglo-American Telegraph Company could both lay new cable and repair the old.

The link across North Atlantic waters spurred competitive development of cable systems. Britain dominated worldwide systems for several reasons. On the demand side, the assemblage of a global empire provided commercial and government traffic for cable systems. Shipping companies could wire instructions to captains as they reached foreign ports. The flexibility inherent in being able to alter a voyage while it was underway gave traders and shipping companies a comparative advantage over competitors. Empire had another demand-side effect. Several British colonies were settled with relatively large European immigrant populations. The existence of these groups created a demand for synchronous, timely news. British newspapers featured stories from the colonies, while colonists maintained interest in homeland developments. Newspapers, and the news services that provided the stories, quickly became major users of global cable systems.[16]

Empire provided supply-side advantages for the British. Wealth generated by colonies enabled entrepreneurs to capitalize expansion of systems. Cable systems required the manufacture of large quantities of continuous rolls of cable, the creation of ships large enough to transport and lay the lines, and financing for worldwide operations. Not until the end of the 1870s could other countries rival Britain's financing of large ventures. The geographic spread of the empire increased the cost of building systems to far-flung outposts, but at the same time systems could link geographic locations in such a way that traffic rarely flowed through territory of another country.[17] The resulting system, called the All Red Line because contemporary maps tended to show British holdings in red, dominated worldwide communication. Bombay first connected to Saudi Arabia and, by 1870, directly linked to London through the Eastern Telegraph Company. By 1872 messages could travel from London to Australia by routing through Bombay, then Singapore or China, and on to the Australian continent and New Zealand. A line across Canada and under the Pacific formed a second route to Australasia that became operational in 1902.

Economic policy at the end of the nineteenth century held that prosperous countries needed worldwide markets and global sources of supply. The United States, as well as other countries, sought to duplicate the success of the British Empire. Alfred Mahan proposed in 1890 that an industrial power required access to markets in other countries, an undertaking that could only be protected by a large, modern navy.[18] A navy ranging over the globe required a communications system. U.S. companies began laying cables, as did German and French firms. British cable companies continued to dominate the North Atlantic long-distance cable market until 1911 and much of remaining markets until the 1920s. A single British cable manufacturer, TC&M, produced more than half of the cable laid in the nineteenth and early twentieth centuries. The majority of cable-laying ships were British.[19]

Cartels formed to protect hegemony. The Anglo-American Telegraph Company owned seven cables crossing the North Atlantic in 1904. Its market power forced rivals to share revenue and carry traffic for other cartel members in the event of cable failure. Revenue-sharing agreements buffered price competition. Anglo-American Telegraph Company simply bought potential competitors. It acquired *Societe du Cable Transatlantique* and its cable from Brest to Newfoundland and Direct United States Telegraph Company by 1900. *Compagnie Francaise du Telegraph de Paris a New York* created a technologically superior cable system connecting Brest with Cape Cod. Unable to compete on a technical level, Anglo-American reduced rates by 84 percent until its rival joined the cartel. Western Union, after creating its own cartel with the German government-subsidized *Deutsch-Atlantische Telegraphengesellschaft* (DAT), joined the price-fixing arrangement to end a rate war. News agencies reflected the importance of international information to the developing world economy. Between 1835 and 1851 three international agencies began operations: Havas (later AFP) in France; Wolff in Germany; and Britain's Reuters. All were subsidized by governments. Associated Press formed in the United States in 1848 but did not establish international operations until around 1900. Wolff, Havas, and Reuters established a cartel in 1870 that divided the world into coverage territories that occasionally overlapped.

Daniel Headrick and Pascal Griset calculated that at the end of the nineteenth century more than 63 percent of the cables in the world were British; one conglomerate operated half of them.[20] Private companies benefited from policies founded in the belief that efficient transmission of information constituted a decisive factor in economic growth. The United States could not create a globe-encircling set of imperial dependencies as the British had, so it sought foreign markets it could exploit. The United States engaged in economic imperialism sustained by communication networks that functioned as political tools wielding economic power.[21]

New global enterprises required global communications. The need to "modernize" a foreign land into a unit of economic activity seamlessly integrated with economic aims of major powers fostered a global media system. Julius Reuter exemplifies the creation of a cable-dependent worldwide news organization. Reuter recognized that news services depended on the availability of cable communications, so he invested in cable companies. He expanded the news-service end of the business only after cable companies developed a dependency on his services as customers themselves. Similar relationships developed around the world. The *New York World* was linked through its owner, Jay Gould, to Western Union, also owned by Gould. Gordon Bennett controlled both the *New York Herald* and the Commercial Cable Company. Newspaper-cable combines formed vertically integrated information collection and distribution systems.

The development of radio communication challenged the domination of British cable companies over the transmission of information. Guglielmo Marconi demonstrated the feasibility of transatlantic information transfer without wires in 1901. Although the Wireless Telegraph & Signal Company, later the Marconi Company, exploited Marconi's patents on radio to the extent that their operators refused to respond to radio messages sent on other systems, British interests treated radio systems as an interesting side show that would never challenge the dominance of cable. The United States, by contrast, fully developed radio systems at the same time that they improved telephony. Just as Britain originally dominated cable, the United States came to be the primary advocate for telephone.

Capital investment necessary to operate a radio system equaled a minor percentage of the investment required to lay and operate cable. Radio equipment could be produced relatively inexpensively in mass quantities. Radio waves did not incur the expensive landing charges assessed on cable companies where undersea cables came ashore. Since radio transmissions did not respect international borders, U.S. entrepreneurs began to understand that radio constituted a technology that could challenge the British-dominated cable systems for information transfer.[22]

Interference by transmitters using identical frequencies motivated twenty-eight nations to meet in Berlin in 1906 to allocate frequencies. The largest use of radio at the time was by navies. Dominated by countries with large navies, the 1906 International Radiotelegraph Conference approved a system in which a country seeking to use a frequency notified the ITU (then called the International Telegraph Union) of the exercise of its rights under the International Radiotelegraph Convention.[23] In 1912 this became a registration system. The "first use" system of regulation favored richer nations with the ability to make capital investments in radio technology over poorer ones.[24]

World War I disrupted the global communication system physically and politically. Britain's reliance on the All Red Line allowed it to cut German cables with impunity. The All Red Line did not route cable traffic through foreign territory, depriving the Germans of any means to retaliate. Cutting German cables, however, meant that U.S. business could not communicate with Germany until repairs were completed in 1920. The disruption reinforced American business interest in challenging the British hegemony. At the same time, progressivism in the United States challenged the economic necessity for cartels. The Federal Trade Commission Act in 1914 established an independent agency enforcing antirust provisions of the Clayton Act, also passed in 1914.[25]

British economic decline after World War I created an opportunity for U.S. world expansion. The transition from British hegemony to American economic domination proceeded episodically. Britain regained a measure of control over international information when RCA transitioned into long-range commercial broadcasting by abandoning its relationship with the military in favor of more lucrative arrangements with the British, French, and Germans.[26] British control eroded as AT&T emerged as a monopolist in the international telephony market, a position it maintained as a result of excessive tariffs and favorable ITU rules. Britain maximized its large investment in cable infrastructure in a way that favored wired over wireless communication. Pooling of patents by radio users, plus lower costs of building systems, undermined the British strategy of combining radio and cable systems to perpetuate the monopoly.[27] Testimony before the Congress reported a general belief that radio would never replace telegraph cables.[28] RCA and the

U.S. Navy, however, viewed radio as a powerful trade-promotion tool that undermined the British communications hegemony.[29]

America began asserting that it had a place in world politics; news combines formed the nervous system of an emerging behemoth. Winseck and Pike demonstrate that competition from radio caused cable rates to decrease until market equilibrium was achieved, even though cable carried more than 80 percent of the traffic through the 1920s.[30] Global communication had changed. The integrated British system succumbed to the need to connect to "an interconnected, pluralistic network of networks increasingly dominated by the United States."[31] By the end of the 1940s the British system shifted away from telegraph, dismantled into systems governed by former colonies, rather than from Britain, and connected to U.S. networks.[32]

To Serve Man: International Development Aids the U.S.

The economic need for global communications became enmeshed with the meme that the free flow of information enhanced freedom and democracy around the world. Winseck and Pike quote an 1869 memo from U.S. Secretary of State Hamilton Fish describing U.S. policy "to initiate this movement for the common benefit of the community and civilization of all."[33] The policy established by Fish argued that the free flow of information would engender world peace. The policy was also careful to require access to foreign markets as a consequence of allowing access to markets in the United States.

The challenge to information cartels occurred during a shift in American foreign policy under President Woodrow Wilson, which advocated a more humanitarian approach to world affairs. The new foreign policy initiatives, at least as expressed, emphasized a goal of making the world better for mankind rather than focusing on American commercial interests. Wilson's campaign speeches in 1912, quoted at the beginning of this chapter, urged a foreign policy promoting American democratic beliefs around the world.[34] A Wilsonian focus on "the progress of mankind" assumed that the world would be better if it adopted "American ideals." Exporting liberal ideals required a free flow of information.

U.S. proposals at the 1919 Paris Peace Conference incorporated the idea that communication systems, as well as the markets they served, should not tolerate restrictions by either governments or cartels. Attacks on cartels were consistent with domestic trust-busting policy but also challenged British domination via cartel. Walter S. Rogers, head of the Committee of Public

Information propaganda agency set up by President Wilson in 1917, advised Wilson in Paris to push for "world-wide freedom of news, with important news going everywhere" as necessary for world peace because "the extension of democratic forms of government and the increasing closeness of contact between all parts of the world point to the conclusion that the ultimate basis of world peace is common knowledge and understanding between the masses of the world."[35] High rates charged by cartels constituted the main barrier to information flow, according to Rogers. His solution required nationalization of domestic cable and radio systems combined with international administration of connections between continents to bring low, uniform rates. The proposals remain anathema to American business interests and to Britain.[36] Unable to achieve consensus, the nations gathered in Paris deferred communication issues to a 1920 conference scheduled for Washington.

As much as the United States tried to keep freedom of information on the agenda at the International Conference on Electrical Communications (ICEC), the meeting devolved into extensive wrangling over the disposition of German cable systems seized during World War I. U.S. proposals offering communication at nominal rates met with almost universal opposition, including extensive objections made by American firms operating international systems. The ICEC debacle exposed an inherent contradiction in U.S. aims: providing international information systems that would deliver messages at low costs conflicted with commercial aims of protecting American business interests. Where U.S. business enjoyed preferential treatment, American policy sought to entrench the status quo; where U.S. commercial activity was burdened, as by the British cartels, the U.S. fought for open communications. American policy mirrored Hamiltonian attitudes toward information during the industrialization of the United States, which promoted both free and restricted information transfer, depending on whichever benefited the country more at the moment.

Britain steadfastly maintained cartels in spite of U.S. efforts to establish open world markets. The United States dominated radio in international communication after World War I. Wilson created a federal monopoly over manufacture of radio equipment and its use within the country during the war. Congress refused to extend the monopoly when the war ended despite Wilson administration rhetoric extolling nationalized systems as operators providing low prices beneficial to humankind. The administration circumvented clear congressional interest to develop an open market for international radio transmissions by having the War Department guarantee a monopoly on military communication by radio to General Electric if it would create an operating company for this purpose, establishing a precedent for creation of a private company to control a new communication technology employed again in 1998, when the U.S. Department of Commerce made ICANN responsible for domain names. The new company, Radio Corporation of America (RCA), amalgamated assets owned by the U.S. Navy with resources it controlled after purchasing the Marconi Wireless Telegraph Company of America and the Pan-American Telegraph Company. The United States, through RCA, could control a large number of frequencies under the existing "first use" international regulatory scheme as a result of vast resources capable of using desired bandwidth first.[37]

The United States had proposed the formation of an international agency to simplify rules regarding radio during the 1920 conference on electrical communication.[38] The desire to unify international regulations became reality in 1927, when the ITU adopted a U.S. proposal to assume responsibility for both cable and broadcast operations. ITU had been formed in 1863 to resolve difficulties arising when national telegraph systems using incompatible protocols and equipment attempted to connect across national borders. International communication required that users employ similar technical arrangements in order for messages to translate from one country to another. The expansion of radio communication demonstrated the necessity of allocating frequencies to avoid interference. A 1906 conference in Berlin established the International Radiotelegraph Convention (IRC). The successor to the 1865 International Telegraph Convention merged with IRC in 1932 to form the International Telegraph Union, subsequently renamed the International Telecommunications Union, unifying the allocation of frequencies with standardization of other technical aspects of radio.[39]

The practical consequence of the international communication regulatory scheme was that any country interested in pursuing commerce beyond its frontiers had to connect with the United States. Communications scholar Hills shows that the structure of international communication regulation fostered a U.S. economic empire based on "a system of international relations that puts the United States at the center of a web of international lines of communication, public and private, from which it is intended that the U.S. economy and favored companies shall benefit."[40]

Global economic devastation following World War II required large-scale investments in national economies. The United States, as the country emerging from the war with intact production capabilities, needed reliable sources of raw materials and international markets for its goods. The International Bank for Reconstruction and Development—now part of the World Bank— had been designed to loan money to build up war-torn areas but failed to provide financial capital in quantities sufficient to stimulate lagging economies.

By contrast, the Marshall Plan financed an effective European reconstruction plan. The Marshall Plan was not without strings, however. Industrial operations were to incorporate American methods of mass production. Nations could not institute trade barriers unfavorable to the United States. Each country receiving aid under the Marshall Plan achieved economic benchmarks surpassing 1938 levels when the program concluded in 1952.

The World Bank was not without influence. The bank controlled countries where it did business both by requiring reforms and by increasing the indebtedness of the customer country. Bank operations tended to benefit the United States, such as when loan conditions opened markets. U.S. companies hired as consultants or contractors profited directly from World Bank projects. The location of the bank headquarters in Washington, D.C., combined with the tradition that an American should head the bank, contributed to the perception that the bank operated as an agent of U.S. policy. Hills concluded that U.S. domination was more than a perception: "Because the bank was regarded as a U.S. institution, Congress and U.S. administrations were able to exercise direct and indirect power over the bank's personnel, over its conceptualization of 'development' and its implementation."[41]

The ability of the United States to provide massive infusions of financial capital directly through aid programs like the Marshall Plan and indirectly through institutions like the World Bank empowered the United States to make demands beyond simply insisting on access to markets. In 1943 the United States began asserting a desire for open access to information, including "freedom of ingress and egress of information in all nations."[42] As World War II ended, the United States informed Britain that one requirement in a negotiated peace would be Germany's acceptance of a universal right to acquire and disseminate information.

The ideal of free-information flow permeated American culture. Palmer Hoyt, publisher of the *Portland Oregonian*, epitomized the prevalence of freedom of information as the cure for ills when, in a speech to the Jackson County Chamber of Commerce on September 18, 1945, he linked open information to the avoidance of nuclear war. Hoyt argued, "Yes, there could be but one answer. Mutual understanding between the nations, and this answer to be achieved in only one way—by free flow of news—American style, the elimination of all political censorships and free and equal use of communication."[43] Information not only had to flow freely, but it needed to conform with an American ideal. U.S. information policy myopically conflated freely flowing information with information that benefited American interests as well.

The emerging American hegemony in the communication of information moved forward as a result of a policy shift at the World Bank toward funding projects resulting in the privatization of services provided by governments. Telecommunications infrastructure became a target for privatization using World Bank financing. The bank drastically curtailed lending to governments for telecommunications infrastructure during the 1990s.[44] The amount available for investment in telecoms with private participation expanded. Private investment increasingly emanated from the United States, where companies were attracted to operating telecoms in a location with minimal effective regulation. For example, the U.S.-Colombia Trade Agreement concluded by the United States Trade Representative (USTR) in 2006 guarantees the ability of U.S. investors to completely acquire Colombian telecommunications companies while eliminating duties on information-technology equipment sold into the country.[45] USTR promoted the agreement in terms of its benefits to U.S. businesses: "The U.S.-Colombia Trade Promotion Agreement provides a new opportunity for U.S. operators to gain the legal certainty necessary to either make significant investments abroad or tap into existing telecommunications infrastructure to better expand their businesses."[46]

U.S. leadership in telecommunications investment and in technology is now threatened by the emergence of China as a supplier of information and communications technology. As China expands its network investments internationally, its influence as a telecommunications center increases. China's core network is believed to be comparable to that of the U.S. A paper circulated by the U.S. National Defense University in 2006 emphasized the sources of investment in most of the world: "At the United States and China Telecommunications Summit, June 17, 2004, Secretary of Commerce Evans described the United States and China as the world's primary engines of global telecommunications growth."[47]

Information has been regarded as an important resource since the Industrial Revolution, but the resource itself could not be traded in real time until the development of sophisticated networks dedicated to high-speed transfer of information. The historical linkage in U.S. policy between commerce and access to information developed into a belief that unfettered information access is a necessary condition for participation in the global economy. As Hills stated, "Developing countries also saw data flows as perpetuating economic dependency, but the majority had few resources to undertake the necessary regulation."[48] As we shall see, subsequent U.S. trade policy further undermined domestic regulation of flows by other countries by proposing free-trade agreements designed to eliminate barriers to U.S. entry.

WTO, GATT, and the Commodification of Information

Developing countries employed the communications infrastructure Americans built for them to discuss issues and to collaborate. The U.S. belief that access to information could foster debate proved to be true as more countries adopted positions on global telecommunications policies not always beneficial to the United States. Three events, each connected to the UN, demonstrated that countries could effectively assert their desires to participate in planning and operation of global systems: the two WSIS meetings and the NWICO discussions.

UNESCO fostered discussion about global consequences of communications technology in the context of the Cold War. Smaller countries organized the Non-Aligned Movement of the UN in the belief that a coalition of independent countries could facilitate a redistribution of resources and power away from major power blocs. Nations in the global South recently emancipated from colonial empires affirmed national sovereignty and sought to develop economic security. Communications deficits increasingly interfered with their ability to participate as equals on the world stage. The Non-Aligned Movement coalesced around proposals to reform satellite and communication systems, including increasing the availability of radio equipment and instituting a right to reply to media reports.[49]

The MacBride Commission report encompassing NWICO recommendations became the focus of attacks by newly elected conservative governments in the United States and Britain. Forces opposed to NWICO characterized the report as restricting freedom of the press through government censorship, although nothing of the kind appeared in the report. The two largest sources of funds for UNESCO left the organization, with the United States departing in 1984 and Britain following in 1985. Without funding, the NWICO agenda gradually became less potent, although meetings continued until 1999.[50]

ITU sponsored the World Summit on the Information Society conferences in Geneva (2003) and Tunis (2005) to discuss global telecommunications issues, principally disparate access between rich and poor countries. Milton Mueller, in *Nations and States*, describes the shift from access issues to internet governance, which we explore in depth in chapters 4 and 5.[51] A majority of ITU members, mainly from developing countries, rejected U.S. proposals for governance by the private sector and sought greater government influence, particularly through ITU. While not explicitly raised at WSIS, insistence on intellectual property rights protection for material on the internet and the refusal, on free speech grounds, to discuss any restrictions to online speech divided Western countries (led by the United States) and the rest of the world. The management of internet domain names, by contrast, was explicitly discussed, resulting in de facto recognition of existing institutions, especially ICANN.[52]

WSIS reflected long-standing dissension about the governance of telecommunications. Discord within ITU motivated the United States to seek alternative policies regarding telecommunications. The United States began treating information as a resource that could be governed by trade agreements. In 1947 the United States sought simultaneous execution of bilateral agreements among multiple countries to counter trade preferences extended by Britain. The resulting accord, later called the General Agreement on Tariffs and Trade (GATT), reduced trade barriers and abolished preferences among twenty-three signatories. GATT established something like a trade cartel in which any preference granted to one member must be accorded to the remainder, an effect called "most favored nation" status. Unlike ITU, where the possibility of a formal vote influences negotiations, GATT reached decisions by consensus.

U.S. companies framed obstructions to information flow as trade barriers; developing countries limited data access to safeguard various national interests such as privacy but also political stability or censorship. As countries discovered that infrastructure development using U.S. or World Bank money increased economic dependency, they began to believe that sharing information exacerbated the problem. The United States attempted to stem the development of data-restricting regulation by different countries through the Organization for Economic Co-operation and Development (OECD), which began as an agency administering aid after World War II. Information restrictions persisted, however, because OECD guidelines were voluntary and did not apply to all countries. The Uruguay Round of trade negotiations that began in 1986 created the WTO as the administrative agency for an expanded GATT as well as a newly developed General Agreement on Trade in Services (GATS). GATS reduced barriers interfering with commercial services just as GATT had done with merchandise.

Telephone and telegraph regulations used since 1973 were replaced by International Telecommunications Regulations (ITRs) issued by ITU that removed pricing restrictions on the resale of international leased lines, rendering traditional telecommunications negotiated-pricing models obsolete.[53] The flexibility of the new regulatory scheme allowed the United States to establish private rules governing its information flows through multilateral trade arrangements and consideration of telecommunications issues as provision of services governed by World Trade Organization rules. The United States favored the WTO over the ITU because structural differences could be exploited by the United States. Telecommunications infrastructure investment by developing countries—often encouraged by the United States—inflated the number of smaller countries belonging to the organization. Every member of the UN, except Palau, participates in ITU. One non-UN member, the Vatican State, enjoys full ITU membership. ITU regulations mandate that each member be treated as an equal, with each casting one vote on all issues. As a result, developing countries exercise more power as a group than do developed countries.

At the World Conference on International Telecommunications (WCIT-12) in Dubai, developing countries proposed numerous changes to International Telecommunications Regulations that would have legitimized the regulatory authority of nation-states over the internet or, in the view of the United States and its allies, would have potentially increased ITU regulatory authority.[54] The opposition of the United States and other developed countries to various proposals not related to information flows or telecommunications (such as regulation of mobile roaming prices, reduction of e-waste, or provision of telecommunications to the disabled) reflects an aversion to the establishment of any international controls that might later be expanded to interfere with core concerns about information flows. (WCIT is discussed in detail in chapters 4.)

After the establishment of the WTO, the United States suggested exempting telecommunications from most-favored-nation status to allow bilateral negotiation of telecommunication agreements. Since a bilateral agreement would not automatically extend reciprocal benefits to all signatories, U.S. multinationals could operate in a country with which the United States had concluded an agreement without fear of a foreign multinational setting up shop on equal terms in the United States. Negotiations over the proposed Telecommunications Annex to GATS broke down as the United States continued to resist the application of most-favored-nation treatment to telecommunications services.

In trade negotiations with Mexico and Canada that resulted in the North American Free Trade Agreement (NAFTA), the United States obtained concessions on the regulation of public and private telecommunications networks and establishment of standards without the burden of a most-favored-nation provision. NAFTA included access to data provisions that rewarded large, private networks transcending international borders. Large transnational corporations could operate in any of the three countries with minimal regulation by any of them. NAFTA effectively established a telecommunications trade protocol independent of rules governing the rest of the world.[55] This was not the first time the United States maneuvered to insulate the North American market from world regulation. When in 1973 the United States signed agreements adopted by the rest of the world at the 1952 ITU plenipotentiary meeting, it specifically excluded provisions controlling telephone and telegraph connection with Mexico and Canada.[56]

WTO members finally concluded a basic agreement in 1997 that subjected telecommunications to GATS market-access regulations. The terms of the agreement were interpreted differently by the United States than by other countries, in that the United States took a very restrictive stance on what constituted "basic" telecommunications services.[57] The United States continued to play the WTO against the ITU, and multinational agreements like NAFTA against all. The United States Trade Representative undertook negotiations at a regional level whenever WTO appeared to be headed in a direction contrary to U.S. desires.[58] For example, Malaysia's WTO telecommunications offered permits up to 30 percent equity in basic and value-added suppliers by foreign investment, yet the proposed Malaysia-U.S. Free Trade agreement allowed U.S. companies a 49 percent stake.[59] NAFTA created a continental market modeled after the incumbent system in the United States while preventing Mexico and Canada from regulating American transnational corporations. "NAFTA achieved what the WTO did not," Hills concluded.[60] The United States emerged from negotiations as a stronger power able to deploy inconsistent strategies that keep other countries off balance while protecting its own business interests.

I Will Because ICANN

The participation of civil society groups marked the principal difference between NWICO and WSIS. Whereas NWICO argued for distribution of resources on a state level, WSIS focused less on states and more on establishing a common vision. After the failure of the IAHC initiative, the 1998 ITU plenipotentiary organized two WSIS meetings to discuss issues resulting from disparate abilities of countries to acquire and use communication technologies, particularly the internet. The choice of meeting sites reflected a growing understanding that a divide existed between the global North and the global South. ITU framed the meetings as technical discussions of issues such as network connectivity and the effect of new technologies, but the agenda broadened to consider human rights and cultural issues in 2001, when UNESCO joined. The first conference, 2003 in Geneva, became a forum criticizing U.S. domination of ICANN. The criticism continued in Tunis during 2005. Developing countries complained about the perceived loss of sovereignty as a result of a private corporation—ICANN—making decisions that controlled the operation of communication technology within a country. ICANN, moreover, operated with little transparency or significant participation by governments.[61]

WSIS I formed the Working Group on Internet Governance (WGIG) to prepare recommendations for the Tunis meeting. Forty members, equally split between governments and private parties, participated in WGIG meetings. WGIG proposed that WSIS II both identify a set of priority issues and adopt a multistakeholder framework for internet governance that included governments, the private sector, and civil society.[62] The recommendation contrasted with the ICANN model based on significant participation by private parties at the expense of governments and civil-society organizations. When Iran, China, and Cuba objected to U.S. influence over ICANN, the United States reasserted that it considered ICANN to be the important player. WSIS II was inconclusive: it did not formally adopt the model urged by the United States, but it did not reject it either.[63] The United States' refusal to truly internationalize internet governance motivated multiple proposals to increase intergovernmental control (either ICANN's General Advisory Council [GAC] or ITU or by establishing a new agency) or to develop a parallel internet using a different root file controlled by a multilateral agency. No proposal received sufficient support to be taken seriously.

Immediately prior to the WSIS 2003 meeting in Geneva, the United States insisted that any multinational agreement should contain "a commitment to the private sector and rule of law," include "content creation and intellectual property rights protection," and adopt policies "insuring security on the Internet, in electronic communications, and in electronic commerce."[64] Each of these "pillars," as characterized by U.S. Ambassador David Gross, protected a fundamental U.S. interest. America produced a substantial percentage of internet material, whether accessed legally or not. Intellectual property rights protected an economic and cultural hegemony seen by many as an unfortunate consequence of globalization. Effective intellectual property rights enforcement increased financial returns to U.S. producers perceived as dominating global cultural production. The U.S. statement at Geneva asserted a need to safeguard intellectual property "in order to inspire ongoing content development." As we have noted, U.S. policy securing rights to inventors and creators to stimulate further innovation dates back to information policy during the Industrial Revolution.

The emphasis on security is ironic after revelations that the National Security Agency possesses significant capacity to intercept a sizable percentage of the world's telecommunications traffic (ironic in light of subsequent U.S. refusal at WCIT to consider treaty language calling for international cooperation to improve security). Perhaps the security "pillar" arose from a desire to embed backdoors and vulnerabilities that the developing NSA surveillance colossus might exploit in the future. It is beyond speculation, however, that any proposal improving electronic commerce would inure to the benefit of American multinational companies.

The final pillar is the one examined in depth here and in chapter 5. Gross characterized a commitment to the private sector as important "so that countries can attract the necessary private investment to create the infrastructure."[65] The United States is a major producer of international private investment funds as well as a large-scale supplier of infrastructure systems. The goal of creating infrastructure sounded egalitarian. The implicit promise communicated by the statement held out the possibility of equality between nations in international information systems. Access to information, according to the U.S. litany, promoted democracy, freedom, peace, and almost everything else with a laudable label. That U.S. business profited from creating infrastructure was a pleasant side effect. "Privatization" amounted to institutionalization of a neoliberal economic model for the delivery of communication services—a model that ignored important economic factors such as network effects, network externalities, economies of scale, and public goods.

Another hidden factor motivated the U.S. commitment to the private sector. Privatization facilitated U.S. control. Gross did not point out that a private company, contractually bound to the U.S. government, acted as the fundamental agent through which the United States exercised power over the internet. ICANN possessed the master switch, called the root file. ICANN developed, published, and enforced rules regarding the management of internet domain names and addresses. Its subdivision, the Internet Assigned Naming Authority (IANA), exercised operational control over those resources, while a third U.S. company, VeriSign, operated the root file itself, although all changes had to be approved by the National Telecommunications and Information Agency (NTIA) in the Department of Commerce.[66]

The root file bestows upon its keeper the ability to regulate the use of internet domain names widely used to access information and services over the network. Manipulation of the root file blocks certain services (such as online gambling) or facilitates new services. Theoretically, the operator of the root file could bring down a country-code top-level domain (ccTLD), with significant consequences for services provided under the ccTLD.

ICANN is an American nonprofit corporation organized at the urging of the Clinton administration in 1998 to internationalize management of internet domain names and addresses (see chapter 4 for additional detail). The so-called root file is the master source for top-level domain names that form the right-most portion of familiar names for websites (for example, www.cnn.com). Those names are called Universal Resource Locators—URLs—that are resolved by the domain name system (DNS) to unique internet protocol (IP) addresses (such as 98.37.241.30). The root file functions as the foundational coordinating system translating internet names into the IP numbers needed for transmission of information across the network. ICANN manages the allocation of IP addresses, assignment of protocol identifiers, the assignment of generic (gTLD) and country code (ccTLD) top-level domain names, and management of the root-server system.

The United States refers to ICANN as an international organization. ICANN is not an intergovernmental organization as implied by the term; its structure limits the role of foreign governments. Government officials are prohibited from serving on the corporate board of directors. Instead, international participation was limited to a General Advisory Council (GAC) composed of one member from any country interested in naming a representative, and this created an aura of internationalism. Recommendations of the GAC are nonbinding, leaving the ICANN board free to ignore any that it does not like. A bylaw change in 2002 required ICANN's board to consult closely with GAC, but the power to reject a proposal ultimately rested with the board of directors alone.[67]

WSIS in 2005 again sought to transfer administration of the domain-name system to a truly intergovernmental body. Developing countries (which include transitional economies, such as Russia, in this account) favored ITU, where they exercised more influence than at ICANN, for the governance role. U.S. opposition to any dilution of its power guaranteed that few changes would be made. The ITU Plenipotentiary Conference in 2010 reinforced ICANN's international political position by acknowledging its functions in the operation of the internet while calling for a greater ITU role.[68] The U.S. Department of Commerce maintains ultimate authority over the root file and the IANA function, a situation reinforced by contract, despite its well-publicized calls for proposals to internationalize these functions.[69]

Conclusion

Daya Kishan Thussu identified domination of global information and entertainment by a few nations and multinational corporations as a recurring theme in the study of international communication.[70] This chapter reviewed the progression whereby the United States usurped British domination of global information commerce. U.S. policy to create markets for information by facilitating the construction of information infrastructure in developing nations increased, in those nations, an awareness and understanding of unfair distribution of resources. And so they availed themselves of UN organizations designed to address such concerns, in the process challenging U.S. dominance. Concern over U.S. hegemony set up the debate over whether ITU and ICANN should govern operations on the internet. The conflict is not between these organizations. The debate is over policy and, ultimately, philosophy. U.S. policy argues that the network governance should be privatized, ideally by ICANN, which the United States dominates. Participation by national governments in ICANN is restricted; nations seeking greater equity in telecommunications policymaking therefore favor ITU.

The nature of the governance structure that will evolve cannot be predicted. U.S. information policy will continue to have a profound effect on the development of internet policy and ultimately the ability of people to access information online.

2

The Information-Industrial Complex

As we prepare to enter the new millennium, we are
learning a new language. It will be the lingua franca of
the new era. It is made up of ones and zeroes and bits
and bytes. But as we master it, as we bring the digital
revolution into our homes and schools, we will be able
to communicate ideas and information . . . with an ease
never before thought possible. And so we meet today on
common ground, not to predict the future but to make
firm the arrangements for its arrival. Let us master and
develop this new language together.

—Vice President Al Gore, Superhighway
Summit, UCLA, January 11, 1994

Daniel Guerin introduced the concept of a "military-industrial complex" in 1936 to refer to a "coalition of groups with vested psychological, moral, and material interests in the continuous development and maintenance of high levels of weaponry, in preservation of colonial markets and in military-strategic conceptions of internal affairs."[1] The MIC emerged as a result of the Great Depression and World War II—in short, crises demanded that the government intervene into the marketplace by creating jobs and pushing innovation in areas under threat from international competitors. Some seventy years later, the transition from an economy based on heavy industry toward one grounded in communication technology and information management has resulted in a new "silicon triangle" between policymakers, the information industries, and the American public. Beginning mainly (but not exclusively) in the post–World War II era, new crises—ranging from the Cold War to post-independence movements, to the War on Terror, to the rise of China—have driven government interest in and intervention into various companies involved in the production of information hardware, software, and processing. This has facilitated the development of what we describe as the information-industrial complex.

This chapter outlines how the U.S. government has cultivated a close and codependent relationship with companies involved in information production, storage, processing, and distribution, referred to here as the "information industries." Regular cooperation between U.S. government and private-sector actors has furthered the rise of a global economy driven by information and communication technologies while simultaneously placing U.S. companies at its center. Starting in the early 1940s, the American government invested in building public-private partnerships in the information technology sector that enabled the rise of Silicon Valley.[2] Through various policy mechanisms, including subsidy, domestic and international policy reform, direct investment, and guidance, the U.S. government facilitated the rise of modern information and communications technologies, including, in particular, computers and the internet, funded their advanced technological development, and pushed for governance structures enabling their global reach.

The analogue to the military-industrial complex is not merely descriptive, it is also prescriptive. The codependence that defined the military-industrial complex produced an ineffective model for governments and businesses alike (ineffective for government because its decisions tended to be overly influenced by private companies; ineffective for businesses because they came to rely on easily obtained government contracts, leading in some cases to a loss of competitiveness). Similarly, the symbiotic relationship between the U.S. government and the information sector does not bode well for the future of Silicon Valley or American statecraft. In order to underline these impending dangers, we must begin first with an exploration of the origins and history of its antecedent—the military-industrial complex.

The Military-Industrial Complex

In 1958, C. Wright Mills wrote about the increased concentration of political power in the hands of a "power elite," a term coined to reference the consolidation of power among a small group of political, military, and business leaders in the United States.[3] He contrasted this consolidation of power to the decades prior to World War II, when centralized government powers were limited, and business and military professionals played only a limited role in political affairs. According to Mills, "There is no longer, on the one hand, an economy, and, on the other, a political order, containing a military establishment unimportant to politics and to money-making. There is a political economy numerously linked with military order and decision. This triangle of power is now a structural fact."[4] This shift in power relations away from democratic balancing to one of political manipulation and corruption Mills attributed to the increased focus on global politics wrought by two world wars and the escalating Cold War. As a result, the United States did "not have suitable agencies and traditions for the democratic handling of international affairs."[5] Private actors thus stepped into the breach.

Mills described what is now called the military-industrial complex (MIC), a concept signifying a symbiotic relationship between actors responsible for managing war (the military, the Executive Branch, and Congress) and private, for-profit actors that produce goods and services for war (defense contractors). The relationship is defined by mutual interdependence between the private sector and government, where both sides benefit from and depend on the relationship for their survival. Perceived gains in security through the use or threat of military force are traded, using public resources, for substantial private-sector financial growth. Taken to the extreme, this can even be described as a "war for profit" theory; though at a more fundamental level, the existence of a military-industrial complex signals a weakened separation between the public and private sectors crucial for the efficacy of a democratic system of governance.

The origins of the MIC are illustrative of how well-intentioned public policy can have far-reaching and unintended consequences down the road. After the Great Depression, in the late 1930s, President Franklin D. Roosevelt struggled to rebuild the economy. Facing the possibility of a double-dip depression, Roosevelt aggressively pushed public-private partnerships as a means of reinvigorating the American economy. The idea was to leverage the federal government's considerable resources to support private enterprise directly without being seen as promoting overly centralized, governmental control of the free-market economy. Specifically, the government supported projects that were not sufficiently profitable for the private sector to invest in on its own but salient enough for the projected long-term economic growth to justify government resources. For example, the government established the Rural Electrification Administration (REA), a public-private partnership responsible for providing public utilities (electricity, telephone, water, sewage disposal) to rural parts of the US that were underserviced when left to the private sector alone. Clean energy is another area where government resources were needed to nudge companies towards innovation. Roosevelt (1933) described the Tennessee Valley Authority (TVA) as a "corporation clothed with the power of government but possessed of the flexibility and initiative of a private enterprise."

Incidentally, one public-private partnership is particularly relevant to the modern information and communication technology industry. At the center of Roosevelt's New Deal was the Social Security Act (SSA), a project that promised to provide American workers with long-term financial security in the face of economic uncertainty. The SSA presented unique challenges for the government at the time: How would the government keep track of salaries, wages, and job records for millions of workers? How would it monitor the fund and ensure proper distribution of resources once workers qualified for their Social Security allocation? This would require massive technological expertise and capacity. Roosevelt turned to the only American company capable of handling the responsibility: International Business Machines (IBM). The project was to be "the biggest accounting operation of all time. . . . [In] the process, IBM transformed from a company trying to survive into the global leader in information and technology."[6]

Public-private partnerships led the way for the American recovery, creating private-sector jobs while spurring innovation in infrastructure, energy, and other sectors. During World War II (1939–1945), public-private partnerships expanded into new economic sectors. Again, the partnerships focused on producing goods and services deemed essential for U.S. prosperity that private companies, acting alone, would not produce. During wartime this meant weaponry and other industrial goods to help the Allied war efforts. Government support for military industries grew as the United States formally entered the war in 1941. After the war ended, focus shifted to outcompeting America's newest geopolitical rival, the Soviet Union. The military-industrial establishment, a minor player in U.S. economics and politics prior to the Great Depression, was, by the Cold War, at the center of America politics. According to Mills, by the end of the 1950s "the seemingly permanent military threat place[d] a premium upon them . . ., and virtually all political and economic actions [were] now judged in terms of military definitions of reality."[7]

President Dwight D. Eisenhower referenced the rise of a military-industrial sector in his farewell address, expressing grave concern over the growing influence of military industries in political affairs:

> Our military organization today bears little relation to that known by any of my predecessors in peacetime, or indeed by the fighting men of World War II and Korea. . . . We have been compelled to create a permanent armaments industry of vast proportions. . . . We must not fail to comprehend its grave implications. . . . We must guard against the acquisition of unwarranted influence, whether sought or unsought, by the military-industrial complex.[8]

Despite the authority of his experience in the Oval Office and as an Army general, Eisenhower's message fell on deaf ears.

In a free-market economy, government interventions favoring particular technologies that would otherwise not be pursued by the private sector can backfire. If no broader demand emerges for the favored technology or related spinoffs, the company producing the technology either collapses or demands and depends on sustained government support for its survival. Government intervention into the market carries significant opportunity costs as well. By refocusing an industry's creative and scientific talent away from market demands toward government priorities, the private sector may be disadvantaged when confronted with foreign competition. As Adam Smith noted in *The Wealth of Nations*, "What is the species of domestic industry which his capital can employ, and of which the produce is likely to be of the greatest value, every individual, it is evident, can, in his local situation, judge much better than any statesman or lawgiver can do for him."[9] Public-private partnerships are necessarily distortions in the market and thus risk propping up certain economic sectors or technology firms that may be better served competing for resources in the private market.

In the case of the military-industrial complex, government intervention drove talent in the science and technology toward government projects, leaving purely civilian-oriented research and development to those with less training and experience. Eisenhower was especially concerned with the power the federal government possessed to shape research agendas, cautioning, "The prospect of domination of the nation's scholars by Federal employment, project allocations, and the power of money is ever present. ... [A] government contract becomes virtually a substitute for intellectual curiosity."[10] Despite sufficient warnings, government resources and priorities have driven research and development throughout the U.S. economy, in particular in the information and communication technology sector.

Separate from the growing influence of military actors and industry, the confluence of public- and private-sector responsibilities significantly altered society's expectations and demands from corporations and government alike. Sheldon Wolin suggests that public-private partnerships, and the blurring of responsibilities that necessarily result, are responsible for the rapid rise of corporate influence in modern politics: "The privatization of public services and functions manifests the steady evolution of corporate power into a political form, into an integral, even dominant partner with the state."[11]

Worse, by creating a dependence on the private sector for military goods—products that are necessary for any state's survival—a government actually becomes compliant to private interests. According to Walter Adams, not long after Eisenhower left office the power dynamics had already shifted in favor of private interests over public responsibilities: "Lacking any viable in-house capabilities, competitive yardsticks, or the potential for institutional competition, the government becomes—in the extreme—subservient to the private and special interests whose entrenched power bears the governmental seal."[12]

The comparison to the military-industrial complex is helpful not only in placing current public-private partnerships into a broader historical context but also as a means of predicting the likely trajectory and result of an information-industrial complex in years ahead. In the United States, since 2001, the vast majority of resources for defense and intelligence are allocated to private, for-profit corporations, known as defense contractors. The consequences of such a shift have been profound at the surface level of operations. According to former CIA consultant Chalmers Johnson:

> The end result is . . . a government hollowed out in terms of military and intelligence functions . . . The costs—both financial and personal—of privatization in the armed services and the intelligence community far exceed any alleged savings, and some of the consequences for democratic governance may prove irreparable. These consequences include: the sacrifice of professionalism within our intelligence services; the readiness of private contractors to engage in illegal activities without compunction and with impunity; the inability of Congress or citizens to carry out effective oversight of privately-managed intelligence activities because of the wall of secrecy that surrounds them; and, perhaps most serious of all, the loss of the most valuable asset any intelligence organization possesses—its institutional memory.[13]

Johnson calls attention to the long-term consequences of outsourcing government responsibilities to the private sector. Juxtaposed to FDR's economic success in the 1940s, there is evidence that such partnerships hurt the private sector's competitiveness over the long term, threatening the vitality of the sector itself, as well as the services and products they provide.

The Origins of the Information-Industrial Complex

Communications and information-technology sector growth radically accelerated as the result of government investments in related research and development in the second half of the twentieth century. In response to the Soviet launching of the Sputnik satellite, the DOD established the Advanced Research Projects Agency (ARPA) in 1958 in an effort to ensure future U.S. technological superiority. ARPA's mission, backed by a $3.2 billion annual budget, was to pursue "imaginative and innovative research and development projects having significant potential for both military and commercial (dual-use) applications . . . and support and stimulate a national technology base that serves both civilian and military purposes through technology sharing and collaboration with broad industry segments."[14] ARPA, renamed DARPA (Defense Advanced Research Projects Agency) in 1996, supports many modern-day iterations of FDR's public-private partnerships.[15]

The internet and the information industries that drive—and thrive on—its existence are the result of an ARPA-funded, military-industrial-academic collaboration. The RAND Corporation, launched with capital from the U.S. Army Air Force in 1948, laid the groundwork for modern packet switching in 1960.[16] The world's first operational connectionless packet-switching network—the foundation of the today's internet—was the 1970 Advanced Research Projects Agency Network (ARPANET).[17] DARPA created ARPANET to better connect universities and research laboratories collaborating on various DOD projects, though it wasn't long before ARPANET was adapted for private and nonmilitary use as well. ARPANET's success sparked investments in NSFNET, a civilian spinoff of the DOD's electronic network, which was also foundational in sparking greater interest in the creation of "the information superhighway."[18]

The ARPANET initiative supported research at universities across the country, including UCLA, where Vint Cerf worked on improving the network while completing his PhD in computer science. After graduation, Cerf went to Stanford University and, along with Robert Kahn, designed TCP/IP for the Department of Defense. Short for *Transmission Control Protocol* (TCP) and *Internet Protocol* (IP), TCP/IP was adopted by the DOD in 1982 as the standard for all military computer networks. The private sector followed in 1984. After designing TCP/IP, Cerf went on to work for DARPA, where he developed early iterations of e-mail, an invention he would take to the private sector as vice president of MCI Digital Information Services.[19] Cerf would go on to help found and serve on the board (as chairman) of ICANN, which manages internet names and addresses.[20] In short, the foundational theory, technology, infrastructure, application, and governance of the internet are each directly related to the DOD's research program.

Inspired by a report summarizing ARPANET and NSFNET's limitations and potential, Senator Al Gore proposed the High-Performance Computing and Communication Act (HPCA) in 1989.[21] Introducing the bill—later called the Gore Bill—to Congress, Gore explained its significance for the future of American hegemony: "The nation which most completely assimilates high-performance computing into its economy will very likely emerge as the dominant intellectual, economic, and technological force in the next century."[22] Enacted in December 1991, HPCA allocated $495 million for the creation of a high-speed fiber-optic computer network called the National Information Infrastructure (NII) and established the National Research and Education Network (NREN). Equally important was HPCA's mandate to "promote greater collaboration among government, federal laboratories, industry, high-performance computing centers, and universities" in high-performance computing.[23] One HPCA-funded partnership was the National Center for Supercomputing Applications at the University of Illinois, where to-be Netscape founder Marc Andreessen created the Mosaic Web browser, the technological springboard to the commercial internet. Andreessen later mused, "If it had been left to private industry, it wouldn't have happened."[24]

One year later, Clinton and Gore won the 1992 presidential election in part due to a pledge to improve government support for an ailing private sector weakened from increased international competition. During the election, Clinton and Gore won the support of conservative business leaders by promising to shift government research and development funding away from weapons and energy—relics of the Cold War—toward consumer- and industry-related computer research and development.[25] After the 1992 general election, Clinton's transition team announced its High Performance Computing and Communications Initiative (HPCCI). HPCCI built on the Gore Bill's initial investment by committing increased federal resources to support the information and technology sector, promising the broad dissemination and government application of technological advances, and substantive gains in U.S. competitiveness. By 1995, the initiative had a $1.1 billion annual budget and served as the rubric through which virtually all government research in information technology was conducted.

HPCCI was overseen by the President's Council of Advisors on Science and Technology (PCAST), a team of experts from academia and the private sector. Members included the senior vice president of AT&T Bell Laboratories, the vice president of Ford Motor Company, and the chairman of the board of Hewlett-Packard. Eager to move beyond previous eras of assertive government regulation in the telecommunications sector, the advisors conditioned HPCCI's success on the government's willingness to engage in cooperative partnerships with the private sector. In its preliminary assessment of the initiative, issued in December 1992, the council recommended that "the dialogue between the HPCC program and industry be continued and strengthened as the program evolves." The report concluded with praise, promising that, with sufficient support for public-private partnerships, HPCCI would foster the "transformation of our society through information technologies."[26]

HPCCI reflected a shift in the government research and development away from a Cold War, industrial model that had poorly served the private and civilian sectors for most of the 1980s. The Cold War model had become highly specialized, often supporting military research with little spin-off potential and with relevance only to a selective group among the private sector. As a result, according to government-relations specialist Daniel F. Burton Jr., "for at least half a century the government had indeed been picking winners and losers."[27] The Clinton administration shifted its emphasis toward technology policy, including precompetitive and generic research whose utility would be felt across industries. Precompetitive and generic research, they believed, was critical for improving and standardizing ongoing technological advances that could then be integrated into specific industrial sectors for product-based research and development. This shift was significant for the domestic industries and for trade policy as well. According to Burton, "While industrial policy is often associated with a protectionist trade agenda that shields weak domestic industries from overseas competitors, technology policy is not. . . . [T]echnology policy suggests an approach of ensuring greater openness in overseas markets."[28] Unlike investing in proprietary military technologies, the aim of this new policy was to develop a communication and information technology industry able to export its products to markets around the world.

The administration's focus on developing information superhighways was driven by raw economic logic. In 1992, the information technology sector generated more than $700 billion in revenue. Gore addressed the National Press Club in 1993, noting, "Over half of the U.S. workforce is now in information-based jobs. The telecommunications and information sector of the U.S. economy accounts for more than 12 percent of the GDP. And it's growing faster than any other sector of our economy."[29] Similarly, in 1995 FCC Chairman Reed Hundt predicted that by 2000 the information sector would be the world's single largest industry, with revenues exceeding $2 trillion.[30]

Interest in an information technology revolution did not simply benefit the IT sector. Rather, the Clinton administration foresaw the effect these technologies would have throughout society and eventually on the global economy. According to Gore, "The biggest impact may be in other industrial sectors where those technologies will help American companies compete better and smarter in the global economy. Today, more than ever, businesses run on information. A fast, flexible information network is as essential to manufacturing as steel and plastic."[31]

In 1993, HPCA and HPPCI were synthesized in the administration's flagship economic policy initiative, *Technology for America's Economic Growth, A New Direction to Build Economic Strength.* In it, Clinton and Gore outlined the need to supplement the government's traditional science policy and support for foundational and basic research with a technology policy to strengthen U.S. competitiveness. Specifically, they pledged to establish a 50/50 balance in defense and nondefense federal research and development, a reallocation worth approximately $8 billion to the technology sector. The initiative also pledged to push America's most advanced federal research laboratories (Los Alamos National Laboratory and Sandia National Laboratory, for example) into commercial partnerships, requiring that between 10 percent and 20 percent of their budgets be allocated for new joint ventures with the private sector.[32]

Building on HPCA's initial investment in a National Information Infrastructure, the new policy established "an agenda for a public-private partnership to construct an advanced NII to benefit all Americans." Specifically, the administration outlined five principles that would serve as the foundation upon which future information technology policy would be based: encourage private sector investment; promote competition; provide open access to the network for all information providers and users; ensure universal service; and create a flexible regulatory environment that can keep pace with rapid technological and market changes.[33]

ARPA adjusted its focus quickly, investing heavily in information and communication technology (ICT) research with potential dual-use capacities. Testifying before Congress in 1993, ARPA director Gary L. Denman noted the growing interdependence between economic growth and national security,

> ARPA will seek maximum national benefit from our technology investments. . . . Our mission is to transition to a *growing, integrated, national industrial capability* which provides the most advanced, affordable, military systems and the most competitive commercial products. We are attempting to do two mutually supportive things simultaneously: stimulate economic growth and bring defense and commercial industries closer together.[34]

That same year, the Clinton administration announced the Defense Reinvestment and Conversion Initiative (DRCI), a $24 billion program to invest in converting the U.S. economy away from Cold War military missions toward new and emerging technologies that would drive the country's global economic expansion. A key component of the DRCI was the Technology Reinvestment Project (TRP), which promised direct federal support for commercial technology through industry consortia and other collaborative activities. According to President Clinton, TRP "rejects the reliance on defense spin-offs that has been the core of the Federal Government's technology strategy . . . [and] recognizes that in the years ahead a growing number of defense needs can be met most efficiently by commercial products and commercial technology."[35]

ARPA was asked to lead TRP, which received more than three thousand proposals requesting more than $9 billion in the first year alone. Reacting to the burst of commercial interest in the initiative, the Clinton administration proclaimed, "There appears to be no shortage of good ideas for turning swords into plowshares and bullets into bullet-trains. That means jobs for factory workers, engineers, and scientists alike, as we redeploy the people, skills and technologies that made our defense industry second to none to the commercial industries we'll need to compete in a global economy."[36] Funding for TRP increased throughout the Clinton administration until 1997.[37]

The End of "Adversarial" Regulation

In January 1994, UCLA—one of the four universities where ARPANET was first tested and developed—hosted the Superhighway Summit. The event was the first public conference that brought together all major industry, government, and academic leaders in the field and "began the national dialogue about the Information Superhighway and its implications."[38]

The summit's goal was to help further public-private partnerships on a large scale. It featured speakers from government (U.S. vice president and the FCC chairman), executives from media conglomerates (Walt Disney Company, News Corporation, Sony, and Time Warner), content providers (Walt Disney Studios, Turner Entertainment Group, MTV, BET, Discovery Communications, Nickelodeon, QVC, ABC Television, and Fox), telecommunications (Bell Atlantic, Pacific Bell, and AT&T), internet service provider America Online, cable providers (Comcast and Tele-Communications Inc.), gaming developer Sega, computer technology experts (Apple, Microsoft, Oracle, IBM, Hewlett-Packard, Silicon Graphics, and the Institute of the Future), advertising agencies (William Morris Agency, Ted Bates Advertising, and Quincy Jones/David Salzman Productions), and the financial sector (Bear Sterns). The speakers represented "the highest and most prestigious executives in the world of communication," or as FCC chairman Reed Hundt proclaimed, "the Edisons and Fords of the 21st century."[39] Brian Lowry, writing for the trade paper *Daily Variety,* noted the group's "joint assets could roughly finance an attempted acquisition of most of the Midwest."[40]

The Clinton administration viewed the summit as an opportunity to reach out to media and entertainment industry leaders and encourage their support for regulatory reform and the NII. In his keynote address, Gore outlined the significance of technological changes on industry and government alike:

> Our current information industries—cable, local telephone, long distance telephone, television, film, computers, and others—seem headed for a Big Crunch/Big Bang of their own. The space between these diverse functions is rapidly shrinking—between computers and televisions, for example, or between interactive communication and video. But after the next Big Bang, in the ensuing expansion of the information business, the new marketplace will no longer be divided along current sectoral lines. There may not be cable companies or phone companies or computer companies, as such. Everyone will be in the bit business. . . . Just as communications industries are moving to the unified information marketplace of the future, so must we move from the traditional adversarial relationship between business and government to *a more productive relationship based on consensus.*[41]

Gore was keen to contrast his voluntary mechanism to an "old, adversarial approach" to regulation.[42] Acknowledging the growing role of information services and providers in the global economy, Gore signaled a new era of regulation based on consensual relations between government and industry. Hundt concurred, outlining the FCC's plan to reinvent itself and assist the private sector's efforts: "Our job, as the networks spread like kudzu down the channels of commerce, is to make sure that unfair anti-competitive bottlenecks don't choke off the natural growth driven by market forces."[43]

Central to regulatory reform was a removal of cross-media ownership regulations that had previously prevented telephone, cable, and newspaper owners from owning and investing in any of the other media industries. As the digitization of information increasingly challenged those "sectoral" lines, Gore argued that it was time to "clear from the road the wreckage of outdated regulations and allow a free-flowing traffic of ideas and commerce."[44] This shift from adversarial to cooperative and laissez-faire rule making is a keystone moment in the rise of the information-industrial complex.

Shortly after the *Superhighway Summit* in Los Angeles, Gore took his message to the international community. In a keynote address to the ITU's first World Telecommunication Development Conference, the vice president offered a vision for the Global Information Infrastructure (GII): "Let us build a community in which people of neighboring countries view each other not as potential enemies, but as potential partners, as members of the same family in the vast, increasingly interconnected human family."[45] Gore called on governments to prioritize the exact five policy issues—encouraging private sector investment; promoting competition; providing open access to the network for all information providers and users; creating flexible regulatory environment that can keep pace with rapid technological and market changes; and ensuring universal service—that he and President Clinton had outlined for domestic information technology policy agenda and National Information Infrastructure just months earlier. Put simply, Gore called for the world to adopt America's model of telecommunications regulation, and his proposal was the basis for the ITU's 1994 "Buenos Aires Declaration on Global Telecommunication Development for the 21st Century," leading the way for the private-sector-driven approach to internet governance.

U.S. government support was crucial for the creation, adoption, and structure of the internet, as well as the integration of information technologies into the global economy. According to Ivan E. Sutherland, vice president of Sun Microsystems Laboratories, "The current health of [the information technology] industry has been made possible by decades of consistent federal investment in information technology research. Federally funded research, which has provided many of the innovative ideas and trained people that have ultimately spelled commercial success for companies in their field, cannot be replaced by industry research because of a different timeline and focus."[46]

While improving efficiency and productivity, among many other benefits, the Clinton administration's push to make an industry-leading IT sector had clear international implications as it quickly expanded trade with countries around the world. In 2010 the Information Technology and Innovation Foundation (ITIF) estimated that the commercial internet had made the U.S. economy at least $2 trillion larger in terms of annual GDP than it would otherwise have been, accounting for approximately 30 percent of U.S. economic growth.[47]

Although American growth led the world's economy for much of the 1990s, in part due to the success of the information technology sector, HPPCI's direct effect on the industry is difficult to quantify. In early 2000 the economy tumbled as the dot-com bubble burst. As technology stocks plummeted, venture capital fled Silicon Valley, leaving few resources for new startup companies. While many people were dismayed by how quickly the sector had fallen apart, one investor saw the bust as an opportunity: the Central Intelligence Agency.

The CIA to the Rescue

In 1999 the U.S. government announced the creation of In-Q-It, a corporation that would "ensure that the CIA remains at the cutting edge of information technology advances and capabilities."[48] In 2000 the corporation was renamed In-Q-Tel in homage to the infamous James Bond technology specialist, Agent Q, and in keeping with the agency's mission—intelligence, or *intel* for short. Estimates place the CIA's investment in the privately held, non-profit corporation between $30 million and $50 million annually. Since inception, In-Q-Tel has financed more than 180 firms and provided at least 280 technology solutions to the intelligence community.[49]

In-Q-Tel's origins can be traced back to former CIA Deputy Director for Science and Technology Ruth David and her deputy, Joanne Isham. David and Isham were the first senior agency officials to champion the information revolution and push the CIA to forge new partnerships with the private sector. George Tenet, the director of Central Intelligence, agreed, naming technology as central to the agency's future in his 1998 Strategic Direction Initiative. Tenet saw a direct link between investments in emerging information technologies and improving the CIA's information-gathering and analysis capabilities. He organized a team of CIA analysts with knowledge of the sector and "entrepreneurial spirit" and sent them to Silicon Valley to network and develop a plan to improve the agency's technology research and development. After meetings with venture capitalists, members of Congress, law firms (the firm Arnold and Porter was contracted to help with the launch), and private-sector consultants, the CIA launched its own not-for-profit venture-capital firm. Former Lockheed-Martin CEO Norman Augustine was appointed as its first CEO. By February 1999 the corporation was established as a legal entity, and in March it received its first contract (funding) from the agency. In-Q-Tel was officially "charged with accessing information technology (IT) expertise and technology wherever it exists and bringing it to bear on the information management challenges facing the Agency."[50]

In-Q-Tel represented an effort to tap into the explosive innovation and creativity in the IT sector, largely concentrated in Silicon Valley. The dot-com bubble, fostered in large part by the excitement surrounding the rapid rise of the commercial internet following the introduction of the more user-friendly World Wide Web in 1994, had generated tremendous private-sector investment, talent, and innovation. The CIA—whose mission centered primarily on gathering and processing certain types of information, or *intelligence*—recognized the information-technology boom as having transcendent consequences for its ability to fulfill its mission. Given the incentives in place in the private sector, the CIA could not compete for talent, and its decades-old bureaucracy made in-house research slow and averse to creative innovation. Certain that it was falling behind in technological innovation, the CIA took a new route and decided not simply to become a buyer of IT but also to be an angel investor. According to Rick E. Yannuzzi, In-Q-Tel's first director of business operations, the initiative was the ideal public-private partnership: "The CIA had to offer Silicon Valley something of value, a business model that the Valley understood; a model that provides those who joined hands with In-Q-Tel the opportunity to commercialize their innovations. In addition, In-Q-Tel's partner companies would also gain another valuable asset, access to a set of very difficult CIA problems that could become market drivers."[51]

Technically independent from the CIA's day-to-day operations, In-Q-Tel is organized like many investment corporations: it has "offices in two locations—Washington, DC, and Menlo Park, CA—employs a small professional staff and a smaller group of business and technology consultants," and is overseen by a board of directors. Its mission is "to foster the development of new and emerging information technologies and pursue research and development that produce solutions to some of the most difficult IT problems facing the CIA."[52] In order to achieve its mission, "the Corporation will network extensively with those in industry, the venture capital community, academia, and any others who are at the forefront of IT innovation."[53] In-Q-Tel promised to be a more hands-on investor compared with other venture-capital firms, offering direct, systematic suggestions on product development from agents and analysts in the field. According to Richard Shaw, CEO of ArcSight (one of In-Q-Tel's early investments), "They are by far the most proactive, helpful investor we have."[54]

The decision to create In-Q-Tel was a significant departure from previous government efforts to tap into private-sector ingenuity. Rather than rely on the standard grants-and-contracts process, as DARPA does, In-Q-Tel can directly invest, establish joint ventures, fund grants, sponsor open competitions, and award sole source contracts, all independent of CIA authorization or approval. According to Yannuzzi, "In-Q-Tel represents a different approach to government R&D. It moves away from the more traditional government project office model in which the program is managed by the government. Instead, the Agency has invested much of the decisionmaking in the Corporation."[55]

Two overarching criteria guide In-Q-Tel investments: the work must be unclassified and have some commercial potential. As the ICT sector rebounded, the CIA saw both similarities and gaps between its technological needs and those of the private sector. In-Q-Tel's purpose was to "bridge the gap between the technology needs of the intelligence community and new advances in commercial technology," focusing on new and emerging commercial technologies that could potentially give the CIA and broader U.S. intelligence community "mission-advantage."[56] Specifically, In-Q-Tel focused on investing in technologies in four primary areas: information security (for example, hardening and intrusion detection; monitoring and profiling of information use and misuse; network and data protection), use of the internet (such as secure receipt of information, non-observable surfing, authentication, content verification, and hacker resistance), distributed architectures (methods to interface with custom or legacy systems, mechanisms to allow dissimilar applications to interact, automatic handling of archived data, and connectivity across a wide range of environments), and knowledge generation (geospatial and multimedia data fusion or integration, and computer forensics).

In-Q-Tel's presence is well known in the ICT private sector. According to the *Washington Post*'s industry reporter Terrance O'Hara, "Virtually any U.S. entrepreneur, inventor or research scientist working on ways to analyze data has probably received a phone call from In-Q-Tel."[57] This is helped, in part, by the extensive connections between its board of directors and the commercial sector. For example, before becoming its current CEO, Chris Darby was vice president at Intel, the world's largest and most highly valued semiconductor computer chip maker.[58]

Despite its connections to the intelligence community, In-Q-Tel is well regarded in the private sector. According to venture capitalist Tim Oren, "It's a chance to look at companies which have already had their technology and capabilities vetted by one of toughest and most sophisticated customers in the world, and which are already receiving cash flow as a result."[59] In-Q-Tel is also seen as a means though which smaller ICT companies can access large-scale government contracts. According to Shaw of ArcSight, "They introduced us and spread our name around the government. I'd say In-Q-Tel is as good or better than any other [venture capital firm] I've worked with."[60]

As a result, In-Q-Tel has emerged as a trendsetter in the ICT venture-capital sector. Other venture-capital firms perceive the government's backing of particular technologies or companies as a strong indicator of their long-term profitability and success. In 2012 every dollar In-Q-Tel invested in the private sector generated nine additional dollars from other investors, which is to say, if In-Q-Tel invests $2 million in a startup, investors will, on average, invest an additional $18 million.[61] In-Q-Tel estimates that its investments are responsible for the creation of ten thousand private-sector jobs since 1999.[62]

The CIA considers In-Q-Tel a tremendous success. Other agencies interested in tapping into and pushing innovative research have used it as a model for their own research and development. In 2002 the Army launched OnPoint Technologies, explicitly modeled after In-Q-Tel. Similarly impressed with the CIA's entrepreneurial approach, NASA launched Red Planet Capital to invest its resources in promising but underfinanced private-sector companies.[63] The DOD also followed, launching the Defense Venture Catalyst Initiative (DeVenCI), a program that connects private-sector venture capitalists, cutting-edge research projects, and military procurement officials.[64] When asked to rate In-Q-Tel's success, former CIA executive director A. B. Krongard said, "On a scale from one to 10, I would give it an 11. . . . It's done so well even Congress is taking credit for it."[65]

In addition to helping to keep the intelligence community ahead of the curve with cutting-edge technology, In-Q-Tel has been remarkably profitable by venture-capital firm standards. As of 2005, with the industry still recovering from the collapse of the dot-com bubble, In-Q-Tel's internal rate of return—the standard measurement for venture-capital funds—was 26 percent. Industry research shows that the average venture fund return on investment from 2002 to 2012 was just 6.1 percent.[66] Moreover, it is likely that some of In-Q-Tel's most lucrative investments haven not yet been fully commercialized, and its revenue stream is likely to continue to grow.[67]

Major companies in the IT sector have acquired startups that received support from In-Q-Tel. In 2005, In-Q-Tel sold 6,425 shares of Google Inc., worth $2.6 million after Google's initial public offering. In-Q-Tel came to own the stock as a result of Google's acquisition of Keyhole, an In-Q-Tel-funded satellite mapping software that became the backbone of Google Maps and Google Earth.[68] Keyhole's EarthSystem allowed users to access large databases of satellite imagery and aerial photography to produce interactive digital models. During the U.S. wars in Afghanistan and Iraq, television networks relied on Keyhole, using publicly available satellite images, to produce virtual flyovers of remote areas of the theater of operations. The Pentagon also relies on Keyhole, using proprietary satellite imaging to support its missions around the world.[69] Google Earth is now the industry-leading platform for visual, 3-D mapping, used extensively in both the commercial sector and by the U.S. military.[70] Google Maps is now used by one billion people, or about half of the world's internet users.[71]

NetApp Inc., the world's second-largest data-storage and security firm, acquired CIA-backed Decru in 2005 to help launch its Cloud-computing data security system.[72] Decru's security systems helped establish industry standards for information security in banking, healthcare, software, and government services.[73]

IBM has also benefited from In-Q-Tel's investments. In 2006, IBM acquired Systems Research Development (SRD), a company that makes data-mining software that enables law enforcement officials to identify significant links between individuals by combing through public and private databases.[74] SRD's software, DB2 Anonymous Resolution, allows government law enforcement agencies and corporations to share information on customers or citizens without revealing their individual identities. The software helps analyze large and diverse data collected across several public and private platforms without violating privacy laws or user agreements.[75]

Intelliseek Inc., another In-Q-Tel partner, has become an industry leader in customized websearch technologies. By providing more refined search possibilities by connecting to user's social media profiles, Intelliseek was able to measure consumer reactions to products and content in real time. In 2006, Nielsen BuzzMetrics Inc., a subsidiary of AC Neilson, bought the company and re-launched it as NM Incite, "the new global standard for measuring and understanding word-of-mouth behavior and influence." Clients, who paid handsomely to access Intelliseek's consumer insights, included Canon, Comcast, Ford, General Motors, HBO, Kraft, Microsoft, Nokia, P&G, Showtime, Sony, Target, Toyota, fourteen of the top fifteen pharmaceutical companies and eight television networks.[76]

In-Q-Tel also invested early in SafeWeb Inc., a free service that allowed internet users to bypass Web censorship by governments and corporations. Using high-level encryption and a global network of proxy servers, its software promised anonymous Web browsing to users as early as 2000. SafeWeb was acquired by Symantec and re-launched as Norton Safe Web in 2008. Norton Safe Web is now an industry-leading application, integrated into current versions of Norton Internet Security and Norton 360, and collectively considered the best suite of consumer internet security products in the world.[77] In 2002, In-Q-Tel invested in Tacit Knowledge Systems, a company that developed employee-monitoring software to measure productivity and identify different types of expertise. Tacit also developed an automated

Table 2.1: Select List of Acquisitions of In-Q-Tel's Investees

Investee	Year of Investment	Acquired by
Silver Tail Systems	2010	EMC
Fetch Technologies	2009	Connotate
Geosemble	2009	TerraGo
Perceptive Pixel	2009	Microsoft
SignaCert	2009	Harris
ThingMagic	2008	Trimble
Asankya	2007	EMC
Forterra Systems	2007	SAIC
FortiusOne	2007	ERS
Pixim	2007	Sony
Polychromix	2007	Thermo Fisher Scientific
COPAN Systems	2006	SGI
Initiate Systems	2006	IBM
StreamBase Systems	2006	TIBCO Software
Cassatt	2005	CA Technologies
Ember Corporation	2005	Silicon Labs
Network Chemistry	2005	Aruba Networks
Nextreme Thermal Solutions	2005	Laird PLC
@Last Software	2004	Google
BBN Technologies	2004	Raytheon
Paratek	2004	Research in Motion (RIM)
Spotfire	2004	TIBCO
Visual Sciences	2004	Adobe Systems
Authentica	2003	EMC
Dust	2003	Linear Technology
Endeca Technologies	2003	Oracle
Inxight	2003	SAP
Keyhole	2003	Google
Language Weaver	2003	SDL
ArcSight	2002	Hewlett-Packard
MetaCarta	2002	Nokia
Rosum	2002	Liberty Media
Decru	2001	Network Appliance
Inktomi	2001	Yahoo!
Intelliseek	2001	Nielsen
Mohomine	2001	Kofax (DICOM Group)
SRD	2001	IBM
Stratify	2001	Iron Mountain
Tacit Knowledge	2001	Oracle
SafeWeb	2000	Symantec
Soflinx	2000	Lockheed Martin

management system, whereby software can route a problem or question to the best person available. Tacit Software was acquired by Oracle in 2008 and now is a main component of its Oracle Beehive collaboration platform. In 2010, Hewlett-Packard bought ArcSight, another In-Q-Tel startup that relied on CIA resources for its field research and its early growth.[78]

In-Q-Tel succeeded by taking advantage of a time when Silicon Valley was on crutches and investors were skittish of losing billions more in a young, unpredictable industry. While the amount of its financial contribution is relatively small, In-Q-Tel's investments signaled the likelihood of profitability and thus became a de facto leader among technology venture capitalists. Its ability to connect technology companies with real-world problems—via its massive intelligence apparatus—enabled investees to benefit from field research that would otherwise be extraordinarily costly and, in many cases, impossible. Most important, with several other government agencies modeling investment firms after In-Q-Tel, and with its ability to leverage massive amounts of private capital, the firm represents a previously unimaginable government intervention into the marketplace.

9/11 and the Rise of Information Assurance

The events that took place on September 11, 2001, sparked an urgent government interest in the information sector, telecommunications in particular. Immediately after the terrorist attacks, the Bush administration and its intelligence agencies went into hyperdrive, attempting to vacuum up any and all information that could potentially help prevent a future attack. Without formally announcing changes in policy, the administration authorized greater surveillance of Americans due to the perceived magnitude of the threat of terrorism on American soil.[79]

At first, a primary concern was identifying and tracking suspects participating in or helping facilitate an operation within the United States. The National Security Agency (NSA), the primary agency responsible for collecting signals intelligence within the United States, reached out to the private sector, requesting assistance in accessing any communications that could be related to future attacks. Lacking a sophisticated profile of likely terrorists or operations facilitators, the NSA pursued a content-based, metadata approach to systematically collect and analyze communications with foreign actors and entities.[80] Virtually all communications infrastructure in the United States is owned and operated in the private sector; thus, this effort called for a new and robust public-private partnership.

Days after 9/11, the NSA reached out to telecommunications providers with an urgent pitch: "National security is at risk, and we need your help to protect the country from attacks."[81] NSA asked telecommunications providers to share call records as well as real-time data regarding who was calling whom. In an effort to work within the parameters of existing privacy laws, the NSA asked that the telecoms hand over the outgoing and incoming phone numbers for every call made on each network rather than personally identifiable customer information. This minor technicality allowed the private sector to cooperate without fear of violating user agreements and the 1934 Communications Act while also giving the NSA substantial data to mine for analysis. While the telecommunications companies technically protected their customers' identities, NSA's extensive databases could easily track down the name, address, and personal information attached to nearly every phone number dialed in the world, thus making the technical protection of privacy functionally meaningless.

AT&T, Verizon, and BellSouth—at that time the three largest telecommunications companies in the United States—all agreed to share calling data with the NSA. Collectively, the three networks covered 200 million Americans, or the vast majority of wired and wireless telephony in the United States. Qwest was the only major telecommunications operator that refused, citing fear of long-term legal and financial consequences. Faced with noncooperation, the NSA "suggested that Qwest's foot-dragging might affect its ability to get future classified work with the government."[82]

Starting in 2002 AT&T—a descendent of the iconic American Telephone and Telegraph Company—agreed to provide the NSA with complete access to its global telecommunications infrastructure by redirecting user internet traffic to data-mining equipment installed in each of its switching centers. According to retired AT&T technician Mark Klein, "Fiber optic cables from the secret room were tapping into the Worldnet [AT&T's internet service] circuits by splitting off a portion of the light signal."[83] AT&T was also providing NSA access to traffic from other domestic and international providers who were connecting the Worldnet in one way or another.

Monitoring and mining internet usage data is not an easy task, even with the cooperation of major telecommunications and internet service providers. The NSA-AT&T agreement relied on the installation of the *Narus STA 6400*, a stand-alone data traffic analyzer that "collect[s] network and customer usage information in real time directly from the message. . . . These analyzers sit on the message pipe into the ISP cloud rather than tap into each router or ISP device."[84] Narus boasts that its Semantic Traffic Analysis technology "captures comprehensive customer usage data . . . and transforms it into actionable information. . . . It is the only technology that provides complete visibility for all internet applications," including email attachments, VoIP, complete rendering of Web pages and file transfer protocols.[85] After an analysis of the results, former FCC technology advisor J. Scott Marcus wrote, "AT&T has constructed an extensive—and expensive—collection of infrastructure that collectively has all the capability necessary to conduct large-scale covert gathering of (internet protocol)-based communications information, not only for communications to overseas locations, but for purely domestic communications as well."[86] As a result of the agreement, NSA could monitor and record the majority of the world's internet communications.[87]

While much of the public spotlight centered on AT&T, a number of ICT companies profited handsomely from government contracts, especially those in the intelligence arena. Oracle Corporation, a technology company specializing in database and enterprise software products (and more recently also offering hardware), is seen by many as a gem of Silicon Valley. Oracle has over 122,000 employees and generates $37.1 billion in revenue annually. Twenty-three percent of Oracle's total revenue, or $8.5 billion, comes from government-related contracts.[88] The company is named after a CIA project that Larry Ellison, Oracle's CEO, and his co-founders worked on prior to its launch. Its first contract was with the CIA. Two months after 9/11, Oracle hired David Carey, former executive director of the CIA, to head its new Information Assurance Center, which was founded to design homeland-security and disaster-recovery solutions and then market them to the federal government.[89] According to industry insider Mike Wilson, "Oracle wouldn't exist if it weren't for government contracts."[90] Government contracts are also responsible for 22 percent of Cisco Systems business, or $10.69 billion of its $48.6 billion 2013 revenue.[91]

Still roiling from the bust of the dot-com boom, Silicon Valley was saved by the rapid investment of government money post-9/11. In 2003, Goldman Sachs predicted that private sector IT spending would decline by 1 percent, far below the 10 percent to 12 percent growth the industry had grown accustomed to during the 1990s. Yet government spending on information technology was skyrocketing. Before 2001, government spending in IT was responsible for 20 percent of the $150 billion/year industry. In 2003 alone, faced with massive restructuring and the creation of the Department of Homeland Security, the government increased its IT expenditures by 9.7 percent to $53.1

billion, or one-third of the entire IT industry's business. Tom Gann, industry insider, noted: "That $53 billion will only continue to expand as technology continues to tackle cross-agency [government] projects."[92]

While few in the industry said so publicly, the new Homeland Security initiative helped pull the information technology industry out of latent recession. Oracle's David Carey was among the few willing to speak frankly about the effect of 9/11 on the IT industries: "September 11 made business a bit easier. Previous[ly], you pretty much had to hype the threat and the problem."[93] In addition to the initial $53 billion in government business in 2003, the Department of Homeland Security spent an additional $37.7 billion for IT to help integrate and streamline its workforce in the subsequent three years.[94] So much government money was being invested in information security and networking that some of the industry's largest companies formed their own homeland security offices, tasked to meet the needs of intelligence and homeland security agencies in order to accrue large government contracts. Industry expert Tom Gann explained the magnitude of the government's investment by adding some historical context: "The last time something of this magnitude was done was 40 years ago, when the Department of Defense was formed."[95]

Conclusion

This chapter outlines the emergence of an information-industrial complex in the United States, tracking the rise of computer and information technology and the modern knowledge economy. We have identified a number of policy mechanisms through which government actors—ranging from the executive and legislative branches to the intelligence community—subsidized, partnered, and otherwise cleared the way for rapid innovation and growth in the information sector. Focused on sector expansion at all costs, policy mechanisms deviated from the traditional regulatory role, rarely monitoring the private sector to ensure compliance with public interest laws. The growth in America's IT sector also created a codependent relationship, whereby government investment was critical to the industry's growth, and the industry's expertise was considered essential for the government's survival. This symbiotic relationship, conceptualized as a "silicon triangle" connecting government, Silicon Valley, and the broader U.S. economy, is similar in structure and scope to the military-industrial complex that emerged during World War II. As the military-industrial complex has shown, a symbiotic relationship between industry and government can have long-term, negative economic and political consequences. This analogue is instructive, not merely to put the information-industrial complex in context but also to foreshadow the likely consequences of continued industry-government codependence: weakened oversight, accountability, and industry vitality and competitiveness.

This historical outline is helpful in thinking through just how NSA's PRISM surveillance program, which depends on extensive public-private collaboration, came to be. PRISM and other government surveillance programs are discussed in greater detail in chapter 7. It also foreshadows a trend that is apparent throughout the book: the re-nationalization of transnational corporations. Discussing the rise of powerful technology companies like Cisco, Oracle, and Ericsson, Google's Eric Schmidt and Jared Cohen foresee "a time when [companies'] commercial and national interests align and contrast with China—say, over the abuse of their products by an authoritarian state—and they will coordinate their efforts with their governments on both diplomatic and technical levels."[96] According to Schmidt and Cohen, competition between private-sector companies from different countries is, thus, inherently geopolitical: "Where Huawei gains market share, the influence and reach of China grow as well." Such trends towards re-nationalization of key elements of the private sector seem natural, given the integral role of information-technology companies in national economies and security.

Finally, connecting to political economy theory, this chapter highlights two critical ways in which digital information is commodified. First, the history of the development and growth of the internet and related digital technologies is one of converting use value into exchange value. For example, ARPANET, developed by DARPA for the purpose of enhancing the speed and efficacy of scientific collaboration, was spun off into the private sector to create a large-scale marketplace for economic activity. Second, in the post-9/11 environment, digital information is commodified through its securitization. Information that was primarily of use value, including phone-call and internet-use metadata, was transformed into having exchange value through the lens of security. In the view of some in the intelligence community, that metadata could be analyzed to track down criminal and terrorist activities. This type of historical analysis is helpful to place current trends in context and to remind us that information is not inherently commodified but rather is transformed into a commodity in very discrete and deliberate ways. Chapter 3 continues this focus, examining how the internet's most powerful actor—Google—is working to commodify all of the world's information, bit by bit.

3

Google, Information, and Power

If I look at enough of your messaging and your location, and use artificial intelligence, we can predict where you are going to go.
—Eric Schmidt, Techonomy Conference, June 2010

It's called capitalism. We are proudly capitalistic. I'm not confused about this.
—Eric Schmidt, in an interview with Brian Womack of *Bloomberg*, December 12, 2012

Central to the internet-freedom movement, and lending legitimacy to the State Department's freedom-to-connect narrative, is Google. In many ways, Google is on the front lines of the cyber war, fighting for increased openness and connectivity around the world, including North Korea, Afghanistan, Pakistan, and Burma. Its work abroad, including helping to expand connectivity in parts of the developing world and lobbying against censorship in authoritarian countries, closely coincides with the State Department's freedom-to-connect agenda. Collaboration between the two was confirmed by a former senior State Department official in an email published by Wikileaks: "Google is getting WH [White House] and State Dept support and air cover. In reality they are doing things the CIA cannot do."[1]

A number of Googlers joined the company after years of government service. In 2004 In-Q-Tel Director of Technology Assessment Rob Painter left the CIA to become Google's senior federal manager, spearheading its acquisition of Keyhole Inc. In 2010 Jared Cohen, a member of the Secretary of State's Policy Planning staff, advisor to Hillary Clinton, and chief architect of the State Department's internet-freedom doctrine, left to become the director of Google Ideas. In 2012 DARPA director Regina Dugan left to join Google as its head of special projects.

Of course, as the information-industrial complex would suggest, a number of former Google employees also left for important positions in government. For example, Google's top policy expert, Andrew McLaughlin, left Google to serve as deputy chief technology officer in the Obama White House. Former Google executive Katie Stanton joined the State Department as its director of citizen participation and special adviser on innovation. Google.org's Sonal Shah was director of the White House's new Office of Social Innovation and Civic Participation. Sumit Agarwal led Google's mobile product management team before he joined the Department of Defense as deputy assistant secretary for outreach and social media.

Such employee and operational synergies raise the question: Why would Google want to be so closely associated with the internet-freedom movement and in the U.S. government more broadly? One possibility, suggested by Julian Assange, is that "by tying itself to the U.S. state, Google thereby cements its own security, at the expense of all competitors."[2] Google's expanding lobbying presence on Capitol Hill provides evidence to support Assange's hypothesis. For example, in 2012 Google's lobbying expenditures were second-largest of any corporation,[3] and in 2014 it announced the opening of a new Washington, D.C., office roughly the size of the White House.[4]

This chapter explores how Google has established itself as a powerful, if not a dominant, actor as a producer, extractor, refiner, distributor, and marketer of valuable data. Before outlining Google's role in each aspect of the commodification of data, we offer a brief overview of the company's origins and mission. The chapter concludes by connecting Google's stakes in commercialized data services to its support for a global internet-freedom movement.

Data Is the New Oil

Before the internet was a global, commercial entity, Irving Goldstein, former president of Intelsat, predicted in 1995 that information "will be for the twenty-first century what oil and gas were for the beginning of the twentieth century. It will fuel economic and political power."[5] Fast-forward to 2009, when European Consumer Commissioner Meglena Kuneva echoed Goldstein's prediction: "Personal information is the new oil of the internet and the currency of the digital world."[6] In 2010, *The Economist* issued a special report on the rise of big data, noting, "Data are becoming the new raw material of business: an economic input almost on a par with capital and labour."[7]

Analogizing data to oil or gas is, of course, imperfect. For starters, oil and gas are finite resources, and data is potentially infinite. But the broader argument about data's rising value and significance holds true. Michael Palmer, executive vice president for the Association of National Advertisers explains, "Data is just like crude. It's valuable, but if unrefined it cannot really be used. It has to be changed into gas, plastic, chemicals, etc., to create a valuable entity that drives profitable activity; so must data be broken down, analyzed for it to have value."[8] The insight that big data provides about human behaviors and motivations, social trends, environmental change, policy effectiveness, and so many other endeavors is tremendous. For example, by monitoring the frequency of use of search terms on Google, one can more quickly and accurately predict flu outbreaks and unemployment levels than by traditional reporting methods and government surveys. The predictive potential of big data is especially valuable, as it can help to more effectively market consumer goods and public policies. Without question, commercial and political actors have taken note, eagerly tapping into a new industry of big data specialists.

There are numerous, almost endless providers of big data: consumers, governments, corporations, NGOs, and so on. We are, in fact, surrounded by data about others and ourselves. But one actor in particular has approached the emerging big data industry with more clarity and foresight than all others: Google. To come back to the oil metaphor: if information is to the twenty-first century what oil was to the twentieth, then an obvious question is, Who are the miners, extractors and sellers of information today? Analogizing information to oil is not merely a statement of its significance; rather, it also signifies the growth and refined nature of information as a resource with

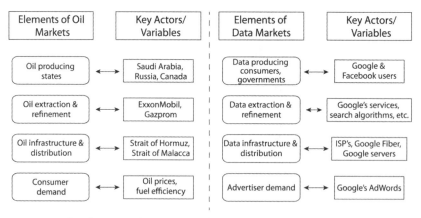

Figure 3.1: Oil and Data Markets Compared

specific and identifiable market value.[9] The analogy also provides a valuable entry point toward understanding how information as a commodity is extracted, refined, shared, and sold.

In oil markets, at a minimum, there are four types of actors that determine the cost of oil—oil-producing states; companies and organizations with the oil-extraction and refinement technology; actors controlling the infrastructure through which oil is transported around the world; and, of course, the consumer. Similarly, in data markets there are data-producing actors (consumers, governments, corporations), actors focused on data extraction and refinement (such as Google and Facebook), actors responsible for the transmission and storage of data (Google's servers, Google Fiber, Amazon's Cloud services) and the consumers of big data, which include a large range of corporate and governmental actors.

Google: An Overview

Google's short corporate history reaches only to 1998, when Sergey Brin and Larry Page established its Silicon Valley headquarters. However, the foundational thinking behind Google dates to Francis Bacon and can be traced through the origins and growth of the field of information science. Google's well-known mission to "organize the world's information and make it universally accessible and useful"[10] is a modern iteration of information science, or the study of the "body of knowledge relating to the origination, collection, organization, storage, retrieval, interpretation, transmission, transformation, and utilization of information."[11] Google collects information around the world; stores data on expansive (and expensive) computer server farms; efficiently retrieves information from its severs; interprets data to classify and analyze for relevance; transmits its systematized archive to internet users through its various services; transforms data into useable, helpful knowledge; and utilizes information about users and the world throughout the process. Each of these functions is critical to the effectiveness of Google's primary service: searching coupled with targeted advertising. If Google can consolidate and classify the world's information and make it accessible and useful, then users will continue to rely on Google for navigating the Web. This, of course, is central to its success and survival.

Google's mission depends on its ability to connect users to useful information, data that users either desire or need. This, of course, is no simple task, and it is what helped Google stand out from its early search competitors. The process requires a careful integration of identifying information of potential interest to users, organizing the information through complex classification schemes, allowing for the creation of algorithmic analysis, and making this information, via search and other Google services, available to internet users around the world. As Larry Page, Google's co-founder and CEO explains, "The perfect search engine would really understand whatever your need is. It would understand everything in the world deeply, give you back kind of exactly what you need."[12] What types of information, you might ask? According to Page, "We've had tremendous focus on really making sure we have very accurate, very structured data about everything."[13] Everything.

How does Google go about paying for such extraordinary services? Providing information to users is only part of the picture. As Page describes, "My job . . . is to create shareholder value and create value for the end users."[14] Like many other information-producing industries, from newspapers to movies, the vast majority (97 percent) of Google's revenue comes from advertising, whereby it connects advertisers with relevant consumers through its various services. So while Google's mission may focus on providing users with the information they want, its business model, and operational capacity, depends on successfully connecting advertisers with *valuable* consumers, or users interested in the message, product, or service offered by the advertiser.

In 2002 Google first developed its proprietary technology that matched advertisements to specific users' informational needs or desires. Although Google lists the advertisements separately from its search query results ("sponsored search"), because the ads were so closely aligned with user demands, many users actually found the advertisements helpful.

Google's second source of revenue stems from building specific, search-related applications (called Google Appliances) for corporate and government clients. For example, Google builds search portals for private intranets, enabling users to search through documents and data from within an organization while using Google's user-friendly interface. The World Bank, NASA, U.S. Department of the Treasury, Apple, PBS, Proctor and Gamble, Timex, Eli Lilly, National Geographic, Cisco Systems, the CIA, and many universities and local governments all use Google Appliances.[15]

In 2013 alone, Google accumulated $55.5 billion in revenue, based largely on its capacity to effectively place the right advertising in front of the right user. The next-largest-grossing internet search engine, Yahoo!, generated $4.68 billion in revenue, less than 9 percent of Google's earnings.[16]

It is nearly impossible to overstate the significance of Google's role in helping users navigate the World Wide Web. On August 17, 2013, for a *single*

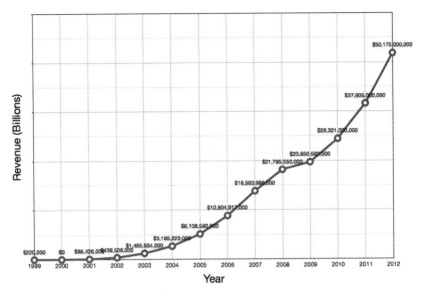

Figure 3.2: Google's Annual Revenue, 1999–2013

minute, between 50 percent and 70 percent of requests to Google's Gmail, YouTube, Google Drive, and Search services went offline. The result of this one-minute disruption was staggering: global internet traffic plunged by 40 percent.[17] This dominance is far from incidental. The remainder of this chapter will explore Google's role as a producer, extractor, refiner, distributor, and marketer of valuable data.

Data Production

Google's business model depends on its ability to produce valuable data about its users. Its ability to connect the right advertisement with the perfect user stems from its tracking and study of user habits. Through a variety of highly popular and increasingly integral Web-based services, including Search, Gmail, Chrome OS, Chrome Mobile, Google Applications and others, Google accumulates tremendous amounts of information on each of its users. This data, amassed over years of internet search, Web, and email use, provides Google with a refined sense of what a user wants when he or she uses its services, thus allowing Google to connect the user to potential advertisers easily. It is important to note that the more user-generated data it gathers, the better Google gets at predicting its users' needs and desires. "Organizing the world's information," Google's mission, doesn't simply describe information "out there"; it also includes information *about its users*.

Google's search query data has the capacity to predict a broad range of activities. According to Eric Schmidt, "If I look at enough of your messaging and your location, and use artificial intelligence, [I] can predict where you are going to go."[18] More important for Schmidt is not where you are going but how Google can use what it knows about your identity, location, and interests to suggest additional information or activities it thinks, based on its complex, patented algorithms, you will enjoy. According to Schmidt, "I actually think most people don't want Google to answer their questions. They want Google to tell them what they should be doing next."[19] Google's ability to track user movement and interests via its services gives the company a tremendous advantage over competitors. Based on its data archive, Google knows things about users that users don't even know about themselves, making it nearly impossible for any competitor to service user demands as adeptly. According to industry specialist Mike Elgan, "This combination of knowledge about you, knowledge about everyone else, artificial intelligence and the ability to learn is something that Google can do better than anyone else. Get used to it. This is the future."[20]

Prediction is central to Google's business model. Ninety-seven percent of its revenue is generated via targeted advertising, which works because of what Google knows about its users' intentions when they type in certain search queries or emails. It shares this data with various groups for a variety of reasons, promising of course to protect user privacy by scrubbing any identifiable personal data.

But what if that were not the case? So much attention has been focused on the specifics of Google's privacy policy: How vigorously does it protect user information from government and commercial investigators? There is a growing and substantial body of research, however, that indicates that simply wiping information that could connect specific users to their search, email, and enterprise data—the promise of anonymous search—is misleading at best. In fact, it is increasingly clear that there is a zero-sum game between keeping data anonymous and maintaining its commercial and political value.

In a 2000 research experiment, Carnegie Mellon's Latanya Sweeney demonstrated that 87 percent of all Americans could be uniquely identified based on three simple bits of information: sex, zip code, and birthdate.[21] Computer scientists have since identified serious flaws behind the basic assumption of "anonymous data": almost all anonymized data, when combined with other bits of relevant information, can be triangulated to a single human being. This idea has a long legal history and goes by the name of "mosaic theory."

Mosaic theory suggests that while some information in specific documents may appear harmless to disclose in isolation, such information may be valuable as part of a mosaic of information collected from a variety of publicly available sources. Mosaic theory is often cited by the government in response to Freedom of Information Act (FOIA) requests, whereby an agency argues that it cannot make public certain information, however harmless it appears to be when examined in isolation, because, when combined with other types of information, national security is potentially breached.

Mosaic theory's roots actually reside in the intelligence community. According to David E. Pozen, expert in national security law and information law and policy, the basic premise underlying mosaic theory—that one can piece discrete bits of information together to predict the likely intentions or actions of others—is central to intelligence gathering: "As more and more items of information emerge about a secret plan or policy, outsiders will have more and more opportunities to draw inferences across the items and to relate them to other items of information they possess. Such analytic mosaic-making is a basic precept of intelligence gathering, used by our government to learn about our enemies and by our enemies to learn about us."[22]

While mosaic theory is typically deployed by the government in FOIA cases to argue against making certain information public, it is beginning to be considered in privacy cases also.[23] In his paper titled "Broken Promises of Privacy: Responding to the Surprising Failure of Anonymization," Paul Ohm argues that as more and more information on all of us is collected and shared online, scrubbing data will become impossible.[24] Ohm predicts that internet companies like Google and Facebook will retain control over "databases of ruin," holding the keys to accessing an aggregate of invaluable information about nearly every one of their users.

In its collection and archiving of user data, Google has embraced mosaic theory. The purpose of the data is, of course, to be able to predict what your wants, needs, and desires are, thus allowing Google to help you achieve your goals by connecting you to a service or product for a small advertising fee. According to Eric Schmidt, "We know roughly who you are, roughly what you care about, roughly who your friends are."[25]

Even in a world where the entire search data is anonymized, disconnected from a specific user or computer, it is still extraordinarily helpful for the purpose of predicting the future. For example, a careful examination of Google search queries in the period leading up to the 2008 election reveals a dramatic rise in search queries for "Obama Muslim" in Tennessee, Kentucky, and Oklahoma, three states where Obama underperformed compared to polls taken just before the election. Similarly, searches for "McCain life expectancy" jumped to unprecedented levels on two occasions: the day he announced Alaska governor Sarah Palin would be his running mate and the day Palin's interview with Katie Couric was nationally broadcast.[26]

Google search queries are especially helpful for identifying trends in attitudes or behaviors that pollsters fail to capture. This is because, "searchers' demonstrated willingness to share their true feelings and unbridled thoughts on Google."[27] Thus, people are much more likely to filter their information when talking to a pollster or doctor than when they enter a Google search query. As a demonstration of Google's predictive power, an analysis of Google's search queries correctly identified trends in voter turnout in 2004, 2006, 2008, 2010, and 2012.[28] While nobody likes to admit that they aren't going to vote on Election Day, those who do vote are more likely to actively seek out information on the location and hours of their local polling station. According to Google data scientist and *New York Times* columnist Seth Stephens-Davidowitz, "This predictive power was significantly stronger than that of other variables we might use to predict area-level turnout, like changes in registration rates or movement in early voting."[29]

Given the volume of searches entered into Google's archives every day, trends in search terms can be used to forecast broader health, social, and economic trends. Eric Schmidt once noted that, based on search data, Google was confident that it could predict the performance of the stock market, quickly adding, "And then we decided that it was illegal. So we stopped doing that."[30] Google's search query servers hold a wealth of data that corporations, opinion leaders, and politicians already pay billions for by way of consumer and public opinion research.

Google also invests in the development of mobile phone applications in order to extract unique information from users and thereby improve the quality of their products. For example, Ingress, a game developed by Google's Niantic Labs for Google's Android mobile operating system, utilizes mobile phone GPS geolocation capabilities to provide a unique, augmented reality-gaming experience. To play, users compete for control over real-world landmarks and monuments, dubbed portals, in their cities. Players are urged to move through the real world, using an android device, to discover objects that are annotated via a layer of virtual information displayed on a user's smartphone. According to the game's description, users "acquire objects to aid in [the player's] quest, deploy tech to capture territory, and ally with other players to advance the cause of the Enlightened or the Resistance."[31] By encouraging users to walk around outside, traveling from point to point within their local neighborhoods, the game documents and sends detailed data about the best possible walking routes in crowded cosmopolitan environments, as well as popular stop-offs along the way.

Thus, in addition to its extensive data collection from user searches and email accounts, Google, by offering free gaming software, is also encouraging users to provide real-world data on how best to get from point A to point B. The game also rewards users for snapping photos of popular landmarks, which Google can later use to refine its visual search capabilities. A review of the game observes, "By wrapping data collection in the trappings of an engaging interactive experience, Ingress is actually fueling a desire amongst its users to provide it with information and giving the company positive coverage to boot."[32]

Offering fun, easy-to-use games for free to its users, Google enables them to behave in ways that creates valuable data integral to Google's improvement of its Maps and Earth applications. This data will be especially valuable for the Google Glass project, where detailed information about what one sees and experiences while walking through a crowded urban environment will improve the functionality of the augmented-reality goggles.

Data Extraction

A tremendous amount of valuable information exists offline, independent of Google's servers. Critical to Google's success and its continued market dominance is the company's drive to identify and extract this nondigital, real-space data into a form that is useable and helpful to its users. Google goes about this process of extraction through the conversion of existing information (books, museum archives, maps, houses, businesses, and so on) into digital, searchable formats. According to Sergey Brin: "One of the important issues with search is, if we don't have it in our index, we can't return an answer."[33]

Early on, Google expanded beyond simply offering search services when it purchased the archives of Deja.com, a company responsible for maintaining millions of Usenet newsgroup discussions that were especially popular in the early years of the World Wide Web. Another example of Google's early interest in identifying and digitizing information was its scanning and archiving of more than fifteen hundred consumer-product catalogs in 2001. Realizing the growing interest in online shopping and product research, Google ventured into consumer shopping, including the scanned pages of consumer goods into its search features, thus allowing users to find products, and where to purchase products, with virtual ease. According to Google's Eileen Rodriguez, the company at that time viewed such a strategy as "an opportunity to maximize [retailers'] outreach and improve search for our consumers." "People who don't have a subscription to L.L. Bean's catalog," she said, "can search its products online."[34] The main purpose of the initiative was to boost Google's ad revenue among some of the biggest advertising spenders.

This process of digitizing content took a new direction with the launch of Google Maps, an online service that provides digitized, searchable maps of the world. The quality of the maps, in terms of up-to-date geographic precision, was unprecedented, though their accuracy is diminished in unstable and less-developed areas of the world. Google's Maps project grew out of its acquisition of Keyhole Inc., a small Silicon Valley startup that had received substantial venture capital from the CIA's In-Q-Tel to help the company develop fast, accurate, and searchable digital maps for the U.S. Armed Forces. Google's acquisition of Keyhole did not change that—Google Maps, the modern iteration of Keyhole's original mapping platform—continues to be used in theaters of conflict in Afghanistan and elsewhere. But Google was also interested in developing the civilian side of the mapping technology, aiming to help users access current, free interactive maps to better find their way to the places they want to be.

Google Maps undertakes digitizing a wide range of data and converting it into information that is both searchable and helpful to users. At a minimum, the process extracts information from the real, physical world and places it on Google's network. The mapping project also aims to photograph the world's streetscapes, creating current digital images of every address searchable in its map systems from multiple angles. What seems ubiquitous now was entirely revolutionary in 2001, when the *Telegraph*'s Kamal Ahmed noted, "Using Street View technology to take images of the pictures which are more detailed than when seen with the naked eye, people will now be able to take virtual tours of the galleries from their living rooms."[35]

Google's Street View project was originally thought to be snapping images of roads, but in 2010, when confronted by the German government, Google revealed that the cars were equipped to do much more. The German investigation found that the Street View cars were also programmed to gather information from local wireless networks in order to improve location-based searches. According to an FCC report, Google's vehicles extracted all unencrypted information sent from homes by computers, including emails and internet searches. Even if a user was not working on a computer at the moment the car passed, if the computer (or other device) was on and the network was unencrypted, the Street View car could collect all sorts of user information. This unauthorized data collection took place for three years, from 2007 to 2010.[36]

At first, Google claimed that the "mistake" was the result of a coding error by a single engineer. But an FCC investigation revealed that the so-called payload data collection was not the result of a rogue engineer but rather a team of engineers who collectively worked on the project and understood the scope of the data being amassed. The original project-design document, written by the Google engineer thought responsible for writing the code into the program, is fairly clear on the scope of its data-gathering mission: "We are logging user traffic along with sufficient data to precisely triangulate their position at a given time, along with information about what they were doing."[37] According to Al Hilwa, former Google software developer, "This is the thinking of an engineer—grab the data and worry about filtering it out later. . . . That's the engineering mind-set, especially at Google."[38]

In October 2004, Google announced it would be adding a new service: Google Print. The idea was to add excerpts from printed books that related to particular search queries, alongside links to vendors (Amazon.com, BarnesandNoble.com, and others) from whom a user could conveniently purchase the book they were previewing. Penguin, Houghton Mifflin, Scholastic, Blackwell, Hyperion, Warner Books, and Oxford University Press were the first publishers to sign on to the new initiative, contributing excerpts of hundreds of thousands of books to the project. Each publisher determined how much of a book could be viewed by a user, typically allowing a free preview of between ten and twenty pages. Critical to securing an agreement was a promise to ensure the integrity of each book's copyright. For example, users could not copy or print the text of excerpted books. All Google requires is that the publishers send copies of the books to their offices in Mountain View, California, where Google scans and uploads each book's content into its search archive. According to Susan Wojcicki, Google's director of product management at the time, "We're trying to make offline information like books searchable and available online. That's a natural next step as part of Google's mission."[39]

Then, on December 14, 2004, Google announced agreements with five prestigious institutional libraries—Harvard University, Stanford University, Oxford University, the University of Michigan, and the New York Public Library—which each agreed to allow Google to digitize parts of their book collections and include the scanned copies in their search results.[40] The announcement meant that rather than including only those books that publishers sent directly to Google for scanning, large parts of the libraries' collections—more than fifteen million volumes from the five major libraries—would soon be archived and accessible via Google Search. While the books were made available only through Google Search, they were also made available to students of the contributing institutions via localized digital archives at each library. Books still covered by copyright will be searchable, but only a sentence or two would be accessible via search. Older books in the public domain would be available to be read or searched in their entirety on Google, but they would not be readily available for printing. The *New York Times* described the announcement as "only a step on the long road toward the long-predicted global virtual library."[41] The project cost Google (at its inception) approximately ten dollars per volume scanned and archived, or more than $150 million.[42] It was estimated in 2006 that to scan thirty million volumes from the five libraries could cost $750 million.[43] Leonid Taycher, a Google Books software engineer, estimated in 2010 that 129,864,880 different books have been published.[44] Google wants to scan all of them.

Google Print's public announcement traced the program back to Brin and Page's days at Stanford, where they were working on an NSF-supported digital libraries project prior to launching Google. According to Page, "We dreamed of making the incredible breadth of information that librarians so lovingly organize searchable online."[45] The head of Stanford University's library, Michael Keller, praised the program, proclaiming, "Within two decades, most of the world's knowledge will be digitized and available, one hopes for free reading on the Internet, just as there is free reading in libraries today."[46]

At the same time, the Google Print (renamed Google Books in November 2005) had clear commercial value to the company too. As its competitors—Yahoo! and Microsoft in particular—became increasingly skilled at search themselves, Google Print offered the company a way to promise users access to additional information that its competitors' search engines could not retrieve. By digitizing millions of print volumes and adding the scanned books to its archive, Google was seizing access to offline information in order to ensure a competitive edge. According to the *Financial Times*, "The project can be viewed as Google making its first serious move as a content provider, bringing structured information assets into its database."[47] According to co-founding editor of *Wired* magazine John Battelle, the initiative promises to be a lucrative endeavor: "There's a ludicrously large backlist in books and this could mean a massive new revenue stream. You are going to see some interesting new hits that haven't sold a copy since 1782. This really does fulfill a model of enlightened capitalism."[48] On August 9, 2006, Page and Brin announced that more than one hundred libraries located throughout the University of California system had agreed to join its Google Books Library Project. Google's Print initiative is exemplary of the company's aim to extract real-space information to cyberspace in order to attract more users to its services.

Google is working to digitize more cultural content as well. In 2011 the company announced the Google Art Project, including agreements with the Tate Britain Gallery in London, the Uffizi Gallery in Florence, and the Metropolitan Museum of Art in New York to digitally catalog their collections and make them available to Google users around the world. The project allows users to tour museum collections virtually while adding deep historical information about the works. Users can also compile their own collection, and a "walk-through" feature allows users to wander through a museum virtually, as if they were physically there. The images of the artworks are produced using state-of-the-art image-capture technology, including gigapixel images (an image containing more than one billion pixels).

After a favorable initial reception, Google began expanding the project the next year, increasing the number of partnering institutions from the initial nine to more than 151 venues spread across forty countries. It currently features more than forty-five thousand pieces from 250 institutions and is available in eighteen languages.[49]

Data Refinement

Google's Search is a glorified, scientifically based means of data refinement. In 1998, as Larry Page and Sergey Brin were testing what would become the backbone of Google's search engine—the PageRank algorithm—they wrote several research articles addressing the question of search-engine bias. At the time, advertisers were paying to influence the results of a user's search query in order to increase the likelihood that they would visit their Web site and purchase their goods and/or services. Page and Brin found this practice to be horribly unethical: "[It's] much more insidious than advertising, because it is not clear who deserves to be there, and who is willing to pay money to be listed."[50] For Page and Brin, the growth of advertising dollars in the search business meant that search engines "will be inherently biased towards advertisers and away from the needs of consumers."[51] They set out to create a search engine based in the scientific study and organization of information, uninhibited by the influence of corporate support or advertising dollars.[52]

Google's search results are based in part on its patented PageRank technology, an algorithm that determines exactly what publicly accessible Web content is closest to what a user desires when he or she enters a particular query into a search field. In addition to the results from the World Wide Web, Google's Search may also return up to twenty-nine special features to connect users with the desired information quicker. Examples of this special feature include: synonyms, weather forecasts, time zones, stock quotes, maps, earthquake data, movie show times, airports, home listings, and sports scores. Each is featured at the top of one's search results, in a separate box, in order to provide what Google thinks is the most relevant and helpful information "in just one click."[53]

The reach of Google's Index is important, as no search engine can completely index the entire World Wide Web. In fact, every search engine intentionally does *not* index the entirety of Web content, for technical, economic, and legal reasons. The parts of the Web that are not searched by Google's spiders are called the invisible web, deep web, or dark matter. The invisible web contains Web pages that are disconnected URLs (where no other Web page links to it), proprietary databases (such as Lexis-Nexis), dynamic (constantly being updated and changed, and thus too burdensome for crawlers to index), and password-protected pages or those that are simply un-indexable due to the technical nature of the content enclosed (for example, Web sites containing only [Adobe] Flash-based content or executable files). Other portions of the Web that are not indexed, or sites that are at least down-ranked so that they don't show at the top of search results, are sites that contain illegal material—for example, copyright-infringing material.[54] The vast majority of the invisible web remains invisible to the vast majority of users not because of inherent technical limitations in search technology but rather because search engines deliberately decide to exclude or down-rank certain types of content.

What makes Google's Search so much better than its competitors? According to Schmidt in 2011, "Google devotes significant resources and manpower to constructing, updating, and maintaining a highly sophisticated crawling and indexing system. Independent analysts have confirmed the superiority of Google's index."[55] To stay competitive and improve user experience, Google tweaks and adjusts its search algorithms to ensure search queries are matching user expectations. "In this rapidly changing industry, Google has evolved to operate at lightning speed," Schmidt said, "our engineers test more than ten thousand changes per year and ultimately make more than five hundred changes a year to our search algorithms, or one to two changes per day."[56] A 2011 study by Alan Bleiweiss found that Google indexes ten times as many pages as Bing.[57]

While search is driven primarily by Google's computer-operated algorithmic equations, human, legal, and political elements can influence search results too. According to Schmidt, "There are a few, limited instances in which we may utilize manual controls—spam, security, legal requirements (copyright, child pornography)."[58]

Copyright, in particular, has become an issue over which Google has faced increasing scrutiny. Users searching for access to copyrighted movies, songs, and literary work have used Google Search to try and locate pirated works. Rep. Debbie Wasserman Schultz (D-Florida) accused Google of helping users break the law: "Your auto-fill brings up things that are not appropriate, and are facilitating illegal content and illegal products."[59] So, at the request of Congress, Google altered its auto-complete search function to exclude certain popular search terms that may encourage a user to locate copyrighted content on the Web. Schmidt outlined the changes in a letter to Congress: "We have begun working to prevent several piracy-related terms from appearing in autocomplete and have asked content industry representatives to suggest other terms for consideration."[60] In 2012, Google went a step further by changing its rankings to demote sites that had been accused of piracy, with the exception of YouTube, which is owned by Google.[61]

Data Infrastructure and Distribution

Central to all of Google's operations, and its success, is the physical infrastructure the company has built to store, transfer, and retrieve information from around the world, otherwise known as the Googlenet. According to *Wired* magazine, "Google's success [is] its ability to build, organize, and operate a huge network of servers and fiber-optic cables with an efficiency and speed that rocks physics on its heels."[62] As of January 2012 it was estimated that Google has around 1.8 million servers housed in its thirty-five data centers worldwide. According to an industry specialist, "It turns out that the Google platform has more computational power than the world's largest supercomputer. A lot more."[63] A 2010 study by Arbor Networks found that if Google were an ISP, it would be the second-largest in the world, the largest being Level 3, which serves more than 2,700 corporations in 450 markets with more than 100,000 fiber miles. Google's data centers consume, on average, 1.5 percent of all the electricity in the entire world.

This multi-billion-dollar infrastructure allows the company to index twenty billion Web pages a day; handle more than three billion daily search queries; conduct millions of ad auctions in real time; offer free email storage to 425 million Gmail users; broadcast millions of YouTube videos to users every day; and even deliver search results before the user has finished typing the query. And the Google platform continues to grow. Experts predict the addition of another five hundred thousand servers in 2014. The system is designed to be able to cope with a total of ten million servers. In a few years' time the Google platform should be sufficiently powerful to run a complete simulation of a human brain, including displays of intelligence and self-awareness.[64]

Google operates two separate networks: one for consumer services like Google Search and Gmail, and another connecting each of the Google servers located around the world. The networks operate independently because they function in very different ways. The consumer-services network requires smooth and consistent data exchange demanding the highest standards of data integrity, but it also slows down and speeds up, depending on time zone and demand. The internal backbone, on the other hand, is not always operating at peak capacity; at it times requires massive transfer of data to occur across great distances, immediately. For example, every time Google updates its webpage index, it needs to transfer the package—a considerable amount of data—to each of its servers around the world.[65]

In 2005 Google started developing its own networking hardware and software—based on OpenFlow standards—that increased the efficiency of the network. Starting in 2010, the company upgraded its backbone, using the new hyperefficient networking technologies and enabling the company to achieve a near-100-percent utilization of its entire network. Industry standards typically consider 30 percent to 40 percent of network utilization to be a reasonable payload, so Google's upgrade makes its network two to three times faster than its competitors.' The new hyperspeed network enables Google to crawl and archive the world's Web pages, spread the data over tens of thousands of servers using its proprietary Google File System, and (using MapReduce) leverage the processing power of its massive networked supercomputer to quickly produce a compressed, single, searchable index.

Essential to Google's competitive advantage is its ability to allow multiple users to access data simultaneously from anywhere around the world. Previously, such networked collaboration was hampered by the challenges in sharing data in real time between servers placed throughout the globe, perhaps tethered to clocks and electricity systems that themselves could be off, if even by a few nanoseconds. To solve the problem, Google engineers started installing atomic clocks and GPS antennas on each server, thus syncing each unit to universally precise and correct time. According to Jeff Dean, Google's head engineer, the system, called Spanner, "allows for a storage and computation system that spans all data centers."[66]

In the early years of the twenty-first century, Google took advantage of a number of troubled telecommunication operators, buying up abandoned fiber-optic networks for pennies on the dollar. Through continued acquisition, exchanges, and development, the company built a "global empire of glass."[67] The high-speed fiber-optic network aimed to help handle the demands of millions of YouTube users from around the world who were trying to watch video at the same time. According to industry expert Steven Levy, "It would be slow and burdensome to have millions of people grabbing videos from Google's few data centers."[68] Instead, Google built local capacity around its core user bases and kept an actual copy of the most accessed content in its data centers closer to the physical location of its users. Google installs its own server racks in various outposts of its network—mini data centers, sometimes connected directly to ISPs such as Comcast or AT&T—and uploads popular videos and webpages, thus decreasing the burden placed on its core, global network. This "proxy cache" was, according to Schmidt, "a tremendous technological achievement."[69] (This technology is also called Content Delivery Networks [CDNs].)

It is difficult to overstate the importance of Google's internal network to its success, today and for the future. According to *Wired* Magazine's Cade Metz, Google

> treats its globe-spanning infrastructure as the most important of trade secrets. The web giant believes much of its success stems from its ability to craft software and hardware capable of juggling more data, more quickly than practically any other operation on Earth. And, well, that's about right. The Googlenet is what so much of the computing world looks to as the modern ideal. Occasionally, the company will reveal pieces of its top-secret infrastructure—which now spans as many as three dozen data centers—and others will follow its lead. The followers include everyone from Facebook, Yahoo, and Twitter to the NSA."[70]

Of course, Google's internal network is not the only potential bottleneck slowing users down. Independent of the Googlenet are local internet infrastructures, operated by the internet service providers (ISPs) that consumers subscribe to in order to surf the Web. These ISPs—Comcast, AT&T, Time-Warner, for example—own the local fiber-optic networks that determine the speed of a customer's connection.

In the United States, Google is eager to see these networks improved. In 2010 the company launched Google Fiber, a super-fast, fiber-optic broadband network that would provide users with upload/download speeds of up to one gigabyte per second—a hundredfold increase over what most Americans can even subscribe to and a thousand times faster than AT&T's basic DSL connection. The Google Fiber initiative aims to encourage experimentation with the ways hyperfast connection could improve consumer and business practices. In particular, Google is keen on developing the next generation of applications, new infrastructure development techniques, and an open-access, nondiscriminatory, transparent network.

An unstated purpose for launching Fiber was to challenge the dominant ISPs—AT&T, Comcast, and Verizon, in particular—to improve their networks and lower their costs. According to *Wired's* Ryan Singel, "When Google enters a market, it usually destroys traditional ways of making money. ISPs want to find ways to measure internet traffic, and charge users by levels—even as their own upstream bandwidth costs continue to plummet. The rhetoric used to justify those decisions to consumer[s] and lawmakers just won't hold up."[71]

Internationally, Google is also working to build better infrastructure, enabling more users to access its services with sufficient speed and reliability. In 2012 Google's philanthropic arm, Google.org, funded the Internet Society to "establish a methodology to assess internet exchange points (IXPs), provide training for people to operate the IXPs, and build a more robust local Internet infrastructure in emerging markets." IXP's are crucial to accessing the World Wide Web in the developing world, as they allow network operators to exchange traffic locally, decreasing costs and improving energy effectiveness. These points also speed up transmissions and improve the overall network performance. IXP development also helps to promote local internet technical expertise.[72] Google supported the establishment and growth of internet exchanges in Nigeria, the eastern Caribbean, and the Middle East. It has also invested in building open-access Wi-Fi networks in Nairobi, Kenya, as a proof-of-concept project that could be scaled to improve internet access throughout the developing world.

Google's interest in enhancing global connectivity goes beyond standard industry practices, too. In 2013, it launched Project Loon, proposing a ring of internet-enabled balloons circling the world via stratospheric winds while providing internet access to populations below. According to the announcement, "We've built a system that uses balloons, carried by the wind at altitudes twice as high as commercial planes, to beam Internet access to the ground at speeds similar to today's 3G networks or faster. As a result, we hope balloons could become an option for connecting rural, remote, and underserved areas."[73] Pilot balloons have been tested in New Zealand and Brazil, as Google's engineers work to improve the stability and longevity of the proposed system.

In South Africa, Google is working with local partners to transform "white space"—spare channels in the TV broadcast spectrum—for use as a delivery mechanism for broadband internet access for schools in rural parts of the country. Operating from Stellenbosch University, Google expects to broadcast 2.5 Mbps speeds up to a ten-kilometer area in the Cape Town area.[74] The six-month trial period ended in September 2013, and the network remains operational, providing connectivity to schools throughout the area. According to Google's Public Policy Manager Fortune Mgwili-Sibanda, "White Space technology is gaining momentum around the world. . . . We hope the results of the trial will drive similar regulatory developments in South Africa and other African countries."[75]

Demand

Googlenomics, a term coined by Steven Levy, refers to Google's two-pronged strategy for gaining users and attracting revenue. The macro side of the approach focuses on developing industry-leading applications and services (Gmail and Google Search, for example) to attract larger and larger audiences, and to encourage them to integrate Google products into all parts of their lives. By giving away products with terrific functionality, such as the Android OS, Google is able to get its products in the hands of billions of users who would rather not pay a premium for services they have grown accustomed to having for free. The micro side of the approach focuses on selling ads and optimizing ad relevancy. For Google, ad relevancy is crucial for two reasons: optimizing relevancy is important for maximizing the click-through-rate, thereby increasing revenue, and relevancy increases in importance over time because users are more likely to click on future advertisements once they learn from experience that it is likely to be relevant. This means that all ads on Google's network need to be highly relevant to users because "a single irrelevant ad can have a lasting impact on revenue."[76]

The success of Google ads thus depends on collecting large quantities of accurate, longitudinal user data. To amass this data, Google offers a variety of products and services that intersect with multiple facets of everyday life, from the personal (Gmail, Search) to the professional (Google Enterprise, Google Drive). Using tracking-cookie technology, Google is able to track user behavior on its own services, as well as its network partner Web sites and services, thus providing a fairly wide window into users' interests.

From an economic perspective, Google is simply a transaction platform whose primary purpose is to match buyers and sellers. The larger the potential market of buyers and sellers, the more able Google is to find a good match. For advertisers, this means that the more viewers accessing a network, the more likely the network is able to connect with likely customers, especially for advertisers selling niche goods and services. The reverse is also true: more advertisers increase the likelihood of connecting users with relevant ads. This network effect explains why reach is crucial to the successful implementation of Google's ad program, as advertisers and users both benefit by using the intermediary with the widest reach. According to Optimizely's Arthur Suermondt, "'Googlenomics' has had and continues to have a significant impact on business model development in the internet industry and Silicon Valley."[77]

Google revolutionized the advertising industry in 2000 when it launched AdWords, an auction-based system for matching text ads to specific search queries. By giving advertisers the ability to match their ads to specific types of search queries, Google could promise a greater return on investment than the typical ad placed in, for example, a newspaper. As well, the auction-based system flattened the cost of advertising, allowing small and large firms alike to set their own price points. Finally, in addition to offering advertisers a pay-per-display rate (cost-per-thousand-impressions or cost-per-mille rates), previously the industry standard, Google's AdWords also offered a cost-per-click service, which charges advertisers only when a user actually clicks on the advertisement and visits a sponsored Web page.[78] This final development allowed advertisers to measure the actual success of particular ads in near-real time while decreasing the overall cost of advertising. Using this system, in 2013 Google made $50.5 billion in advertising revenue.[79]

AdWords offers several features that allow advertisers to get a maximum return on investment. For example, Google offers IP address exclusion, whereby particular messages can be excluded from appearing on any range of IP addresses—addresses that typically reflect a particular geographic location (read: demographic), allowing for greater narrowing of targeted users. AdWords also allows for "frequency capping," whereby an advertiser places specific limits on the number of times ads appear to the same unique user on the Google Content Network. Placement-targeted advertisements (formerly site-targeted advertisements) allow advertisers to enter keywords, domain names, topics, and demographic targeting preferences, and Google places the ads on what it determines as relevant sites hosted within its content network.

All AdWords content appears on Google.com alongside Google search results; advertisers can also choose for their ads to appear on Google's partner search networks, which have included Yahoo!, AT&T, AOL Search, Ask. com, *New York Times*, Netscape, and others. In 2012, there were five billion ad impressions on Google every day worldwide, translating into more than $100 million *per day* in revenue for Google from its AdWords program.[80]

Separate from search-related ads, Google's AdSense program, launched in June 2003, allows for any Web site to monetize itself by allowing Google to place ads automatically in designated places on their Web pages. Web sites that opt into the program become part of Google's Display Network, which scans each Web site to determine what types of ads would best appeal to a user visiting the site. AdSense publishers may select channels to help direct Google's ad placements on their pages in order to increase performance of their ad units. There are many different types of ads that can run across Google's network, including text ads, image ads (banner ads), mobile text ads, and in-page video ads. In 2010, to increase the effectiveness of AdSense ads, Google started using a user search history to match a particular user with appealing ads rather than merely relying on the content of the Web page that a user visits. In 2011, AdSense accounted for just under $10 billion, or approximately 28 percent of Google's total revenue.

By March 2004, Google's advertising program comprised more than one hundred thousand advertisers worldwide and was the fastest growing in the industry. A press release celebrating Google's rise noted that Google's online ads were five times more effective than its competitors' ads: "Users see the most relevant advertising first and advertisers are rewarded with average click-through rates at least five times higher than the industry average for traditional banner ads."[81]

Google dominates the online advertising market. In 2013, Google accounted for more than 33 percent of the total online advertising market and 56 percent of mobile ads. The second-largest actor in the digital advertising sector, Facebook, controls just 5 percent of the market. Google publishes more ads worldwide than any other firm—31.91 percent of all ads; Facebook shares 5.64 percent of the market.[82] To help put these figures in perspective, in 2012, Google made more money on advertising than the entire U.S. print media industry combined.[83]

Google's online advertising programs place it as a leader in the advertising industry more broadly. Leveraging the success of its AdWords system, its search algorithm, the growth of digital advertising, and its brand, Google is the most important advertising company in the world. ZenithOptimedia declared in 2013 that Google was, for the first time, the world's largest owner of advertising media, surpassing News Corporation.[84] ZenithOptimedia measures media revenue as "all revenues deriving from businesses that support advertising, not just the advertising revenue itself."[85] In other words, Google employs its search engine and other user-attracting services, such as You-Tube, to create an audience for its advertisers. Google's domination of online advertising coincided with a shift that saw digital media advertising exceed the value of national TV advertising, with a 23 percent market share.[86] According to Will Margiloff, CEO of Denstu's Innovation Interactive, "Google has become the remote control for the world; it's the first stop, not TV." To put Google's $50.57 billion of annual advertising revenue for 2013 in context, the largest and most successful advertising company, WPP, earned just $18 billion in revenue in 2013.[87]

Google's advertising programs extend the economic impact of the company's operations well beyond the revenue it generates every quarter. According to its Economic Impact Assessment, in 2012 Google's search and advertising tools helped provide more than $94 billion in economic activity for 1.9 million businesses, website publishers, and nonprofit organizations across the United States.[88]

Google and Internet Freedom

This chapter examined Google's aims to dominate the global market for information services and data. Drawing from the suggestion that "information is the new oil of the internet and the currency of the digital world," we describe how Google's various endeavors seek to control each facet of the data market: production, extraction/refinement, infrastructure, and demand. Building on the analogy of the historical significance of the oil industry, it is important to note that there is no equivalent company that has ever been capable of dominance in each facet of the oil economy to the extent that Google leads in the data economy. While much of this chapter is descriptive, such analysis is required to convey the sheer scope of the company's operations. The model proposed here, separating four distinct aspects of the data economy, is helpful in not only analyzing Google but also in assessing other actors competing in the data economy. It may also facilitate thinking about the type of regulatory intervention required to prevent the monopolization of the entire sector.

There is an additional analogous economic variable that shapes virtually every market and plays a crucial role in determining the cost of oil (and any other hard commodity): taxes. Over the course of the oil production and dissemination process, a variety of governments levy taxes on its extraction, refinement, processing, shipping, and, of course, sale. For example, Russia, Saudi Arabia, and Canada require companies to pay hefty tax rates and royalties in order to extract oil or gas from their land. Yet, in the data economy, governments have been slow to impose similar tariffs, due in large part to fear of being accused of disrupting the free flow of information. In particular, no government taxes companies for data extraction or for data imports/exports, both of which are heavily regulated aspects of markets exchanging other valuable commodities. This is not meant to be an argument in favor of greater taxes. Rather, it is included to call attention to the irregular way in which the global data market is regulated compared to other valuable commodities, an irregularity that is explained in part by the power of the internet-freedom agenda to legitimize a particular set of economic practices.

This analysis of Google's market dominance also offers a detailed assessment of the processes by which information becomes commodified in the modern internet economy. While the entirety of Google's business model is based on processes of commodification of information, its efforts to digitize information that was previously only accessible in "real space" for inclusion into its content and advertising network are especially potent examples of the underlying logic driving Google's operations.

So much coverage of Google's grand initiatives, from Project Loon to its Art Project, portrays the company in a positive light, simply pursuing its commitment to not "be evil." As a result, Google remains at the forefront of the internet-freedom movement. The company's founders and its current leadership routinely espouse the economic and political benefits of a free flow of information between people and countries. According to Eric Schmidt, "We [at Google] clearly have a strong view that more information is better."[89] While it seems clear that Googlers do genuinely support freedom of expression as a fundamental human right, there is little evidence that this is the reason the company pursues greater global connectivity. In fact, there are numerous examples of Google's complying with law enforcement agencies in India, Pakistan, Turkey, Egypt, China, the United States, and other countries to restrict content deemed illegal by local authorities. Emails obtained from FOIA requests indicate Google's interest in spreading access to the internet exclusively on its own terms. For example, during the WCIT negotiations, Aparna Sridhar, Google's Telecom Policy Counsel, wrote to the rest of the U.S. delegation, "We are also extremely concerned about the resolution to foster an enabling environment for the greater growth of the Internet."[90]

It is thus difficult to suggest that the company's desire for freedom of expression is driving its global business strategy. Instead, this chapter suggests a more compelling explanation for Google's interest in internet freedom and connectivity: the simple fact that its survival (in the political-economy sense of the word) depends on getting more and more people online to use its complimentary services.

It should therefore come as no surprise that Google has been highly critical of efforts to regulate the flow of digital information across borders. Google's fear of regulation of the internet is genuine, as greater discretion regarding how governments control the flow of information within, into, and outside its geographic space is of tremendous import to the future of Google's business. Similar to how the industrial revolution and the rise of the middle class was central to the economic success of American car manufacturers, a "free and open" internet, accessible around the world—tax free—is central to Google's business model. Every user is a potential target for the company's highly effective advertising, as well as its data, which can help refine and improve its search services. Moreover, closed or heavily regulated access to data in other countries would make it increasingly more difficult for Google to index data located in those countries, making its search and advertising algorithms less effective. Internet regulation is the equivalent, in Google's mind, to trade barriers: unfair restrictions that distort the marketplace in favor of other, domestic actors. In truth, this characterization is accurate—if Google continues to flounder in China, for example, Chinese companies like Baidu will continue to improve their search engines, making it harder and harder for Google to compete in the long term. But, similar to the realities of trade, one must also consider the arguments in favor of limiting the reach of Western corporations. The following chapter explores this dynamic in detail through the lens of internet governance, and the International Telecommunications Union (ITU) in particular.

4

The Economics of
Internet Connectivity

Censorship by some countries creates an unfair environment for online business and stifles competition.

—U.S. Ambassador David A. Gross, U.S. Coordinator for
International Communications and Information Policy, U.S.
State Department, Washington, D.C., December 20, 2006

We will continue to actively participate in these discussions and to reiterate the importance of private sector
leadership and support for the privatization of the
technical management of the domain name system as
envisioned in the ICANN model. That multi-stakeholder
model has served the United States and the global digital
economy well.

—U.S. Ambassador David A. Gross, U.S. Coordinator for
International Communications and Information Policy, U.S.
Senate testimony, Washington, D.C., September 30, 2004

Robust debate continues regarding the potential for "connective technologies" to cause transformative democratic change or reinforce existing autocratic institutions via enhanced surveillance and endless, mindless entertainment for their citizens. It is highly unlikely that the U.S. government would announce and implement a new foreign policy doctrine based on such a contested theoretical framework. There is, however, another rationale that policymakers, industry, and civil society actors all agree on: the global, deregulated internet is good business for the American economy.

At a basic level, U.S. internet policy can be boiled down to getting as many people using the network of networks as possible, while protecting the status quo legal, institutional, and economic arrangements governing connectivity and exchanges online. From the global infrastructure facilitating exchanges of data to the creation of unique content and services online, American companies are dominant, extraordinarily profitable, and, in most cases, well ahead of foreign competition. Building on chapters 1 and 2, this chapter traces how economic logic continues to drive U.S. policy. From this perspective, the real cyber war may not be over offensive capabilities or cybersecurity but instead over legitimizing existing institutions and norms governing internet industries in order to assure their continued market dominance and profitability.

This chapter proceeds with two central foci: the uneven relationship between connectivity and economic growth; and the economic motivations behind criticism of the International Telecommunication Union's (ITU) potential role in internet governance. In the first three sections we examine how the U.S. government, with the aid of its private sector, wired the world and profited handsomely as a result. We also discuss how economies of scale strongly favor established actors in the internet economy, challenging the idea that increased connectivity is equally profitable for all. The final three sections examine the controversy surrounding the World Conference on International Telecommunications (WCIT), outlining how the negotiations were shaped by economic concerns. We argue that, contrary to popular coverage of the event, the United States left the treaty-making process gloriously successful, protecting its private-sector and economic interests at the expense of the majority of the world's concerns about the status quo governance structure. This analysis identifies how the United States government leverages the private sector to tilt international negotiations in its favor and offers a critique of the multistakeholder process that too often operates as a proxy to ensure private-sector voices and interests dominate international fora. This section concludes with a discussion of economic externalities, the basis for a "network effect" theory, suggesting an alternative framing to the neoliberal, modernization, and "information sovereignty" discourses that often dominate debates surrounding internet governance.

Global Information Infrastructure and Beyond

How did the internet become a global communications medium in such a relatively short time? Whereas chapter 2 ("The Information-Industrial Complex") discussed how the internet came into existence with the help of government/private-sector collaboration, and chapter 3 utilized Google as a case study for documenting private-sector efforts at the commodification of data, in this chapter we are concerned with documenting the outcomes of this collaboration. Out of this system of collaboration has emerged a thoroughgoing and consistent pattern of cooperation between the U.S. government and the private sector aimed at preparing and nudging the world toward accepting and embracing the internet as the connective tissue of the twenty-first century.

In 1994, the Clinton administration embarked on the Global Information Infrastructure (GII) initiative, an ambitious project to wire the world based on the deregulation of the telecommunications sector, removal of trade protections, and a surge in foreign direct investment by Western companies and institutions in global communication infrastructure. Vice President Al Gore formally announced the initiative at the ITU's 1994 World Telecommunication Development Conference in Buenos Aires, calling on delegates to support the GII and "circle the globe with information superhighways on which all people can travel. These highways—or, more accurately, networks of distributed intelligence—will allow us to share information, to connect, and to communicate as a global community."[1] According to Gore, the GII would spread the principles of participatory democracy far and wide, allow for greater sharing of knowledge between cultures, and promote international cooperation and peace. Gore was also keen to argue the economic possibilities of an enhanced global information infrastructure, noting, "The global economy also will be driven by the growth of the Information Age. Hundreds of billions of dollars can be added to world growth if we commit to the GII."[2]

Gore acknowledged that the GII could not simply be wished into place. Despite the lofty rhetoric, Gore was aware that GII implementation would take considerable coordination. Noting that "a primitive telecommunications system causes poor economic development," Gore promised that investments in telecommunications infrastructure would have ripple effects throughout the developing economies.[3] It was a modern-day articulation of the modernization paradigm of economic and political development discussed in detail in the introduction to this book.

In order to facilitate the development of a global, interoperable network of networks, the United States committed to global assistance in the form of aid from USAID and the World Bank to support robust telecommunications growth, while noting that "regulatory reform must accompany this technical assistance and financial aid for it to work."[4] These reforms were merely extended versions of the Clinton administration's domestic regulatory priorities, emphasizing the opening of new markets to competition, privatization, and the implementation of robust protections for intellectual property.

In his keynote address at the 1994 conference, Gore called attention to the U.S. Telecommunications Training Institute (USTTI) as a means for telecommunications professionals around the world to learn from the American model. Ambassador Michael Gardner, U.S. representative to the ITU

Plenipotentiary Conference in Nairobi, Kenya, with the support of William McGowan (founder of MCI Communications), Joseph Charyk (first president of COMSAT), Charles Wick (director of the USIA), and Dick Nichols (vice president of AT&T International) founded the USTTI in 1982 as a public-private partnership. "Dedicated to aggressively sharing ICT knowledge with women and men" managing "the communications infrastructures in the developing countries of the world," the institute continues to provide tuition-free training for communications professionals, regulators, and entrepreneurs from the developing world.[5] By 2012 the Institute had graduated 8,774 professionals and regulators from 171 developing countries.

The courses offered at USTTI draw from a mixture of American public-sector and private-sector expertise, with instruction from officials at the FCC, NTIA, the private sector, and academia. The State Department assists by identifying communications professionals abroad, offering scholarships to participants to cover the costs of traveling to and from the workshops as well as room and board. As outlined in Table 4.1 (USTTI Board of Directors), the Institute's board of directors, which oversees operations and decides course curricula as well as who is admitted, currently includes representatives from Facebook, AT&T, Cisco Systems, Comcast, Ericsson, FCC, Google, 21st Century Fox, IBM, Intelsat, Inmarsat, Intel, Internet Society, Microsoft, Walt Disney Company, GSM, Qualcomm, NTIA, NASA, U.S. Department of State, and Verizon. These board member companies also provide training space at corporate and government facilities, and finance the overhead costs for the institute.[6]

The composition of the board shapes the content and purpose of the training courses. According to industry insider Dave Burstein, the USTTI is run by industry lobbyists whose "heavy corporate agenda" is "unlikely to effectively see what's needed in less developed countries."[7]

Ambassador Michael Gardner, one of the USTTI founders, was the U.S. representative to the ITU Plenipotentiary Conference in Nairobi, Kenya. The institute has been an unofficial partner of the ITU's since its inception in 1982. In 2004, the partnership was formalized, including ITU support for the institute's programming. According to ITU secretary general Hamadoun Touré, the agreement represented "the culmination of two decades of cooperation between ITU and USTTI in bringing state-of-the art courses to telecommunication professionals in developing countries and LDCs. The multiplier effects of such high-quality training on the way telecommunications is provided and managed in Member States make it well worth the long-range investment by ITU."[8]

Table 4.1: USTTI Board of Directors (2014)

Name	Position
Michael R. Gardner	Chairman, USTTI, The Law Offices of Michael R. Gardner, P.C.
Rebecca Arbogast	Vice President, Global Public Policy, Comcast Corporation
Ellen Blackler	Global Public Policy Group, The Walt Disney Company
Kathryn Brown	President and CEO, Internet Society (ISOC)
Mark Cleverley	Director, Strategy, IBM
Gonzalo de Dios	Assistant General Counsel, Intelsat
Belinda Exelby	Head of Institutional Relations, GSM Association
Bruce Gustafson	Head of Government and Industry Affairs, Region North America, Ericsson
Eric Loeb	Vice President, International External Affairs Team, AT&T
Paul Mitchell	General Manager, Technology Policy, Microsoft Corporation
Christopher Murphy	Vice President, Government Affairs, Inmarsat
Dr. Robert Pepper	Vice President, Global Technology Policy, Cisco Systems
Peter Pitsch	Executive Director, Communications Policy, and Associate General Counsel, Intel Corporation
Michael Regan	Executive Vice President, Global Public Policy, 21st Century Fox
Jacquelynn "Jackie" Ruff	Vice President, International Public Policy and Regulatory Affairs, Verizon Communications
Hon. Harrison H. Schmitt	Aerospace Consultant and Director, Former Chair, NASA Advisory Council, Former U.S. Senator and Astronaut
Daniel L. Sepulveda	Ambassador, U.S. Coordinator, International Communications and Information Policy, Verizon Communications
Aparna Sridhar	Policy Counsel, Google
Lawrence E. Strickling	Assistant Secretary of Commerce for Communications and Information and Administrator of NTIA, U.S. Department of Commerce
Tom Wasilewski	Vice President, Government Affairs, Qualcomm
Tom Wheeler	Chairman, Federal Communications Commission
Sarah Wynn-Williams	Director, Global Public Policy, Facebook

As the USTTI's training programs expanded throughout the 1990s, the U.S. government pursued additional assistance initiatives in order to increase the scope and speed of global telecommunications development. Beginning with the George W. Bush administration, internet-freedom programs were used as a means to further synchronize global telecommunications standards and practices, allowing for greater transnational movement of technologies and capital. Recent USTTI programs integrate technical training with lectures that emphasize the importance of multistakeholder processes in internet governance.[9]

In 2003, the Bush administration issued an executive order establishing the Digital Freedom Initiative (DFI), supporting the transfer of American telecommunications and digital media expertise to ICT entrepreneurs abroad.

The DFI included increased foreign aid directed at ICT development, training by Peace Corps volunteers, and collaboration with major U.S. technology companies. Programs focused on improving rural access to telecommunications services, regulatory reform, infrastructure development, integration of ICTs into small and medium businesses, and expanding the use of technology in healthcare, education, and finance. Between 2003 and 2008, the DFI supported projects in Indonesia (cybersecurity), Jordan (education), Pakistan (telemedicine), Peru (rural internet services), Rwanda (broadband development), Senegal (entrepreneurship), and elsewhere.[10]

Integral to the DFI's implementation was technical and entrepreneurial expertise, provided by the DFI Business Roundtable, a body composed of more than forty U.S. companies, nongovernmental organizations, and academic institutions. According to the 2005 DFI Annual Report, the partners "provide[d] volunteers and other resources that leverage[d] activities supported by the U.S. government; and they collaborate[d] with private sector entities in the DFI host countries to identify and implement activities that promote economic growth and opportunities." Technology and strategy leaders from Cisco, Google, Hewlett-Packard, IBM, Intel, MIT, and VeriSign, among others, participated in the government's programs.[11]

Alongside the DFI, USAID, with support from the FCC and the National Telecommunication and Information Administration (NTIA), launched the Telecommunications Leadership Program (TLP) to provide technical assistance and capacity-building support to developing-country governments aiming to reform their telecommunications policies and practices. Table 4.2 outlines a select list of TLP programs from 2002 to 2007. The reforms focused on synchronizing the trend in privatization to allow for greater Western investment in telecommunications and ICT industries abroad.

By 2005 ICTs had become increasingly central to the work of USAID. According to its annual report, the agency helped expand ICT access and capabilities in more than eighty countries with more than $200 million in government aid, leveraging another $240 million in assistance from the private sector.[12] In addition to the TLP, DFI, and the USTTI, the Bush administration launched the Internet for Economic Development Initiative, the Last Mile Initiative, and the LeLand Initiative for Africa,[13] each of which helped establish telecommunications infrastructures and regulatory environments favorable for Western companies to invest and expand into new markets around the world.

The driving force behind these initiatives was the desire to create opportunities for market expansion and economic growth for United States and other

Table 4.2: Select list of Telecommunications Leadership Program (TLP) Events

Dates	Focus	Participants	Location	Outcome
April 2002	Telecommunications Regulatory Workshop	USAID, Moroccan Telecommunications Regulatory Agency, Yemeni officials	Rabat, Morocco	Workshops on liberalization; training
April 2002	NTIA's Caribbean Telecom Workshop	US experts and officials from Dominica, Grenada, St. Kitts/Nevis, St. Lucia, St. Vincent and the Grenadines, Dominican Republic, Jamaica, Barbados, and Trinidad and Tobago	Bridgetown, Barbados	Workshops on spectrum licensing and management, interconnection, enforcement, Internet topography
May 2002	USTTI Seminar on International Telecommunications Union's Plenipotentiary	US Telecommunications Training Institute officials along with officials from El Salvador, Guatemala, Honduras, Jamaica, Mali, Moldova, Russia, Thailand, and Uganda	Washington, D.C.	Workshops on governance, competition, and regulations
June 2002	African VoIP Conference	AFCOM International hosted conference on Voice-Over-Internet Protocol for Gambia, Ethiopia, Swaziland, Burkina Faso, Uganda, Namibia, Rwanda, Nigeria, and South Africa	Atlanta, Georgia	Training
August 2002	APEC "Legal Frameworks for Combating Cybercrime" Workshop	APEC telecom ministers	Moscow, Russia	Discussions on deterring cyberattacks
November 2002	AFCOM 2002	FCC officials and Ghana, Mauritius, Mauritania, Mozambique, Nigeria, Gambia, and Senegal	Washington, D.C.	Presentations on integrating into the digital economy
November 2002	E-Commerce and Small Business Development in Southern Mexico Workshop	EB/CIP officials Mexican small and medium-sized enterprises	Villahermosa, Tabasco, Mexico	Advice on how to use information technology in southern Mexico
November 2002	Implementing E-Government Conference	USAID, U.S. Trade Development Agency and 25 developing countries	Washington, D.C.	Workshops on harnessing power of information technology

Continued

Table 4.2: *Continued*

Dates	Focus	Participants	Location	Outcome
November 2002	Training for Afghanistan Telecom Officials	Afghanistan Ministry of Communications Officials and FCC officials	Columbia, Maryland	Training
April 2003	E-Logistics Forum on Electronic Commerce	US EB/CIP and Hungarian government officials	Budapest, Hungary	Deregulation of related industries; lower trade tariffs
May 2003	Digital Bridge to Africa Roundtable	NGO Digital Partners Institute officials and U.S. experts	Accra, Ghana	Roundtable on capacity and financing
August 2003	Central American Free Trade Agreement Trade Capacity Building Workshop	Telecom regulators from Costa Rica, El Salvador, Guatemala, Honduras, and Nicaragua, and USAID and FCC officials	Washington, D.C.	Trade capacity building workshop
February 2004	Connected for Development Workshop in India	Digital Partners (NGO), development officials, and local government leaders	Baramati, India	Training
March 2004	West Bank and Gaza Telecommunications Regulatory Authority Capacity Building	Palestinian Authority communications officials, USTTI officials, and University of Montana officials	Washington, D.C/, Missoula, Montana, and Silicon Valley, California	Training
March 2004	AFRINET Conference on Rural Access to Telecommunications	U.S. government experts and West African telecom regulators	Washington, D.C., Missoula, Montana, and Silicon Valley, California	Discussion of competition and liberalization
March 2004	Arab Telecommunications Regulatory Network (ATRN) and Arab Regional IT Association (ARAITA)	United States, Jordan, Morocco, Saudi Arabia, Iraq, Kuwait, Palestinian Authority, and Syria	Amman, Jordan	Liberalization; training
May 2004	Morocco Free Trade Agreement Capacity Building	Moroccan telecom officials and FCC experts	Washington, D.C.	Training

Dates	Focus	Participants	Location	Outcome
September 2004	Training through Telecommunications Leadership Program	Andean telecom officials	Washington, D.C.	Training
July 2005	Last Mile Training	FCC and NTIA officials and Colombian Telecom Regulator and Ministry	Bogota, Colombia	Training
September 2005	Telecommunications Regulatory Workshop	Ukraine and U.S. officials	Kiev, Ukraine	Training
September 2005	Workshops	FCC officials	Johannesburg, South Africa	Workshops
December 2005	Consultations with Moroccan telecom officials	Telecommunications Leadership Program and Moroccan counterparts	Rabat, Morocco	Consultations
December 2005	Telecom Meetings	Telecommunications Leadership Program and Algerian counterparts	Algiers, Algeria	Training
February 2006	Telecom Meetings	Telecommunications Leadership Program and counterparts at Independent Communications Authority of South Africa	Pretoria, South Africa	Training
February 2006	Workshop on interconnection, pricing, competitive access and regulatory principles that promote investment	TLP experts and regulators from 14 nations of the Telecommunications Regulatory Authority of Southern Africa and Common Market for Eastern and Southern Africa	Dar es Salaam, Tanzania	Training; liberalization
February 2006	Talks on development and liberalization of Kenya's telecom sector	Officials from the State Department and Kenya's Ministry of Information and Communication	Nairobi, Kenya	Telecommunications liberalization
January 2007	Workshops on Universal Service Funding and Remote Communities Wireless Broadband Initiatives	Telecommunications Leadership Program officials and officials from Vietnam and Cambodia	Hanoi, Vietnam	Training to supplement Last Mile Initiative
April 2007	USTDA Conference	TLP experts and officials	Almaty, Kazakhstan	Workshops and training

Data gathered from FOIA requested information regarding the TLP provided by the State Department.

Western companies. Put simply, the greater congruence between regulatory environments and technical standards, the more able Western corporations are to expand confidently into new markets and quickly turn investments into revenue. The following section outlines how the global connectivity enabled by these reforms became an impetus to American economic growth.

It's (Still) the Economy . . . Stupid!

The economic significance of the internet's ascendance is unprecedented. According to U.S. Secretary of Commerce Gary Locke, "The internet is becoming the central nervous system of our information economy and society."[14] In 2010, global online transactions totaled $10 trillion, and by 2020, internet-based transactions will exceed $24 trillion.[15] A 2011 report prepared by McKinsey Global Institute (MGI) found that "the internet is, and will remain over coming decades, one of the biggest drivers of global economic growth."[16] MGI focused on thirteen countries constituting over 70 percent of the world's Gross Domestic Product (GDP) and found that internet-driven commerce and productivity are responsible for 21 percent of GDP growth in mature economies from 2006 to 2011. If internet consumption and expenditure were a discrete industry, its contribution to GDP would be greater than energy, agriculture, and several other critical sectors. The internet's total contribution to the Gross World Product (GWP) is larger than the GDP of Spain or Canada, and it is growing faster than Brazil's economy.[17]

How, exactly, does the internet contribute to economic growth? Seventy-five percent of the internet's economic contribution stems from its role in industries not directly linked to ICT. By lowering the costs of materials and administrative tasks, and increasing market reach and overall productivity, the internet, coupled with computerization, has become fundamental to almost every industry in the modern economy. According to the Organization for Economic Co-operation and Development (OECD), broadband and ICT networks may have a greater effect on productivity than any other technology to date, including electricity and the combustion engine.[18]

Moreover, researchers at the OECD found that internet maturity correlates strongly with a $500 increase in per capita GDP.[19] To put this growth in perspective, whereas the commercial internet has existed for less than twenty years, it took the industrial revolution more than fifty years to achieve the same level of economic impact. MGI found that internet maturity saves consumers money in each of the countries studied, resulting in an annual net consumer surplus of $10 billion in France and $64 billion in the U.S. in 2009.[20] These consumer savings are, in most cases, reinvested into the local economy. Testifying before Congress, David Fisher, vice president of ADC Telecommunications, put it simply: "Communications networks have become quite literally an essential strategic resource in most countries of the world, on a par with labor and capital in making a real difference in peoples' lives. The global information infrastructure is a necessary part of growth in every economic sector."[21]

At the center of the global internet economy is the United States. According to Fisher, "The United States is the indisputable world leader in telecommunications technological innovation and development."[22] Thirty-eight percent of the production needed to build internet-related hardware, software, and content originates inside the fifty contiguous states. The next largest contributor is Japan (14 percent), followed by China (10 percent). The United States also captures 35 percent of global internet connectivity (telecommunications) revenues and more than 40 percent of net income generated online.[23] MGI concludes, "The United States remains the largest player in the internet supply ecosystem."[24] This position is due to strong growth and sales in software and services, hardware, telecommunications, as well as the U.S. position as global leader in cultural exports.

As a result, U.S.-based technology companies dominate the global internet industry and are a critical driver of American economic growth. The internet is also spurring job creation in the U.S. digital commerce, and IT jobs grew by 26 percent between 1998 and 2008—projected to grow an additional 22 percent by 2018. This growth is, on average, four times faster than in any other sector of the American economy.[25] In 2010 the ITIF estimated that the commercial internet had made the U.S. economy at least $2 trillion larger in terms of annual GDP than it would have otherwise been, accounting for approximately 30 percent of U.S. economic growth.[26]

Increasingly, the export of internet technologies, provisions, and services are crucial to the continued strength of the American information economy sector. According to a report from the Bureau of Economic Analysis (BEA), ICT-enabled services accounted for 45 percent of U.S. exports in 1998;[27] by 2010, they accounted for 61 percent, generating $324 billion for the U.S. economy.[28] Royalties, license fees, and intellectual property exports accounted for $106 billion in exports in 2010. To highlight just two examples, in 2012, 54 percent of Google's revenue resulted from its international operations, or just over $23 billion.[29] And more than $19 billion of Cisco System's 2012 revenue stemmed from sales and services abroad.[30]

As more people access the internet, the companies that provide the internet's backbone will profit from its use. Who exactly profits from internet use depends on the location of the visited Web site. If a user visits Facebook, for example, which is hosted primarily in the United States, foreign ISPs that connect their customers to Facebook's servers pay a connection fee to one of the Tier 1 internet bandwidth providers, such as AT&T, Verizon, or Level 3. In 2012, according to one ranking service, 43 percent of the world's million most popular Web sites were hosted within the United States. The nearest competitors trail well behind this figure: Germany (8 percent), China (5 percent), and the United Kingdom (less than 4 percent).[31] According to Martin N. Bailey, Schwartz Chair in Economic Policy Development and senior fellow at the Brookings Institution, "Countries that helped put in place the internet infrastructure and promoted usage reaped the benefits of their efforts and saw a larger growth contribution."[32]

American market dominance in the internet economy is not incidental. According to Cameron Kerry, general counsel for the Department of Commerce, "Today the internet is central to our mission to promote growth and retool the economy for sustained U.S. leadership in the twenty-first century."[33] Kerry's supervisor, Secretary of Commerce Gary Locke, agrees, noting, "This is the future of the global economy. And it's a sector where the United States has demonstrated tremendous innovative capacity. . . . The sheer volume of economic activity today directly translates into yet more opportunities for entrepreneurs as well as keeping our larger companies competitive in the aggressive global economy."[34]

Critical to continued growth of the internet and its maturity in markets like China, India, Russia, Brazil, and elsewhere are the polices governing internet usage and development. Like any industry, regulations (or their absence) have a tremendous influence on the size, scale, and significance of internet-related commerce in a given country. According to MGI, "The context in which business operates is critical to the growth of the internet ecosystem and will hold back its growth if the environment does not encourage expansion of usage, encouragement of innovation, and business investment and participation."[35] The potential growth in countries with less-established internet industries is substantial. While the internet accounts for about 6 percent of GDP in established economies, its contribution to emerging economies is significantly lower (Brazil, 1.7 percent; India, 2.1 percent; Russia, 1.9 percent).[36]

These emerging markets, however, have the potential to fuel the Western-dominated internet industries for the coming decades, but only if they play ball. Domestic controls on access and content are thus not simply questions of freedom of expression; many American businesses consider them "digital protectionism." According to Jake Colvin, president of global trade at the National Foreign Trade Council, "Barriers to technologies which enable access to the internet are simply tariffs. . . . Even where policies are designed to support legitimate objectives, national security, law enforcement, privacy, businesses can be at a disadvantage when those rules are unclear or arbitrarily, non-transparent or unevenly applied."[37]

The effect of local policies is not lost on American policymakers. According to Secretary Locke, "We know that overseas barriers to online transactions can frustrate and impede our innovators here at home. When this happens, our competitiveness is diminished and potential job growth can fail to materialize. . . . [A]rtificial restrictions are simply methods of promoting or protecting local businesses"[38]

Foreign information policies can directly impact the bottom-line of American corporations in three ways. First, U.S. companies have difficulty interpreting and ensuring proper enforcement of arbitrary or nontransparent restrictions on certain types of speech, violations of which open them up to costly litigation; worse, in order to compensate for ambiguity in foreign censorship laws, U.S. corporations are likely to over-censor in an effort to avoid litigation, putting them at a competitive disadvantage vis-à-vis locally or regionally based corporations more familiar with the ambient legal and cultural norms. Second, Western corporations that follow requirements regarding government access to consumer data (surveillance, for example) incur accusations of failing to protect user rights. As Yahoo! Inc. can testify, even a few limited infractions in one country can result in a domestic and global public-relations disaster.[39] Third, requirements for the localization of data and servers leave corporations vulnerable to cyberattacks. Given the nature of cloud computing today, a successful cyberattack on a company's server in one country may corrupt its entire network, threatening proprietary information, customer data, and operational readiness. According to Daniel Weitzner, former White House deputy chief technology officer for internet policy, "These risks can constitute a price so high that U.S. companies may avoid doing business altogether in such environments."[40]

Economies of Scale and the Internet Economy

While many pundits, politicians, and corporations trumpet the economic benefits of internet connectivity, it is important to note that its significance and effect will not be universally enjoyed. In highly developed countries, there is little doubt that connectivity is likely to increase economic productivity and reduce inefficiencies. This is largely attributable to the fact that developed economies are primed to incorporate internet-based services and technology to support existing institutions, organizations, and infrastructure.

The effect of connectivity in the least-developed countries is not necessarily associated with similar trends. Economist Eli Noam argues that improved access to the internet and internet connectivity—solutions to the so-called "digital divide"—could exasperate the global rich-poor gap. Noting that developing countries account for only 5 percent of commercial websites and receive only 2.4 percent of world internet revenues, Noam predicts that as connectivity increases, "twelve countries will account for almost 85 percent of e-commerce and eight countries will account for 80 percent of e-content."[41]

Noam's prediction is based on the simple fact that that e-commerce and internet-based goods and services operate on strong economies of scale and, like the telecommunications industry before it, deviate from several fundamental, underlying assumptions of perfect market economics in several crucial ways: the cost of services decrease as the scale of production increases (economies of scale); the higher the number of users, the more valuable the service (network effects); the cultivation of a critical mass of users is required before an operation is economically self-sufficient (barriers to entry); and in some cases there can be only one economically viable supplier (natural monopolies).

Put another way, the fixed costs of e-commerce operations are high, resulting in high barriers to entry for new competitors. At the same time, the variable cost of spreading the service to the world is incredibly low and can be implemented incredibly fast. Once successfully tested in a sample market, services and products are relatively easy to scale up to broader, transnational markets. Further, on the demand side, there are clear positive network externalities associate with larger user communities, resulting in huge advantages to being large. These tributes are commonly observed surrounding so-called "natural" monopolies.[42]

Thus, as governments and transnational corporations work furiously to wire the world, increasing connectivity and data transmission speeds while reducing costs, they create "the highways and instrumentalities for rich countries to sell to poor countries."[43] According to Noam, as commerce and businesses move online,

> U.S. firms will be the most successful. They will be technologically at the leading edge, with risk capital at their disposal, with the advantage of being an early entrant and having a large home market. Once a firm establishes a successful model for the U.S. market, invests in the fixed costs, and secures

nearly non-existent transmission prices, there is no reason to stop at the border. The implications are that e-commerce will be dominated by firms from the US and other electronically advanced countries.[44]

Without question, greater internet connectivity will enable all sorts of innovation and e-commerce in developing countries. The classic anecdote of a local craftsman being able to market and sell her handmade goods around the world holds weight; and there are thousands, if not millions, of examples to back it up.

But what the local-craftsman anecdote overlooks is how important a complex, tested, secure, trusted e-commerce portal is for her success. It is expensive to operate and certainly not as simple as running a Web site with a shopping cart. It requires systems, backup systems, security, and a host of technical knowledge beyond the capacity of most savvy computer users. Things like "supply chain electronic data interchange, payment systems, integration with financial institutions, fulfillment systems, customer data mining, production, customization, community creation and the creation of community lock-in by additional features" all require expertise and resources.[45] These complexities and security risks are only increasing as more and more people are brought online. Broadband complicates things even further, as consumers come to expect clean, sophisticated Web sites. According to Noam, "Text and still images will not be sufficient in a competitive environment, and expensive video and multimedia will be required."[46]

As a result, the production costs for attractive and trusted e-commerce sites are high, and established actors dominate the internet economy. While new competitors will always arise, Western corporations have a relative advantage due to familiarity with the required systems, institutions, regulations, and access to large pools of human and financial resources. Contrast this with small-scale success stories in the developing world achieved through the use of mobile phones, which do not require sophisticated underlying infrastructures, such as fishing in parts of India (where fishermen, in mobile contact with merchants on shore, can react at sea to market conditions so as to reduce waste)[47] and financial transactions.[48]

The dominant actors in the internet economy typically acquire the few portals offering possible alternatives before they can truly disrupt the market, typically for the talented human resources and intellectual property driving the competition in the first place. Google, for example, has acquired a total of 161 companies, averaging more than one acquisition per week since 2010,[49] and as a result dominates online markets for search and mapping. The cost of importing technology is another consideration. According to UNCTAD, in 2010, ICT goods accounted for 12 percent of world merchandise trade, and as much as much as 20 percent in developing countries[50].

What can World Bank and ITU data tell us about the relationship between connectivity and economic growth? The studies referenced above from MGI, the Boston Consulting Group, and the OECD focus on the internet in growing, established, and/or transitioning economies with significant ICT infrastructures, including widespread deployment of personal computers and corporate computing systems.

In Africa, the economic benefits of connectivity are far from clear. Both Kenya and Senegal are among the weakest economies in Africa, but both have greater internet penetration and connectivity than 85 percent of the continent. At the same time, some of Africa's wealthiest countries, including Botswana, Equatorial Guinea, and Gabon, have extraordinarily low internet penetration rates.[51] Fewer than 5 percent of the citizens of Lesotho, a small, landlocked country in Southern Africa, are connected to World Wide Web, and yet its per capita GDP has doubled since 2009.

The "connectivity spurs economic activity" hypothesis is also challenged by the case of Tanzania, one of the world's poorest economies, based on per capita income. Modeled after Sweden's national internet program, Tanzania's $250 billion national backbone initiative (supported by a soft loan from China) established a ten-thousand-kilometer high-speed fiber-optic cable network connecting rural villages, towns, and cities to the Web.[52] The initiative is part of a national ICT policy aiming for "Tanzania to become a hub of ICT infrastructure and ICT solutions that enhance sustainable socio-economic development and accelerate poverty reduction both nationally and globally."[53] The quality of the network and the speeds it offers are among the best in the world. Yet despite its availability and relative affordability compared to other networks of similar quality, less than 10 percent of its capacity is being utilized. A 2012 study found that virtually no citizens outside of government and multinational corporations had accessed the high-speed network, adding, "Few people even know it exists."[54] Despite the existence of the network, only 4.4 percent of Tanzanians use the internet.[55] A Tanzanian participant in a USTTI training course echoed these challenges, expressing concern for the economic sustainability of internet access: "Tanzanian citizens are faced with a choice to feed their families or spend their income (2 to 3 dollars a day) on telecommunication services. Economically they cannot afford Internet access at the expense of eating to survive."[56]

More broadly, a careful analysis of *global* internet penetration rates and trends and economic growth only further muddies the waters. Between 2006 and 2011, five countries experienced shrinking GDP: the Bahamas, Ireland, Antigua and Barbuda, the United Kingdom and Iceland. Iceland is the world's most connected country, with more than 97 percent of its citizens accessing the World Wide Web, yet its economy shrank by nearly twenty percent over the five-year period. The United Kingdom ranks in the top twenty nations in terms of global connectivity, with 82 percent of its residents online. Yet its economy shrank by 3.8 percent. Similarly, the three remaining countries witnessed similar declines in GDP despite increases in internet connectivity: Bahamas (9.5 percent), Ireland (7.8 percent), and Antigua and Barbuda (6.2 percent).[57]

Conversely, a number the world's poorest countries experienced rapid economic growth despite below-average internet penetration and below-average growth in internet connectivity. Turkmenistan, Iraq, Mongolia, Lao PDR, Liberia, Timor-Leste, Kyrgyz Republic, Tajikistan, Nepal, and Papua New Guinea each achieved a 95 percent or greater increase in per capita GDP between 2005 and 2011, with internet penetration increasing by less than 10 percent in each country, well below the global average for that six-year period.[58]

Needless to say, there are many other factors driving these economic trends, including the great recession and the acquisition of in-demand natural resources. These examples do, however, challenge the logic behind the modernization paradigm that drives so much of contemporary internet policy. Internet connectivity is not necessarily an on-ramp to modernity, as Secretary Clinton suggested in her 2010 internet-freedom address.

None of this is to say that the internet is not having a profound effect on the modern global economy, reshaping industries and driving innovation and efficiency across sectors. It clearly is and will continue to do so. But, like any new market for goods and services, there will be winners and losers and the transfer of wealth between competitors. Given the dubious correlations between internet penetration and economic growth documented above, and the real positive effect of mobile technologies in the developing world, the modernization paradigm governing internet policy debates takes on a new light. The following sections focus on the current and historical efforts of established actors with clear-cut economic and geopolitical interests in maintaining existing regulatory ambiguity, favoring large, dominant actors, all through the language of supporting a multistakeholder process predicated on the promise of global and *distributed* economic growth.

The International Telecommunications Union

The International Telecommunication Union (ITU)—originally named the International Telegraph Union—was founded in 1865, in Paris, France, and is the world's longest surviving intergovernmental organization. Its founding purpose was to facilitate and manage international interconnection of national networks, which it achieved by supporting and protecting an international cartel of national telecommunications monopolies for most of the twentieth century.[59] In 1947 the ITU became a specialized UN intergovernmental agency, codifying a system whereby governments around the world collaborate to ensure a reliable and accessible system of international communications. Today, the union purports to oversee "the whole ICT sector, from digital broadcasting to the internet, and from mobile technologies to 3-D TV."[60]

The ITU has two types of membership: governments and sector members. Governments have full membership and voting rights, while sector members, which include companies and industry groups, pay an annual membership fee of approximately $35,000. In return for the annual fee, sector members contribute to ITU's technical work, but not to its administrative or policy work, and they do not have formal voting rights (but votes are rare for technical work). The inclusion of the private sector goes back to 1871, when privately held telegraph companies were allowed to participate (but not vote) in the union's 1871 meeting in Rome. Recognizing the essential role that Britain's private sector was playing in establishing and maintaining the infrastructure for international communication, and the highly technical nature of much of the union's work, governments agreed to accept this limited multistakeholder format.[61]

Today's ITU boasts membership of 193 countries and more than seven hundred private-sector entities.[62] In total, the organization's projected 2013 budget was just over $165 million.[63] The private sector entities, the majority of which are American companies and trade associations, contribute roughly 20 percent of the ITU's annual budget, and the United States contributes an additional $10.4 million, or 7.7 percent of the total budget, each year.[64] Australia, Belgium, Denmark, Finland, France, Germany, Hungary, Italy, Lithuania, the Netherlands, Spain, Sweden, Switzerland, and the United Kingdom each recently cut back their annual contributions to the organization.[65] The only country contributing on a similar scale to the United States is Japan.

The ITU's formal inclusion of the private sector stands out among other intergovernmental organizations. Although sector members are not allowed to vote, the vast majority of ITU decisions are made at the level of the committee and do not require formal voting by all member states. ITU secretary-general Hamadoun Touré explains the union's proclivity to avoid formal voting processes as follows: "We never vote because voting means winners and losers and you can't afford that."[66] As a result, the committee decisions that constitute the majority of the union's rulemaking are based on consensus (as opposed to majority rules), where private-sector input can often be decisive. Testifying to Congress, Vonya McCann, former U.S. coordinator for international communications and information policy, argued: "U.S. companies . . . are world leaders in communication technologies and services [and] have a profound influence on ITU activities. . . . [A]s a result of the tremendous participation of the U.S. private sector . . . many in the ITU feel that we already dominate the organization."[67] Further, in practice, corporations are able to influence the positions of their governments, whereby state representatives focus on defending their private-sector interests.

The high profile of American companies has deep historical roots. In the ITU's original formation, only governments whose telegraph systems were publicly owned and operated could participate, and so the United States and the United Kingdom were required to send representatives through private companies. According to the ITU's historical account, "The United States took full advantage of this," driving the organization's early agenda through its private-sector proxies.[68]

As the ITU evolved, the organization provided a crucial mechanism for the U.S. government to assist and protect American telecommunication and information service companies as they expanded abroad. At a 1997 congressional hearing assessing the value of the ITU, Lon C. Levin, then-president of XM Satellite Radio, highlighted the essential role the organization plays in providing a policy forum for the dissemination of telecommunications norms like deregulation and privatization: "The ITU is the ideal place for that kind of discussion. . . . It resulted, I believe, in each country feeling more comfortable with these global systems."[69] Offering a concrete example, Levin noted how the satellite industry—which generates $85.9 billion in annual revenue for the U.S. economy[70]—depends on the ITU to coordinate frequency allocations and procedures for launching and operating regional and global systems. Decisions made at "past ITU conferences," Levin said, "paved the way for . . . the development of Direct Broadcast satellites, the Low Earth Orbit (LEO) mobile satellite systems, Digital Audio Radio Satellites, and the newly proposed high-speed data satellites."[71] Testifying at the same hearing, ADC Telecommunications vice president David Fisher was eager to see greater U.S. involvement in ITU proceedings, noting, "The United States cannot afford to bypass the opportunity to assert its rightful role as the World leader in telecommunications by ignoring participation in the ITU standards setting bodies."[72]

The U.S. ITU Association, representing such companies as Cisco Systems, Boeing, Comcast, Verizon, AT&T, Lockheed Martin, Sprint, and Lucent Technologies, aims to coordinate private-public strategic planning in order to mold favorable policy outcomes at ITU meetings. As the association noted in 2005, "The U.S. economic and technical successes at the ITU have in large part been due to the availability of policy and technical expertise from the private sector. . . . The traditional role of private sector experts on U.S. Delegations has been, is, and will continue to be, a critical factor in the advancement of any U.S. Administration's telecommunications agenda."[73] Similarly, in a 2009 letter, the U.S. ITU Association reminded President-elect Barack Obama, "The ITU and related multi-lateral policy fora . . . are critical organizations for the United States. The output of these organizations results directly in the promotion of U.S. technologies, the growth of the U.S. telecommunications and high-technology industry, and the international promulgation of U.S. principles."[74]

Given the history of U.S. dominance in the ITU and the robust presence of its private sector in its decision-making processes, one would assume the government's support for a renewed ITU mandate. This, however, was not the case.

The WCIT

The ITU met in Dubai on December 3, 2012—its first summit since 1988—empowered to revise the International Telecommunication Regulations (ITRs). First negotiated in 1988 as a successor to the Telegraph Regulations and the Telephone Regulations (which themselves are successors of the original 1865 ITU Convention), the ITRs are a treaty that established the rules for how traffic flowed between different telecom networks and how charges would be calculated for traffic exchanged between carriers in different countries. However, contrary to its predecessors, the 1988 ITRs included clauses that, in effect, favored liberalization of international interconnection and enabled the subsequent growth of the internet.[75] Much of the media coverage of the WCIT (pronounced "wicket") negotiations framed the ITU as attempting to "take control over the internet," implying that its state-centric governance structure would allow for greater control over the free flow of information by nondemocratic governments.[76] Such accusations are, on their face, disingenuous.[77]

First, the vast majority of ITU member states, including Japan and EU governments, agree that the ITU's authority already extends to regulating internet-based services. In 2006 the American ambassador to the ITU, David Gross, said as much: "One of the great things about the ITU is it has changed over the years, from telegraph to telephone to Internet. We don't want a major international institution to become obsolete just because it couldn't change as the world changes."[78] In fact, the ITU has been involved in discussions regarding standardization and development of the internet protocol stack, including the mechanisms of data transmission, and telecommunications cables and switches, for decades.[79] ITU Council Resolution 1305, adopted at the seventh Plenary Meeting with unanimous consensus, recognized "the scope of work of ITU on international Internet-related public policy matters," including: multilingualization of the internet, the economics of connectivity, the management of domain names, cybersecurity, combatting spam, privacy and consumer rights, and building internet capacity in underdeveloped parts of the world.[80] Internal documents from the NTIA show that the U.S. government recognizes at least thirty-five separate ITU resolutions and programs, providing the ITU with a relevant mandate to discuss internet-related public policy issues.[81]

Second, the ITU itself has no regulatory power or enforcement mechanism. Compliance with the ITRs is entirely voluntary on the part of each member nation, and governments often fail to implement parts of agreements they don't support. So what was all of the hype about?

Many states saw the WCIT negotiations as a means to, in part, enhance norms in favor of greater state authority over transnational information flows, in particular with respect to financial and security issues, including how information is routed. This movement to bolster the international legitimacy of the regulatory power of the governments emerged as a clear threat to the U.S. internet and telecommunications companies. American technology corporations and key sectors of the U.S. government, including members of Congress and the State Department, saw WCIT as a crucial battleground for the future of internet governance and a threat to the American economic interests. According to Eli Noam, "Right now, the foundations are being laid for a great new economic system and for a new generation of business empires."[82] Of the ninety-five-delegate team led by Ambassador Terry Kramer, fifty-nine members were from the private sector and only thirty-six were public servants (approximately ten of whom were from the defense and intelligence communities). Kramer described the delegation as "a Dream Team of policy and technical experts, representing a cross section of government, industry and civil society groups in the fields of international telecommunications and the Internet."[83] Before his appointment at the State Department, Kramer spent twenty-five years as a telecommunications executive at Vodafone and Q Comm International. Government delegates represented numerous executive-branch departments and agencies, as well as the FCC. Among the nongovernment delegates, the ratio of private sector to civil society delegates was 10:1 in favor of the private sector.

Headed into the WCIT negotiations, the official U.S. perspective was crystal clear to all involved: the internet should "require no global regulatory regime and that all these systems will thrive wherever there is free and open access to content and information."[84] From the American perspective, the role of national governments, and the ITU by extension, was to promote market-based solutions, including deregulation, liberalization, and market-based competition. Such a strategy would, according to the State Department, ensure fast growth and investment in services and technologies. The government officials coordinated closely with members of the private sector in the lead up to and during the WCIT negotiations, including at times pressuring nongovernment stakeholders to support the government's position.[85]

Google played a particularly important role in the negotiations. The internet giant launched a Web site in advance of the summit, under the headline "a free and open world depends on a free and open web," warning users against governments seeking "to use a closed-door meeting of the International Telecommunication Union to increase censorship and regulate the web."[86] Google saw the possibility of a renegotiated ITR—whereby governments had greater authority over Google's operations and services inside their own countries—as a problem. Asked about what the most significant threat to Google's future business model might be, the company's European head of public policy, D. J. Collins, fingered the ITU as its principle adversary, arguing that the ITU "is looking at mandatory regulation of the web."[87]

Moving beyond the fierce rhetoric surrounding the ITU's alleged power grab, what was driving the tensions surrounding WCIT, and what was at stake?

Historically, the majority of the ITU's operations focused on technical aspects of coordinating international communication infrastructure and establishing norms for data exchange, including financial aspects of international interconnections. With the growth of business, government, and societal dependence on networked communications for daily operations, internet governance and ITU rulemaking increasingly intersect with important geopolitical issues. Many governments outside the West—including most in Africa, Asia, the Middle East and Latin America—favor an expanded place for ITU oversight in internet-based international communications as a means of slowing the perceived onslaught of Western technology companies around the world. This group of eighty-nine countries—a majority of WCIT participants—includes many that support an "information sovereignty" approach to international communications, as outlined in chapter 1.

There were three primary issues at stake at the WCIT: the distribution of the economic rewards resulting from internet proliferation; the development of proper standards and protocols for securing internet-based communication; and deciding which actors and which forum should be responsible for internet governance in the future. The remainder of this chapter focuses on the economic stakes of the WCIT treaty and addresses the U.S. arguments in favor of a non-ITU, multistakeholder model for the future of internet governance.

The Economics of Internet Governance

For most of the twentieth century, the ITU thrived as the primary mechanism for coordinating the economic costs and benefits of international telecommunications. The ITU's Telegraph Regulations and Telephone Regulations outlined how an outgoing call from Washington, D.C., for example, would connect to a receiver in Jakarta, Indonesia, and which telecommunications provider would pay for the cost of the service. In short, the ITU's regulations created a stable international context for the growth in international telecommunications, while also ensuring that telecommunications providers and their governments received a fair distribution of the revenue. These regulations were often de facto protections for domestic telecommunications providers around the world, which enabled them to compete and grow vis-à-vis foreign competition. The residual effects of these regulations are visible around the world, where local telecommunications providers continue to dominate the market despite the liberalization of telecommunication regulations and the rise in foreign competition. In fact, there are few transnational industries that continue to be dominated by national firms in such a fashion. The telecommunications industry is something of an anomaly in terms of the global economy, defying the theory of comparative advantage, largely due to the effectiveness of regulatory protections for domestic industry and the fact that some portions of the market are no doubt natural monopolies.[88]

Toward the end of the twentieth century, the monopoly hold of the telecommunications sector over the circuits of communication began to wane. As internet-based services became more sophisticated and ubiquitous, they began to appropriate many of the services previously garnered by telecommunications providers. For example, whereas Turkcell, Turkey's leading telecommunications provider, profits from connecting an incoming call from an American-based AT&T caller, no analogous Turkish company profits when that same American connected with her Turkish friend via Skype using high-speed broadband connections. As telecommunications becomes less and less about circuit-based voice communication and more about IP-based networks, local telecommunications companies lose a critical component of their business model: fees assessed for connecting international callers to local citizens. While no study has documented the actual scale of the losses, they are substantial. The ITU estimates that from 1993 to 1998, settlement payments from developed countries to developing countries amounted to approximately $40 billion, a significant transfer of wealth that promises to decline.[89]

As the potential revenue from internet-related commerce crystallized, governments around the world grew wary of the increasing transfer of wealth from domestic industries to transnational corporations operating the backbone of the global internet. As internet-based services have increasingly supplanted telecommunications providers, demand has grown for the ITU to help develop more equitable systems for managing internet-based services revenue that would mirror the systems it developed for international telephone rates and services. By 2006 many, including the United States, argued that the ITU's International Trade Regulations (ITRs) were in need of substantial reconsideration. One central question for the 2012 WCIT negotiations centered on a proposed redefinition of the boundaries between telecommunications and information services. If governments interpreted "telecommunication" to include internet services, then the services could be subject to certain forms of national regulatory control as well as certain provisions of the ITRs. Several proposals for revising the ITRs aimed to establish interconnection arrangements among ISPs that would limit the dominance of U.S.-based companies.[90]

Put another way, as internet-based services increasingly dominated the world of telecommunications, and the growth of internet-based services revenue far exceeded that of telecommunication operators for nonmobile services, developing country governments sought to use the ITU as a forum to establish rules that would facilitate or at least legitimize national measures to rebalance shifting revenue streams.[91] As industry expert Dave Burstein notes, "At ITU/WCIT, the Africans are trying to recover that revenue by a (presumably modest) 'boundary tax' on termination. The U.S. is fighting back, demanding our companies not pay. That's an ordinary mercantile fight over national interest that the State Department is portraying as a battle of principle. . . . It's part of a century-long battle between North and South over 'terms of trade.'"[92] Governments that view the internet as a means for extending American hegemony "logically gravitate to the ITU as a counter-hegemonic vehicle for collective action."[93] Its "one state, one vote" governance regime, as opposed to the existing multistakeholder model, offers a potential check on the private sector's ability to influence governance.

Thus, for much of the developing world, the WCIT negotiations were primarily about the economics of internet expansion.[94] While internet penetration rates in developing countries quintupled from just 4.6 percent in 2002 to 31.2 percent in 2014, increasing their share of the world's total number of internet users from 4.3 percent to 32.4 percent, ISP costs skyrocketed.[95] Due to the lack of standards regulating the exchange rate between "enhanced services networks," local ISPs in the developing world bear the whole cost of international internet transit, resulting in hefty connection fees to connect users to Western Web sites. According to Pauline Tsafak Djoumessi, Cameroon's head of market research for the Ministry of Telecommunications, accessing international bandwidth accounts for 80 percent of costs for internet access providers in Africa and "constitutes a significant bottleneck for internet development in the developing countries."[96] As a result, "on the internet, the net cash flow flows from the developing South to the developed North."[97] From this perspective, internet providers and users in the developing world are in effect subsidizing the maintenance and growth of the global, Western-owned internet backbone.

Worse yet, fees assessed for accessing the international internet backbone are not evenly applied. Connections established between many developed countries—where most of the internet's content is hosted—have established private-sector arrangements (in other words, peering agreements) that allow for a mutual transfer of data at no charge. According to Pedro Oliva Brunet, senior telecommunication expert at the Cuban Ministry of Computer Science and Communications, "Developing countries continue to pay the full cost of the interconnection links and ports for the access to this network while operators in developed countries use these facilities for carrying their traffic without paying anything in return."[98]

In 2013, there were twelve "Tier 1" internet providers, defined as a network able to reach every other network on the internet without purchasing IP transit or paying settlements: AT&T, CenturyLink (formerly Qwest & Savvis), Deutsche Telekom, GTT, Level 3 Communications, NTT Communications, Sprint Nextel, Tata Communications, TeliaSonera International Carrier, Verizon Business, XO Communications and the Zayo Group. Combined, the companies generated more than $689 billion in revenue in 2013, a figure greater than Switzerland's GDP ($650.8 billion).[99]

To summarize, countries entering into the internet economy late, with little original content created and hosted locally, are forced to pay high fees to these Tier 1 providers. At the same time, peering agreements facilitate no-cost international transmission of data between Tier 1 providers, allowing most of the developed world to enjoy low-cost connectivity.

The ITU's primary institutional interest in the WCIT outcome relates to its broader goal of increasing the Web's reach in economically sustainable ways. In an article written for *Wired* a month before the WCIT negotiations, the ITU's secretary-general Touré wrote, "The challenge today is bringing internet access to the *two-thirds* of the world's population that is still offline. . . . If we can achieve this, all the world's citizens will have the potential to

Table 4.3: Tier 1 Internet Providers Annual Revenue

Company	Headquarters	2013 Annual Revenue (billions)
AT&T	USA	$128.8
CenturyLink	USA	18.1
Cogent	USA	0.4
Deutsche Telekom	Germany	60.1
GTT	USA	0.16
Level 3 Communications	USA	6.3
Nippon Telegraph & Telephone Corporation	Japan	106.1
Orange S.A.	France	58.2
Seabone (Telecom Italia)	Italy	51.2
Sprint Nextel	USA	35.5
Tata Communications	India	2.9
Telefónica, S.A.	Spain	83.5
TeliaSonera International Carrier	Sweden	14.7
Verizon Communications	USA	120.6
XO Communications	USA	1.5
Zayo Group	USA	1.0

access unlimited knowledge, to express themselves freely, and to contribute to and enjoy the benefits of the knowledge society."[100] According to Touré, critical to achieving this goal is the development of local internet capacity and infrastructure, which requires capital. One goal of the WCIT negotiations was to allow for a more equitable revenue-sharing system, stimulating investment in nondeveloped markets in order to bring affordable internet access to all. Touré argued that the ITU has a responsibility to check the private sector's profit-seeking agenda: "For big commercial interests, it's about maximizing the bottom line. For me and the ITU, it's about giving people the power to totally transform their lives."[101]

For much of the developing world, doing nothing—the de facto position of the United States—was unacceptable. The legacy of international telecommunications regulation has, from a developmental perspective, been disastrous for the 80 percent of the world forced to choose between expensive telecommunications services or simply not communicating to the outside world for much of the twentieth century. Increasingly, the twenty-first century is looking like the twentieth, as monopoly service providers are allowed to dictate the cost, terms, and range of services provided. For example, market forces have resulted in fixed-broadband internet access for just 9.8 percent of the world's population, and more than 92 percent of people in the world's forty-eight least-developed countries remain unconnected to the Web.[102] Touré's concern is that the current regulations will continue to privilege existing transnational corporations over local actors and leave the vast majority of the world behind, unable to use modern World Wide Web services requiring a high-speed connection.

Such a regulatory shift toward greater tariffs for traffic entering into new and emerging markets can be justified by the theory of network externalities.[103] If two actors consent to an arrangement that affects a third party, that condition is referred to as an externality. Put another way, an externality refers to consequences not taken into account in setting the price of the good or service, thus creating a market dysfunction. Externalities can be positive or negative. For example, an arrangement between two actors allowing for the production and transfer of coal-generated electricity to individual homes and businesses may produce a negative externality of environmental pollution. If the costs of increased pollution are not accounted for in the exchange, governments are justified in addressing the dysfunction, by, for example, levying a tax—called a Pigovian tax, after the economist Arthur Pigou—to compensate for disadvantages suffered.

Transactions in telecommunications and internet economies can produce negative externalities too. For example, the addition of new customers to a mobile telephony provider can increase the level of congestion on the network, decreasing the functionality and, thus, value of the provider's services.

Less understood, and difficult to quantify, are the positive externalities that result from the addition of new users to any given communications network. In 1974 Bell Labs economist Jeffrey Rohlfs outlined the likelihood and significance of positive externalities in the telecommunications industry. Rohlfs wrote: "The utility that a subscriber derives from a communications service increases as others join the system. This is a classic case of external economies in consumption and has fundamental importance for the economic analysis of the communications industry."[104] For example, the value of having a telephone increases as the number of other people with telephone numbers increases. This increase in the value of the network itself, as a result of an additional telephone user, is the classic case of a positive externality.

Today we describe this theory of interdependent demand as the "network effect," referring to the external value added to a communications network from the addition of new users/consumers. Yet while the need for government intervention to correct market imbalances that result from negative externalities is fairly well established, little consensus exists on what the appropriate action should be to correct for market disruptions that result from positive externalities. In theory, positive network externalities should be a source of network development, maintenance, and expansion. This is to say, as a network expands and user demands increase, a network provider should reinvest revenue into developing additional infrastructure to continue to support network expansion and innovation. Ideally, service providers would exploit network externalities to develop faster networks, reaching more and more people and providing more sophisticated services.

But what happens when network providers do not reinvest revenue generated from these positive externalities evenly—or at all? Economists describe a situation where the benefits of consumption are not properly accounted for as a market failure, resulting in prices that are either too high or too low, and either the over- or underproduction of a particular good or service. One possible solution is to institute a tax on, for example, international traffic, requiring the core network to pay additional fees in order to add consumers to its network. Economists from Côte d'Ivoire estimate that a 5 percent network premium on international traffic going into developing economies could result in a balanced global communications infrastructure by 2027.[105]

In 2007, OFCOM, the United Kingdom's broadcast regulator, implemented a network externality surcharge (NES) on termination rates in order to fund infrastructure development for "marginal" mobile telephony users.[106] In preparation for the WCIT negotiations, the European Telecommunications Network Operators' Association (ETNO) proposed the introduction of the principle of "sender party pays" in order to ensure fair compensation for local telecommunications services.[107] Domestically, AT&T has similarly called for a version of "sender pays" in order to compensate cable companies for providing the infrastructure that enables internet companies like Google and Facebook to reach its millions of users (and sell billions of dollars in advertising).[108]

A network externality premium (as opposed to tax) would be especially helpful in two regions in particular, Latin America and Africa, which depend on other regions for their connectivity. In 2012, 82 percent of Latin American internet traffic went through North America, and nearly 90 percent of African connections went through Europe.[109] There are currently no Tier 1 or Tier 2 internet service providers operating in Africa.

Conclusion

The aim of this chapter is not to argue in favor of the ITU's new ITRs or against the U.S. approach to the WCIT negotiations. The vast majority of coverage of the controversy was highly critical of the treaty negotiations, with an emphasis on the UN, as a proxy for the Russian and Chinese governments, trying to "take control of the internet." Congress even issued a resolution, with unanimous support (397–0), for "the consistent and unequivocal policy of the United States to promote a global Internet free from government control." Such fear of greater governmental control over the internet is, without question, justified. At the same time, such declarations are disingenuous and overlook the fact that every government in the world controls information within its borders, including internet-enabled communications, and that the majority of these controls are recognized as legitimate policies of the state.[110] By focusing on questions of regulation and censorship, the WCIT controversy became hyperpoliticized, and legitimate discussions regarding the economics of internet connectivity were sidelined.[111]

By outlining the economic significance of the issue—how economies of scale favor established, dominant actors, and how the current deregulated system enables a handful of Western corporations to profit handsomely from expanded internet connectivity—we attempt to deviate from the modernization and information-sovereignty paradigms that too often dominate discussions of internet governance. While heavy-handed government controls over the internet should be resisted, so should a system whereby internet connectivity requires the systematic transfer of wealth from the developing world to the developed. By focusing on the uneven empirics of the internet's economic significance, combined with a discussion of positive economic externalities and the network effect, this chapter offers an alternative framing of an ongoing debate, and, we hope, a more reasonable path forward.

Post-WCIT policymaker discourse provides compelling evidence of the continued importance of U.S. engagement with the ITU. Despite public rhetoric questioning the continued value of the ITU, the U.S. government sees the organization as crucial for the continued economic success of its private sector. In a policy paper outlining the United States' post-WCIT ITU policy, NTIA's Brian M. Patten noted, "In terms of the funding of the ITU, the United States gets a great deal of value from the ITU-R. . . . The U.S. achieves its goals through presence and leadership"[112] Commenting on the paper, NTIA telecommunications specialist Jonathan Williams agreed, adding, "NTIA, and the United States in general, are heavily engaged in ITU-R due to the importance of the sector described previously, and this long-term investment has enabled both a venue and outcomes that are generally quite favorable to the United States (public and private sector)."[113]

Arguments in favor of continued engagement were not limited to the radiocommunication sector. ITU's development arm was similarly described as a crucial forum for securing American economic interests. According to the NTIA's Office of International Affairs, "Continued participation in ITU-D . . . allows the private sector to examine the market needs and engage in business in these regions more effectively. In addition, many countries, especially those in developing regions, rely heavily on the ITU and ITU-D for advice and best practices when establishing or upgrading their telecommunications networks. Participation allows the U.S. to influence the content and development of those best practices that developing countries use as building blocks of national policy."[114]

ITU-T, the ITU's standardization sector, is similarly seen as crucial for protecting U.S. economic interests. NTIA's official "Trip Report" from the World Telecommunication Standardization Assembly (WTSA-12) touted the large number of Americans elected to leadership positions within the ITU, including representatives from the Department of State, Department of Commerce, AT&T, and Cisco Systems.[115]

The next chapter tackles another element of the internet governance debate, the multistakeholder process, assessing its value in light of historical and empirical evidence.

5

The Myth of Multistakeholder Governance

Imagine for a moment soldiers in jeeps with blue helmets surrounding a building in Marina del Rey, California. What reason, you might ask, would U.N. soldiers have to be in California? They are there to transfer governance of the Internet to the infamous international bureaucracy of the U.N. . . . In order to ensure that the Internet remains a tax-free, efficient, global communications network, I, along with Congressman Rick Boucher, introduced House Concurrent Resolution 268. This bill expresses the sense of Congress that the current management of the Internet's domain name and addressing service works, and that the administration of the Internet should remain in the US under private control.

—Congressman Robert Goodlatte (R-VA), November 4, 2005, Washington, D.C.

Multistakeholderism—the coordination of private-sector and non-profit actors with government authorities—has become central to debates over internet governance since 2003, when the term emerged during WSIS and was formalized in the 2005 Tunis Agenda. The United States, in particular, has adopted the discourse of multistakeholderism as its starting point for any discussion over internet governance. According to Assistant Secretary of Commerce for Communications and Information Lawrence E. Strickling, "The steadfast policy of the U.S. government has been to promote these values of inclusion and participation through our support for the multistakeholder process."[1] While pleasing to the ear, very little research has examined the realities of the processes of inclusion and diverse representation embraced by internet-governance institutions.

Congressman Goodlatte's quote, which introduced this chapter, reflects the widespread fear, held by many American policymakers, of any shift away from the current internet-governance institutions. The discourse mirrors critiques of other international regimes seen as encroaching on American sovereignty. From their perspective, the internet grew out of U.S. government investments in technological development and the authority to oversee its operations should remain fundamentally under American authority.[2]

Of course, the United States no longer has the diplomatic, military, or economic capital to compel international compliance with its unilateral control over the world's most critical communications medium. It recognized as much in 2014 when the National Telecommunications and Information Administration (NTIA) announced its intent to conditionally relinquish its stewardship over the Domain Name System (DNS).[3] Instead, it has organized a system of multistakeholder arrangements to lend increased legitimacy to the institutions overseeing the internet's day-to-day operations.

This chapter explores how these institutions, through multiple layers of governance, reflect dominant political and/or economic interests, deploying discourses of multistakeholderism to legitimize arrangements benefiting powerful, established actors like the United States and its robust ICT private sector. First is a brief discussion of what is actually at stake in debates over internet governance. An overview of the origins and theory of the multistakeholder process (MSP) follows. Then, using three case studies—the Internet Corporation for Assigned Names and Numbers (ICANN), the Internet Society (ISOC) and the Internet Engineering Task Force (IETF)—we explore how seemingly participatory, inclusive, and consensus-driven decision-making structures provide legitimacy for existing political and economic interests.

What's at Stake?

The role of nongovernment entities in deliberating about the future of internet governance has been a crucial sticking point of international negotiations since WSIS and continued to be an issue at WCIT. Internet governance, as defined by the Working Group on Internet Governance (WGIG), refers to the "development and application by governments, the private sector, and civil society, in their respective roles, of shared principles, norms, rules, decision-making procedures and programmes, that shape the evolution and utilization of the internet."[4] This vision of multistakeholder governance is typically juxtaposed to top-down, government-driven regulatory control over the different elements of the network of networks. Debates are then framed as a clash over who has the right to coordinate or oversee the internet: Is it multistakeholder governance institutions or nation-states?

Governance over what, one might ask. Internet governance refers to the core elements that constitute the internet, including: IP addresses and the corresponding domain names; protocols for data transmission (such as TCP/IP and HTTP); and root servers.

The DNS ensures the universal resolvability of domain names to Internet Protocol (IP) addresses, which are required of any device connecting to and communicating on the internet. Every computer on the internet has a unique numerical address (in other words, an IP address, though that address might not be stable over time due to the dynamic allocation of IP addresses), and every Web page must resolve to an IP address. The safe, reliable, and consistent interoperability of the two elements is central to the idea of internet governance.[5] However, according to the WGIG, "The administration of the Internet's names and addresses is much more than the mere allocation of numbers or the assignment of names. It involves integrating technological developments, relevant engineering standards, and related technical policies, as well as the administration thereof."[6]

Translating a domain name into an IP address is referred to as resolving the domain name. The purpose of a single, hierarchical Domain Name System (DNS) is to allow any user anywhere in the world to be able to reach a unique and specific host IP address by entering the address's domain name. Domain names are also used for reaching e-mail addresses and for other internet applications. The data constituting the DNS thus requires a hierarchical, widely distributed set of machines called "name servers." The top of the hierarchy is referred to as the root, and the set of internationally distributed root servers mirror the root and provide redundancy and robustness to the domain-name system.

Control over the root is a critical means of exercising power. According to WGIG, "Domain names determine the visibility and accessibility of a web site or any other service; by removing a domain name, all services associated to it are suddenly made unreachable."[7] Lawrence Lessig's *Code, and Other Laws of Cyberspace* argues that political and social values are inevitably built into the architecture of technological systems.[8] The hierarchical nature of the DNS root server means that power dynamics are necessarily built into any question of governance of the DNS. Yet because internet governance typically relates to highly technical questions of standards and protocols, it is often considered tangential to geopolitics. This is a crucial lapse, as Joel Reidenberg explains: "The Internet Engineering Task Force, the Internet Society, the World Wide Web Consortium and traditional standards organizations like ISO, ETSI, and committees like T1 are the real political centers of" the information society.[9]

The ITU operates using a traditional approach to international governance whereby governments—the parties to the UN charter—come together to discuss the coordination of international telecommunications issues. A criticism leveled by Western countries, and by the United States in particular, is that the ITU fails to include nonstate perspectives, especially those from the private sector. Assistant Secretary Strickling expressed this reservation in relation to the WCIT process in 2012, noting, "Only member states will have a vote at the ITU. A treaty conference, such as the WCIT, can never be a true multistakeholder process where all interests are fairly represented."[10] This perspective fails to acknowledge the long history of American corporate dominance within the organization, as detailed in chapter 4.

Industrialized, developed countries, as well as private sector corporations operating in internet-related industries, support the existing MSPs. Robert Boorstin, formerly Google's director of public policy, praised the MSP, noting, "When was the last time a group of governments got together and decided they didn't want to govern something? This is a big deal. . . . Multistakeholder initiatives will succeed because we have no other choice."[11] Boorstin, like many others in the industry, argues that the decentralized nature of the internet means that efforts to control, censor, or strictly regulate will inevitably fail. Such thinking conveniently overlooks the fact that the DNS is highly centralized and controlled top-down by ICANN. Nevertheless, proponents of MSP argue that, due to the shared, global nature of the internet's operation, any single government's attempt to wall itself off from the rest of the world, even if only partially, will not work, as its citizenry will lose out on critical economic opportunities and political discussions taking place beyond their borders.[12] Many point to the choice of using TCP/IP as the primary language of the internet as a compelling example of the effectiveness of this multistakeholder decision-making process while overlooking the fact that TCP/IP was developed by academics working under contracts with the U.S. Department of Defense, hardly a multistakeholder approach.[13]

For many in the developing world, the ITU is the preferred forum for discussing questions of internet governance precisely because it is based on a traditional UN "one state, one vote" model. Regardless of stakes for the private sector, each state has equal say in policymaking process. It is, thus, an ideal forum to discuss the economics of the internet industries without fear or pressure from internet and telecommunications companies whose interests reside in shaping opinions and rules in their favor. As Levin argues, "Member states are comfortable that the ITU protects their sovereign rights."[14] The ITU's process of establishing industry-wide technical standards also provides a way of ensuring that less-experienced telecommunications regulators are not misled into investing substantial public resources into the wrong technologies by powerful, private-sector stakeholders.

The question of stakeholder inclusion is, in fact, the primary reason the U.S. delegation provided for American opposition to the new ITU treaty. Commenting on the negotiated treaty language, Terry Kramer, U.S. ambassador to the WCIT, announced that the United States would not be signing the treaty because the revised mandates were not compatible with the existing multistakeholder model of internet governance: "Internet policy should not be determined by Member States, but by citizens, communities, and broader society, and such consultation from the private sector and civil society is paramount. This has not happened here."[15] Despite this stated position, U.S. officials privately acknowledge the ITU's role in fostering multistakeholder negotiations.[16] Fifty-four other countries also protested the new treaty language and refused to sign, including all twenty-eight European Union member states and Australia, Canada, Costa Rica, India, Japan, Kenya, and New Zealand.

An alternative framing of the WCIT negotiations could describe it as an effort by disenfranchised governments to reassert their rights in a multistakeholder governing process that is dominated by a small group of actors, most of whom reside in the United States, Western Europe, and Japan. Kramer accurately describes the ITRs as promising an enhanced role for governments in the existing MSPs. For example, the 2012 WCIT Resolution 3 recognizes that "all governments should have an equal role and responsibility for international internet governance." The resolution also provides the ITU secretary general with the responsibility of playing "an active and constructive role in the development of . . . the multistakeholder model of the Internet," suggesting that the ITU's intergovernmental approach be more prominent in future discussions of internet governance.[17]

Table 5.1: List of Countries Signing the 2012 ITRs
*Signatories of the Final Acts: 89

Afghanistan*	Georgia	Norway
Albania	Germany	Oman*
Algeria*	Ghana*	Panama*
Andorra	Greece	Papua New Guinea*
Angola*	Guatemala*	Paraguay*
Argentina*	Guyana*	Peru
Armenia	Haiti*	Philippines
Australia	Hungary	Poland
Austria	India	Portugal
Azerbaijan*	Indonesia*	Qatar*
Bahrain*	Iran*	Republic of South Africa*
Bangladesh*	Iraq*	Republic of the Congo*
Barbados*	Ireland	Russia*
Belarus	Israel	Rwanda*
Belgium	Italy	Saint Lucia*
Belize*	Jamaica*	Saudi Arabia*
Benin*	Japan	Senegal*
Bhutan*	Jordan*	Serbia
Botswana*	Kazakhstan*	Sierra Leone*
Brazil*	Kenya	Singapore*
Brunei Darussalam*	Kuwait*	Slovakia
Bulgaria	Kyrgyzstan*	Slovenia
Burkina Faso*	Latvia	Somalia*
Burundi*	Lebanon*	South Korea*
Cambodia*	Lesotho*	South Sudan*
Canada	Liberia*	Spain
Cape Verde*	Libya*	Sri Lanka*
Central African Republic*	Lichtenstein	Sudan*
Chili	Lithuania	Swaziland*
China*	Luxembourg	Sweden
Colombia	Malawi	Switzerland
Comoros*	Malaysia*	Tanzania*
Costa Rica	Mali*	Thailand*
Cote d'Ivoire*	Malta	Togo*
Croatia	Marshall Islands	Trinidad and Tobago*
Cuba*	Mauritius*	Tunisia*
Cyprus	Mexico*	Turkey*
Czech Republic	Moldova	Uganda*
Denmark	Mongolia	Ukraine*
Djibouti*	Montenegro	United Arab Emirates*
Dominican Republic*	Morocco*	United Kingdom
Egypt*	Mozambique*	United States
El Salvador*	Namibia*	Uruguay*
Estonia	Nepal*	Uzbekistan*
Finland	Netherlands	Venezuela*
France	New Zealand	Vietnam*
Gabon*	Niger*	Yemen*
Gambia	Nigeria*	Zimbabwe*

The proposed power shift not only rubbed the Americans the wrong way, it also troubled powerful nongovernment groups. According to Sally Wentworth, ISOC's head of public policy, "The resolution shifted the emphasis from community and consensus to centralization through government action."[18] Many in the developing world, as well as China and Russia, counter by arguing that the current MSP is a result of a Clinton administration design that continues to benefit American interests. Nevertheless, thus far multistakeholderism has a nice, diplomatic ring to it, while it continues to function as a productive means of furthering raw geopolitical intentions.

Before analyzing how the current MSP replicates existing geopolitical and economic power relationships, this chapter will explore the origins of multistakeholder decision-making processes and identify the underlying assumptions behind such negotiations grounded in multistakeholderism.

Theories of Multistakeholderism

MSPs emerged as a means of resolving conflicts over natural resources, first in the developing world and later as a global phenomenon. Such processes typically occur, according to Steins and Edwards, when "decision-making bodies (voluntary or statutory) comprising different stakeholders who perceive the same resource management problem, realise their interdependence for solving it, and come together to agree on action strategies for solving the problem."[19] The term stakeholder refers to "those who have an interest in a particular decision, either as individuals or representatives of a group. This includes people who influence a decision, or can influence it, as well as those affected by it."[20] Today, MSPs are used to try and resolve any number of "metaproblems,"[21] or complex, public challenges that cannot be solved unilaterally or in isolation due to high levels of interdependence.

Two primary motivations drive state interest toward MSPs. First, when a broad group of actors collectively have more information or knowledge than the central governmental authority, then governments often decide to turn to them for assistance. Second, if states are concerned about the perceived legitimacy of a policy, they can turn to the multistakeholder processes to demonstrate that a decision has broad, democratically instilled buy-in from interested parties. Much of the research on MSPs was based on resource disputes within a particular legal jurisdiction, such as a single federal state (like California) or single country. MSPs focus on creating a consensus among actors, whereby each stakeholder acknowledges that the proposed solution is acceptable, even if it does not reflect its ideal preference.

Multistakeholderism is grounded in a Habermasian conception of rational, ethical, public arguments among interested parties as a means of resolving legitimate ideational differences. It presumes that strategic actors, in the right setting and by embracing shared norms, can disregard their political motivations and pressures to deliberate, listen, adjust perspectives, and come into an agreement regarding a matter of public concern.[22] Researchers often refer to this as the Habermasian ideal speech situation, as real world examples of such conditions are few and far between.[23] Moreover, Habermasian approaches are often criticized by minority groups as being elitist and exclusionary, failing to account properly for disenfranchised stakeholders unable to participate. That said, many continue to point to it as an ideal worth striving for, and its promise of inclusive and deliberative-democratic processes is seen as a means of increasing perceived validity of policy proposals.

Research on multistakeholderism, however, tells a far different story. In their study of the use of multistakeholder negotiations between environmental groups, local populations, and state authorities, Edmunds and Wollenberg found that "multistakeholder negotiations mask abuses of power and more structural, enduring inequity. In doing so, they are prone to exaggerate the level of consensus reached through negotiations and expose disadvantaged groups to greater manipulation and control by more powerful stakeholders."[24] In fact, powerful actors are likely to use the veil of consensus "to mask continuing differences in perspective and discount the input of disadvantaged groups."[25]

In the context of multistakeholderism, the Habermasian model envisions four baseline criteria for any deliberation: stakeholders must accept mutual interdependence; be willing to share information and learn from each other; be willing to work together to address the problems identified; desire a shared, negotiated agreement.[26]

But, this model is just a theoretical construct. Several of the assumptions crucial to its effectiveness simply do not exist in the real world, particularly in international contexts where existing power dynamics cannot be easily cast aside. The suggestion that strategic actors will negotiate in earnest, will be honest, willing, and able to alter their policy preferences based on arguments expressed by others, is empirically troubled.[27] More often we see established actors engaging in inclusive negotiations in order to benefit from the perception of democratic decision making while refusing to engage authentically in the deliberative process. Such an approach allows for powerful actors to benefit from increased support for the negotiated agreement without ever deviating significantly from their true policy preference.

Moreover, an ideal negotiation process requires the full disclosure of information by all parties involved, a condition that, again, is rarely met in real-world scenarios. For example, requiring area experts to divulge certain expertise about a topic as a prerequisite to entering an MSP may weaken a constituent group if that knowledge is crucial to their negotiating leverage. In the context of internet governance, there is a high risk of such a scenario, given the governments' collective dependence of other, private-sector groups for the know-how required for the smooth and secure operation of the internet. For example, one could argue that the open, deliberative nature of debates over the encryption online enabled the National Security Agency (NSA) to weaken international security standards and, eventually, crack the encryption altogether.[28]

Conversely, powerful actors may have an incentive to control information so as to not reveal their true intentions or previous mistakes. The United States, for example, has refused to volunteer information regarding its global surveillance activities, despite its direct relevance to questions of internet governance. If information is not shared equally and transparently, then the marketplace of ideas is necessarily skewed. Particularly in situations where information is valuable, or not previously shared, the requirement for equal sharing could in itself be a power grab by those in positions of authority to take away one of the few negotiating chips a disadvantaged (or nonadvantaged) group may have.

Thus, multistakeholderism can also hurt the negotiating power of disadvantaged groups. In her study of the adoption of multiculturalism as official Canadian policy in 1971, Evelyn Légaré found that powerful actors—in this case, white Canadians—used the veil of consensus and shared identity to deny any special claims of rights for disadvantaged groups like the aboriginals. Of Légaré's findings, Edmunds and Wollenberg observe: "Powerful groups often manipulate seemingly neutral terms that are quickly agreed to in meetings, but then are used in ways that meet each stakeholders' own needs."[29] Based on her fieldwork, Légaré cautions against the perceived neutrality of the language of consensus building and multistakeholderism, noting how easily the process can be manipulated by established groups to further their strategic interests.[30]

The Tunis agenda's call for "enhanced cooperation" on public-policy issues pertaining to the internet provides a more topical example. Intended as a euphemism for reducing unilateral U.S. control over ICANN, "enhanced cooperation" was subsequently interpreted by the United States and its allies as referring to greater interagency cooperation. The resultant debate has dragged on since 2005, giving rise in 2013 to the creation of a dedicated UN group to resolve the matter.[31]

Despite this, multistakeholderism has taken hold in many international fora as a means of resolving contentious differences between interested parties. In the area of internet governance, multistakeholderism is often presented as the panacea to what is otherwise a geopolitically driven negotiation among traditional state actors. Given the internet's historical dependence on private- and nonprofit-sector expertise, many consider it crucial that it be governed through a process that includes these nontraditional perspectives in determining ideal policy.

At the same time, few dispute that all stakeholders should be consulted when making policy; the disagreement lies in how to make decisions in cases of conflicting interests. Proponents of multistakeholderism argue that decisions should be made only by full consensus of all stakeholders participating with equal rights. Opponents argue that decisions regarding matters of public policy should be made by states. Framed as such, it is easy to understand why private companies and states that benefit from the status quo favor the multistakeholder model, particularly given that such states would be in a minority in any formal UN-style voting process.

But it is more instructive to examine how these multistakeholder dynamics play out in negotiations over internet governance. The remainder of this chapter reviews three case studies of multistakeholderism related to internet governance. Each case study represents a different aspect of the MSP. Combined, they demonstrate how multistakeholderism reinforces existing disparities in power rather than providing voice to nontraditional and historically disenfranchised groups.

ICANN

ICANN's emergence as the central actor in modern internet governance, which was supported by narratives of privatization and self-regulation, and avoidance of alleged potential heavy-handed, top-down, bureaucratic international control, offers a cautionary tale about the language of multistakeholderism. To start, it highlights the important but often overlooked question of why powerful actors engage in multistakeholder negotiations in the first place. Why would a government with substantial legal and economic power agree to sit and negotiate away their power? One possibility is that a desire for legitimacy is deemed substantial enough to engage in a MSP, even if it means certain concessions. A second possibility is that the negotiations are simply a political cover for more aggressive and controversial tactics. The story of ICANN's origins and its hands-off, deferential regulatory approach exemplifies how these concerns play out in the area of internet governance.

ICANN is a corporation, physically headquartered in Los Angeles, California, and responsible for managing the system of unique identifiers that underpins the global internet. These responsibilities include: coordinating the internet protocol address spaces IPv4 and IPv6; assigning address blocks to regional internet registries; maintaining a database of the different internet registries of internet protocol identifiers; and managing the top-level domain space, the DNS root zone, including the operation of one root name server.

But how did ICANN assume these responsibilities? Until 1998 the administration of the internet was coordinated through a series of Department of Defense (DOD) and National Science Foundation (NSF) contracts with the Information Sciences Institute (ISI) at the University of Southern California (USC), Internet Assigned Numbers Authority (IANA) and Network Solutions, Incorporated (NSI).[32] According to a 1998 NTIA policy paper, "The U.S. Government has played a pivotal role in creating the Internet as we know it today. . . . [M]ajor components of the domain name system are still performed by, or subject to, agreements with agencies of the U.S. Government."[33] Why would the DOD be interested in decreasing its control over the administering of the internet?

As the internet transitioned from a primarily research-driven network to a global medium for communication exchange and commerce, there was widespread recognition that its management also needed to transition. According to the NTIA, "An increasing percentage of internet users reside outside of the U.S., and those stakeholders want to participate in Internet coordination." In order to enhance the legitimacy of its role in overseeing the internet, the Clinton administration agreed, in principle, to shift responsibility to the private sector. ICANN was thus established, at the urging of the Clinton administration, to combat a shift in control over the internet's DNS from the U.S. government to what could have been a truly international and multistakeholder group as proposed by the International Ad Hoc Committee (IAHC), with ITU acting as the depository for the parties participating in that group.[34]

Prior to the transfer of authority, in June 1998 the Department of Commerce issued a white paper proposing the creation of a private, not-for-profit corporation that would manage the various DNS functions outlined above. The proposed organization would reflect the broad interests of international stakeholders from both the nongovernment and public sectors, and it would be transparent and accountable to the broader internet stakeholder communities. At the same time, the white paper was clear that, before the U.S. government would agree to transfer responsibilities to another organization, certain criteria would have to be met. According to internet governance expert Milton Mueller, insiders knew that "the content of the white paper could be interpreted as a mandate."[35]

These criteria included a promise of maintaining a single, authoritative root system, as well as a new DNS management system that would prioritize the implementation of a "comprehensive security strategy." The paper also specified that "the new corporation should be headquartered in the United States" and that the new corporation would "restrict official government representation on the Board of Directors." Of course, the U.S. government's interests were naturally reflected in the corporation's official charter. While the new organization was to be representative, open, and transparent, the paper argued in favor of its (and not any other organization's) clear and unquestioned authority over internet's administration: "The commercial importance of the internet necessitates that the operation of the DNS system, and the operation of the authoritative root server system should be secure, stable, and robust."[36]

The Clinton administration framed the transition as a model of industry self-regulation, whereby the various private-sector stakeholders would come together, agree upon the proper membership and protocols for the new entity, and then assume responsibility for governing the internet, its root servers, and related protocols. In November 1998 the Department of Commerce officially recognized ICANN as the organization that would assume responsibility for managing the internet.[37]

Despite the language of self-regulation and the Clinton administration's promise of a hands-off approach to internet governance, one year later—on the anniversary of ICANN's founding—Mueller found that "most important long-term policy decisions are still being made by means of privately negotiated contracts with the U.S. government that bypass ICANN's organic processes."[38] Mueller added, "Control of the internet's centralized coordination mechanisms could be exploited or abused to attain regulatory powers over internet users and suppliers."[39]

Of course, the self-governance narrative was strategic, perpetrated at the expense of government interests around the world. Mueller explains:

> Corporate and governmental participants on the U.S. side wanted to short-circuit European desires to turn over internet governance to a formal, intergovernmental body. If internet governance was taken over by a 'private sector'

organization, the US could pretend that it was not responsible for the outcome, and hence, European demands for the participation of other governments in the decisions could be finessed. Of course, if the 'self-regulatory' process was firmly in the hands of U.S.-based interests such as IANA, ISOC, IBM and MCI WorldCom, the U.S. could have the best of both worlds.[40]

The white paper, according to Mueller, "reflected a behind-the-scenes agreement that IANA-ISOC and their corporate allies would be the ones in control of the new organization and that a specific program acceptable to the trademark lobby, the U.S. Commerce Department and the Europeans would be executed."[41]

The name "ICANN" was first proposed by IANA and NSI—two government contractors—in September 1998. Industry partisans with clear ties to IANA, IBM, and ISOC dominated the initial board of directors. Its CEO was Mike Roberts, former head and charter member of ISOC, discussed in detail below. According to Mueller, Ira Magaziner—the behind-the-scenes, senior advisor for policy development for President Clinton—and the Commerce Department "had already tacitly anointed [IANA] as the nucleus of the new corporation. It is clear that Magaziner himself, as well as IBM and foreign governments, had been involved in vetting the initial board selections."[42] When ICANN encountered early financial difficulties and struggled to establish a sustainable business model, Vint Cerf solicited $650,000 in corporate donations from MCI and Cisco to keep the institution alive.

A September 1999 agreement between NSI, ICANN, and the Department of Commerce required NSI to "continue to operate the root server system in accordance with the directions of the U.S. Department of Commerce."[43] The trope of industry self-regulation[44] was simply a ruse, placating powerful stakeholders just enough while still retaining substantial regulatory authority. The agreements required by the Department of Commerce before officially handing off day-to-day operational oversight to ICANN "clearly assert the U.S. government's intention to maintain 'policy authority' over the root indefinitely."[45] According to Mueller, "The 'self-regulatory regime' being constructed by ICANN is actually far more centralized and controlling in nature than the pre-ICANN internet."[46]

Again, in 2005, the U.S. government decided it was not prepared to delegate full decision-making power to ICANN. According to a NTIA press release, "Given the internet's importance to the world's economy, it is essential that the underlying DNS of the internet remain stable and secure. As such, the United States . . . will therefore maintain its historic role in authorizing changes or modifications to the authoritative root zone file."[47] In July 2012

ICANN signed an extended seven-year contract with the Department of Commerce's NTIA that confirmed its commitment to operate and administer the internet according to the rules laid out by the U.S. government.[48] Despite promises to hand over total control to the private sector once and for all, the Department of Commerce consistently retained final regulatory authority over ICANN's control of the root servers.

The process of establishing ICANN and supporting it as the legitimate organization to represent the global internet community interests was crucial for quelling growing concern over U.S. government control over the internet's backbone and root server. Research on multistakeholder processes shows that, once involved in the multistakeholder process, participants are encouraged to reach a consensus and overlook dissenting views.[49] Stakeholders who balk at the established consensus, dwelling on minority concerns, are often accused of negotiating in bad faith, working against the collective good of the group. Thus, once legitimized, groups were pressured into working through ICANN, an organization that is on its surface international but in practice reflects U.S. government and corporate interests.[50]

This criticism becomes clearer by juxtaposing ICANN's promises of participation and inclusion to the organization's record of accountability. For example, ICANN describes its policymaking process as a "bottom-up, consensus driven, multistakeholder model" that begins at the grassroots, allowing for inclusion of a "broad representation of the world's perspectives" where "all points of view receive consideration on their own merits."[51] Yet, despite the promise of participation, there is no guarantee that ICANN actually listens to or acts upon the contributions from the participant-driven, multistakeholder model. In fact, in 2009 Mueller found that ICANN lacks any substantive mechanism for accountability:

> Although it takes in a large and growing amount of revenue and stands at the center of a number of highly contentious commercial interests, it has no competitors, nor does it have corporate shareholders with the legal right and the economic incentives to see that it performs properly. Unlike government, it has no citizens enfranchised to share in its power through election and representation. Unlike an intergovernmental organization, it is not composed of member-states with direct forms of accountability over it.[52]

Participation thus creates legitimacy, even in the absence of actionable mechanisms of accountability. According to Mueller, "The large amount of staff and financial resources and public relations activity ICANN invests in inviting public comment and participation allows ICANN to achieve great public legitimacy; this in turn helps it avoid more direct, harder forms of accountability."[53]

As a result, foreign governments and civil-society actors increasingly see ICANN as a puppet for American interests. The NTIA's authority to approve changes to the root server requested by ICANN means that it is accountable to no one.[54] According to Mueller, the U.S. government is a big part of the problem with ICANN's accountability and process. "U.S. government involvement sets up a privileged 'back channel' for influencing ICANN decisions so that powerful interests . . . can get their way while bypassing the procedures everyone else has to use."[55]

If ICANN reflects the powerful commercial and governmental interests, then who is reflecting nongovernment and civil-society perspectives in the multistakeholder process? Civil-society groups are supposed to keep the governmental and corporate interests in check. In lieu of a formal global democratic system, civil society represents the global public interest, offering both technical expertise and real-world knowledge with regard to the role of the internet in societies around the world. The following section will analyze the largest and most powerful representative of this global civil society—ISOC—providing background on its origins and examining the intent and legitimacy of its efforts to represent civil-society groups in the MSP.

The Internet Society

ISOC was founded on January 1, 1992, by Vint Cerf and Bob Kahn, two of the researchers who helped found the internet. Despite the defeat of the IAHC proposals regarding the future of internet governance (ISOC was one of the sponsors of IAHC), ISOC was well positioned when ICANN took over in 1998. It lobbied the NTIA and Department of Commerce throughout the transition, praising the Clinton administration's white paper as "excellent" and supporting the decision to "leave internet governance to users and the private sector instead of governments."[56] When ICANN launched, it was overwhelmed by the sheer number of stakeholders and perspectives connecting to the internet's operation. As a result, it turned to ISOC to help facilitate dialogue with the host of government and nongovernment stakeholders.[57]

ISOC's origins and rise as a critical node in the MSP is closely aligned with its historically close relationship with the U.S. government, on the one hand, and the American private sector on the other. For example, the Clinton administration, IBM executives, and the European Commission helped select ISOC's initial board of trustees.[58]

The Internet Society (ISOC) functions as a nonprofit organization whose mission is to ensure the "internet stays open, transparent and defined by you." Its website touts the organization as "the world's trusted independent source of leadership for internet policy, technology standards, and future development." According to its 2011 annual report, the ISOC "help[s] build the communities and expertise required for self-sustaining internet development and growth in every part of the world." In 2013, Assistant Secretary Strickling praised the organization (among others), saying, "The internet we enjoy today—this marvelous engine of economic growth and innovation— did not develop by happenstance. It emerged as a result of the hard work of multistakeholder organizations such as the Internet Society, the Internet Engineering Task Force, and the World Wide Web Consortium."[59] ISOC has consistently characterized the internet as a multistakeholder realm. Its Global Internet Report 2014, for example, concluded, "The multistakeholder model that was central to the creation of the Internet has evolved and grown to encompass Internet governance and key development projects such as IXP creation."[60]

Critical to ISOC's credibility is its international reach. In 2014 the nonprofit boasted over 65,000 members, 100 chapters, and more than 145 organizational members around the world. With this broad constituency, ISOC claims it is "uniquely positioned at the intersection of development-oriented (technical) groups, public policy, and technology activities [to] serve as the hub of a global network of individuals and organizations."[61] Due to its historical role of interfacing with important civil society actors, the ISOC say that it "plays a unique role in advancing technology and policy on key areas for the Internet's development, providing a neutral position, often able to gain access where others cannot, and recognized as carrying (credible) perspective from other groups."[62]

Research on multistakeholder processes urges caution when any organization claims to represent a broader coalition of actors, especially one as large and influential as ISOC. Historically, powerful actors are likely to "exaggerate the level of agreement reached through negotiations and expose disadvantaged groups to more manipulation and control by more powerful stakeholders."[63] Such a criticism raises the question, If it's not working for its global internet-using communities, what is ISOC advocating for? The organization's leadership structure and funding offer some answers.

To begin with, ISOC's leadership positions are filled with former private-sector executives from telecommunications, technology, and internet companies, as well as former industry liaisons from the Department of Commerce, FCC, Department of State, ICANN, ITU, the French Prime Minister's Office, and the Canadian Office for International Telecommunications Policy. Table 5.2 details the previous affiliations of the ISOC senior staff. ISOC's Board of Trustees Executive Committee also includes a Comcast senior executive

Table 5.2: Select ISOC Senior Staff (2014)

Name	Position at ISOC	Previous Professional Affiliation
Kathryn Brown	President and CEO	Verizon; Clinton Administration
Constance Bommelaer	Senior Director, Global Policy Partnerships	French Prime Minister's Office
Paul Brigner	Bureau Director for North America	Motion Picture Association of America; Verizon
Eric Burger	Board of Trustees	BEA Systems; MCI Telecommunications
Narelle Clark	Board of Trustees	Vodafone
Jane Coffin	Director, Development Strategy	NTIA; USAID
Keith Davidson	Board of Trustees	ICANN
Gihan Dias	Board of Trustees	LK Domain Registry
Hans Peter Dittler	Board of Trustees	BRAINTEC Netzwerk-Consulting
Frédéric Donck	Bureau Director for Europe	European Commission; ETNO
Hiroshi Esaki	Board of Trustees	Toshiba Corporation
David Farber	Board of Trustees	FCC; Presidential Advisory Board on Information Technology.
Bill Graham	Senior Policy Consultant	Canadian government; ICANN
Bob Hinden	Board of Trustees	Nokia and Sun Microsystems
Scott Hoyt	Vice President, Strategic Communications	IBM, Stratos
Michael Kende	Chief Economist	Analysis Mason, FCC
Jason Livingood	Executive Committee, Board of Trustees	Comcast
Sofie Maddens	Senior Director of Global Services	ITU
Scott Mansfield	Advisory Council Officer	Ericsson
Desiree Miloshevic	Board of Trustees	Afilias
Karen Rose	Senior Director, Strategic Development and Business Planning	FCC; NTIA and the Department of Commerce
Walda Roseman	COO	FCC
Christine Runnegar	Director, Public Policy	Australian Government
Theresa Swinehart	Executive Committee, Board of Trustees	Verizon; MCI; ICANN
Sean Turner	Board of Trustees	International Electronic Communication Analysts; Booz Allen Hamilton
Rudi Vansnick	Board of Trustees	ICANN
Sally Shipman Wentworth	Vice President, Global Policy Development	U.S. Department of State
Russell White	Advisory Council Officer	VeriSign
Bert Wijnen	Board of Trustees	Alcatel-Lucent; IBM

(Jason Livingood) and a former Verizon executive (Kathryn Brown). In fact, the organization's advisory council does not include a single person from academia or other nonprofit organizations.[64]

With its board and operational leadership so closely connected to established political and corporate institutions, one may question how effectively ISOC is able to represent noncommercial, global, civil-society perspectives during multistakeholder negotiations. This is exacerbated by the fact that ISOC policy papers are prepared by the staff and approved by the leadership: there is no formal consultation of the ISOC membership (although the staff does purport to take into account views expressed by the membership on various ISOC mailing lists). Thus it cannot be said that ISOC policies are made using a "bottom-up" process.

Another perspective suggests that ISOC is more similar to a traditional lobbying group than an advocate for global civil society. But what is it lobbying for, and on behalf of whom?

In October 2002 ISOC successfully bid for the .ORG registry and formed a separate but connected entity known as Public Interest Registry (PIR) to operate the .ORG domain. At the time, a press release reported: "The acquisition of .ORG marks a turning point in ISOC's history. It puts the organization on much sounder financial footing."[65] Today, .ORG is the third-largest generic top-level domain in the world (10.3 million registrants at the beginning of 2014) and, via its direct control over PIR (its board of directors is appointed by ISOC), ISOC expected to receive just under $30 million, according to its 2014 budget.[66] PIR was budgeted to contribute more than 75 percent of ISOC's $39.9 million in annual revenue. The remainder of ISOC's annual revenue comes primarily from corporate donations and from IETF sponsorships funded through registration fees paid almost entirely by corporations. Corporate sponsors include Afilias, Alcatel-Lucent Technology, AT&T, CERN, Cisco Systems, Comcast, Cox Communications, Ericsson, Facebook, France Telecom Orange, Google, Hitachi, Huawei Technologies, Intel, ICANN, Juniper, Microsoft, National Cable and Telecommunications Association, NBC Universal, Nippon Telegraph and Telephone Corporation, Nokia, Nokia Siemens Networks, Panasonic, PayPal, Qualcomm, RIAA, Rogers Communications, The Walt Disney Company, Time Warner Cable, the Department of Defense, VeriSign, Verizon and Yahoo![67] ISOC filings with the IRS on September 30, 2013, explained, "The Internet Society has a corporate membership dues structure, and is continuously seeking to expand its base of corporate members. The Internet Society also has more than 52,000 individual members around the world. It does not charge membership dues to individuals since many of them are located in developing countries, but the Internet Society does seek and receive contributions from individuals."[68]

To maintain its nonprofit, tax-exempt status, ISOC's promises on its 990 Form tax return denies engaging "in any lobbying activities."[69] In practice, it is a powerful lobbyist aiming to shape internet policies. ISOC's annual review lists "expanded advocacy efforts on government and industry policy," as well as "advanced ISOC's positions at World Economic Forum and other public policy events, and in key European media outlets" as crucial achievements in 2011.[70] It also touts how the organization "influenced global policy makers in forums such as the OECD and the G8 summits."[71] ISOC's 2012 annual report discloses expenditures of $2.3 million for public policy programs.[72]

ISOC claims that its accomplishments include increasing internet connectivity in Africa as well as assisting in attracting ISPs and foreign investment on the continent. For example, the organization touts its focus "on increasing interconnection among African networks and especially IXPs because they're a key factor in the Internet's development in Africa," adding, "They're also likely to attract investment from content providers."[73] ISOC engaged the African Union in 2012 "to support the establishment of IXPs across 30 African Countries."[74] The organization spends millions per year increasing internet connectivity. It is not a coincidence that the growth of .ORG arises largely from non-Western countries. From 2010 to 2012, for example, registrations from Asia and the Australian Pacific grew by 47 percent, Africa by 23 percent, and Latin America by 25 percent.[75] Its advocacy efforts toward greater global connectivity directly benefit the organization's bottom line, as ISOC's subsidiary PIR is financially rewarded when new users go online.

ISOC's outreach and goodwill efforts toward the broader internet community are leveraged in favor of PIR's business interests. It publicly recognized as much in its .ORG application to ICANN, noting, "ISOC has earned the respect of the Internet and noncommercial communities, which will help PIR,"[76] adding, ISOC's "standing in the noncommercial community makes it particularly well suited to manage a domain dedicated to an extremely large and varied community, the needs of which can best be understood by a fellow member."

Without question, ISOC's work to connect parts of the world often ignored by commercial internet providers is praiseworthy. The purpose of this case study is not to argue that the organization is doing harm, nor is it necessarily a criticism of its business model. Much of its advocacy work against surveillance and censorship online would not be possible without ISOC's substantial corporate backing and, via PIR, commercial operations. That said, this brief analysis argues that ISOC's commitment to representing civil-society interests and groups in the MSP depends on and is perhaps driven by its commercial interests. Thus, despite the inclusion of civil society groups in the MSP, the case of ISOC demonstrates how easily such inclusion can get co-opted by powerful, corporate entities.

In addition to its advocacy role, ISOC also supports the Internet Engineering Task Force (IETF) and the Internet Architecture Board (IAB), two groups that play leading roles in shaping the technical standards and protocols upon which the internet operates. The following case study analyzes how the IETF reinforces existing political and economic interests despite its commitment to a multistakeholder, deliberative, and inclusive structure.

Internet Engineering Task Force

Established in 1986, the IETF is the primary organization responsible for the development and maintenance of technical standards for the internet. According to Alvestrand and Lie, IETF has "the largest influence on the technologies used to build the internet."[77] The standards upon which the internet operates—TCP/IP, for example—are critical to its functioning. Agreed-upon and shared standards make the internet interoperable, allowing for its massive growth and use across numerous legal and cultural divides. Shared standards are also essential for the internet's stability, as they determine the required security protocols. The IETF's basic mission is to "make the internet work better," though who defines exactly what is "better" remains an open question.[78] IETF is often associated with a cyberlibertarian ideology, seeing state interventions as barriers to innovation by individual developers. Decisions are made through "rough consensus," referring to a process whereby the collective judgment of IETF experts with "real-world experience in implementing and deploying our specifications" becomes "code" unless a participant strenuously objects.[79] While the IETF allows anyone to participate in their meetings, in order to contribute to IETF documents or standards making, a participant must be "technically competent."[80]

Who, exactly, is involved in the IETF? Its original sixteen members were each U.S. government-funded researchers. Today, a typical meeting is attended by fifteen hundred networking professionals, the vast majority of who are "employees of networking equipment companies, internet service providers, or researchers in internet technology."[81] Despite its being open to all, "it's a small core of about 100 people, predominantly old-timers, who are still getting the work done."[82]

While the IETF is relatively unknown compared to organizations like the ITU, ICANN, or even its parent ISOC, its decisions and publications are normative and thus of vital significance for the internet (IETF standards are, like most standards, adopted voluntarily, but if they are widely adopted, as is often the case, they become de facto mandates). By establishing the standards upon which internet-enabled applications and hardware function, the IETF embodies what communication theorist Manuel Castells describes as programming power.[83] According to Joel Reidenberg, "The power . . . to embed non-derogable, public-order rules in network systems is not benign. Once a technical rule is established at the network level, the information policy rule is both costly and difficult to change. All participants in the network must adopt and implement any new rule."[84] In fact, an argument can be made that the IETF wields more power than a traditional regulator. As Peng Hwa Ang explains, "In place of officially mandated sanctions from government, the penalty for non-compliance with an IETF standard is the electronic equivalent of the death penalty—the device does not work and the user is denied existence in cyberspace."[85]

Several of the current hot-policy issues regarding internet governance, including spam and surveillance, relate to the relative lack of security provisions in the original internet standards—which made sense at the time, because, as already noted, the internet was originally conceived as a closed network, not a public network.[86] Given the cost and political implications of adding security features, it is clear how technical decisions made long ago have significant influence on current policy debates.

Formally, the IETF is as close to the Habermasian ideal-speech situation as it gets, if one accepts that participants must be fluent in English and in technical jargon. The organization is notoriously open to include anyone interested in participating; due to its roots within the original internet pioneers, it ideologically rejects making decisions based on meritocracy. According to one participant, "In the IETF, there's a kind of direct, populist democracy that most of us have never experienced: Not in democratically elected government, where too many layers of pols and polls and image and handling intervene."[87] Participants espouse the organization's decision-making purity, noting, "We don't allow caucusing, lobbying, and charismatic leaders to chart our path, but when something out on the Net really seems to work and makes sense to most of us, that's the path we'll adopt."[88]

Yet, a more detailed look at the IETF's leadership—composed of the Internet Engineering Steering Group (IESG) and the IAB—shows a shocking lack of gender, geographical, or social diversity (see Table 5.3). In fact, according

Table 5.3: Internet Engineering Steering Group Members (2014)

Name	IETF Position	Professional Affiliation	Citizenship
Jari Arkko	IETF Chair	Ericsson	Finland
Alia Atlas	Routing Area	Juniper Networks	USA
Mary Barnes	IAB Liaison	Polycom	USA
Richard Barnes	Real-time Applications and Infrastructure Area	Mozilla. Previously BBN Technologies (Raytheon)	USA
Benoit Claise	Operations and Management	Cisco	USA
Alissa Cooper	Real-time Applications and Infrastructure Area	Cisco	USA
Michelle Cotton	IANA Liaison	ICANN	USA
Spencer Dawkins	Transport Area	Huawei Technologies	USA
Adrian Farrel	Routing Area	Juniper Networks	UK
Stephen Farrell	Security Area	Tolerant Networks and Trinity College Dublin	UK/Irish
Sandy Ginoza	RFC Liaison	Association Management Solutions	USA
Brian Haberman	Internet Area	Johns Hopkins University, previously IBM	USA
Russ Housley	IAB Chair	Vigil Security, LLC	
Joel Jaeggli	Operations and Management	Zynga and Fastly	USA
Barry Leiba	Applications Area	Huawei Technologies, previously IBM	USA
Ted Lemon	Internet Area	Nominum	USA
Kathleen Moriarty	Security Area	EMC Corporation	USA
Alexa Morris	IETF Executive Director	Association Management Solutions	USA
Pete Resnick	Applications Area	Qualcomm Technologies, Inc.	USA
Martin Stiemerling	Transport Area	NEC Laboratories Europe (NEC)	Germany

to an open letter sent to the IESG, the IAB, the IETF Administrative Oversight Committee (IAOC), and the ISOC Board, despite the rapid growth in non-Western internet users, the IESG's diversity is in decline:

> Ten years ago, in February of 2003, there were 25 members of the IETF leadership (12 IAB members and 13 IESG members). Of those 25 members, there was one member of non-European descent, there was one member from a country outside of North America or Europe, and there were four women. There were 23 companies represented in the IETF leadership (out of a total of 25 seats). In February of 2013, there were 32 members of the IETF leadership (12 IAB members, 15 IESG members and 5 IAOC members). Of those 32 members, there was one member of non-European descent, there were no members from countries outside of North America or Europe, and there was only one woman. There were only 19 companies represented (out of a total of 32 seats).[89]

Particularly notable is the decline in the range of companies represented among the organizations leaders. Outlined in Table 5.3, a handful of corporations with direct business interests in the outcome of the IETF's discussions dominate, including CISCO, Huawei, and Ericsson.

The open letter sparked an energetic debate on the IETF forum, soliciting 121 responses. A former IETF board member, Keith Moore, noted, "One aspect of IETF leadership diversity that seems to have considerably decreased over the years that I've been working with IETF is the number of people from academic/research relative to the number of people from the commercial sector. . . . Our processes are considerably biased against anyone who is not funded by a large company."[90]

Another forum participant suggested that the increased dominance of certain corporations was due to the fact leadership positions in the organization required substantial time commitments, and only a handful of corporations were willing and able to employ staff who spend the majority of their time on IETF business. According to Cullen Jennings, "Most people who take on positions of authority within IETF have companies paying their salaries, companies that can afford to have them doing much less company work in the short term so that the company can benefit in the long term."[91] Dave Cridland, another participant, agreed: "People from large commercial organizations are dominating, and I'd argue that this is due to the cost (in time and financially) of doing reasonably high level IETF work. This also restricts the available pool, and furthermore means our leadership is at most as diverse as those large commercial organizations."[92] Martin Rex also concurred: "The monetary and time resources necessary to fill an I* position adequately appear quite significant to me, and I believe it would be hard to fill them without strong support from an employer which covers the monetary investment."[93]

Melinda Shore summarized the debate by noting the structural nature of the problem: "I'm convinced there's a problem but I'm equally convinced that we can't make progress on it given current organizational constraints."[94] Shore also argued the result of concentration in sponsorship at the top level would have a spiral effect on the IETF's work, noting, "If everybody serving that gatekeeper function comes from a similar background (western white guy working for a large manufacturer) it's going to tend to create certain biases in the work that's taken on."[95]

Reflecting on the significance of the lack of diversity, former IESG member Keith Moore suggested, "Far too often, our standards aren't serving the Internet community so much as serving the interests of a few large companies."[96] John Klensin took the argument a step further, arguing that the level of corporate collusion may even be unlawful: "We have had years in which company af-filiations, presumed sponsorship, and industry sectors have been much more concentrated, possibly enough so to be fodder for antitrust actions."[97]

A review of the forum's comments section found no response to the accusation that particular corporate interests were dominating the IETF's leadership. It seemed to be the only thing the group could actually agree upon.

IETF's challenges go beyond its close association to its corporate supporters. Even the open, inclusive, and democratic discursive rules themselves reflect a bias in favor of a particular type of engineer who has a particular type of pedigree and experience. In response to the open letter, one IETF member described how, when he tried to play a leadership role, "the management and some participants (i.e. maybe companies also) did not like that for some reasons, and said that is wrong style, so I got a warning for such inputs (volume, style, disruptive-to-managers)."[98] Put another way, the "rough consensus" that the IETF bases its decisions on inevitably exudes certain cultural preferences as to what constitutes a reasonable or technically competent argument.

Moreover, the close-knit IETF exerts strong social pressure, whereby dissent is unlikely to be expressed in situations where it would possibly cause disruptions to the status quo. According to Alvestrand and Lie, "The society of internet engineers is a *social* environment. The people who work on Internet systems know each other, and they care what their peers think of them."[99] At times the IETF even encourages a quieting of dissent among participants in order to achieve a contingent agreement. According to Dave Crocker, a member of the IETF's administrative and legal oversight bodies, "Even at what seems like an impossible stalemate, IETFers will look to graceful principles to arrive at a resolution; diversity of opinion might be resolved by an agreement to make some decisions, for instance, in the belief that 'agreement about parts may lead to agreement about wholes.'"[100]

Conclusion

By incentivizing inclusion and consensus, MSPs risk stifling legitimate dissent from external actors who have no interest in lending legitimacy to the façade of an apolitical negotiation. By linking legitimacy to the inclusion of all stakeholders, pressure is exerted on actors to get involved, leaving very little place to legitimately criticize the outcomes of negotiations. If groups participate and then criticize, they will be labeled as hypocrites, pandering to constituent interests after the fact. And if they decline to participate and then criticize afterward, they are called out for not voicing their concerns in the right time and place. And indeed the United States (and its allies) regularly call for everybody to participate in MSPs and even succeed in embodying such calls in formal outputs agreed by consensus.[101]

According to Edmunds and Wollenberg, "The focus on involving all stakeholders in a process, especially in a process with a goal of achieving agreement, encourages us to regard all those who refuse to participate as having relinquished their moral authority to speak on the issues."[102] Disadvantaged groups may also have limited resources to challenge negative representations of themselves in the mainstream media—representations that are reinforced when disadvantaged groups are left out of the mainstreaming process. It is crucial to remember that withdrawal is a potent form of protest against "the tendency of the system to exact participation, communication, the acceptance of one's assigned place in society as an effective processer of information."[103]

As Hintz and Milan note, nontraditional civil-society groups, including grassroots media activists, radical technology collectives, and alternative internet service providers, are not significant participants in the multistakeholder internet governance process.[104] These groups contribute to innovation in the development of online infrastructure and services, and they are also affected by policy changes in both straightforward and subtle ways.[105]

The veil of legitimacy that is created through the existence of these (and other) multistakeholder processes and groups makes it harder for groups marginalized in the current processes to speak out with much credibility. According to Edmunds and Wollenberg, "Groups may be labelled biased or ideological for not accepting the rationality of a negotiation process, particularly when facilitators of negotiations have invested heavily in the neutrality of the process and their credibility is at stake. Dissident groups are then forced to remain outside that process and miss the possible benefits of engagement with other stakeholders, or dampen their criticism of the persistent politics within the process."[106] In the case of internet governance, the multistakeholder processes mask the deep and systematic economic and political agenda embedded into the existing power arrangements.

Over time, ICANN, ISOC, IETF, and other multistakeholder organizations have provided legitimacy for a process that has allowed continued U.S. control over the many critical aspects of the internet. When the existing internet governance institutions were challenged by developing countries (who have proposed a range of alternatives, such as reinforcing government influence in ICANN, shifting international policy responsibility to ITU, and creating a new UN organization), exactly what theory predicts happened: the United States and other stakeholders deeply invested in the status quo processes labeled the alternatives disparagingly as trying to "take over the internet" and "placing the internet under the control of non-democratic countries." Emails obtained via Freedom of Information Act (FOIA) requests outline members of the American WCIT delegation endorsing this framing as a means of pressuring ITU Secretary General Toure during the negotiations.[107]

In the aftermath of WCIT the United States is doubling down on the multistakeholder model. According to Ambassador Terry D. Kramer, head of the U.S. delegation to the WCIT,

> The United States will use its leadership position to effectively listen to developing countries, identify effective public-private sector approaches and support multistakeholder organizations and forums. Where needed, the United States will explain and advocate the multistakeholder model to other countries, because we know it works and already is contributing to the ever-accelerating growth of internet access around the world.[108]

Not surprisingly, while the United States and other Western countries may have walked away from the WCIT and the ITU, opposition to the current multistakeholder model of internet governance is mounting. In particular, Brazil is eager to operationalize the role of governments in internet governance[109] and has become especially active in pushing for reforms to existing multistakeholder fora to ensure adequate "participation of governments."[110] Brazil convened an international conference, NETmundial, in April 2014 to encourage a pivot in internet governance toward a system less susceptible to U.S. influence. NETmundial failed to change governance structures and was widely considered to be a failure by civil society groups.[111]

The next chapter details how governments around the world are beginning to treat the internet not as a shared resource but instead as a traditional mechanism for sharing information that is within the sovereign jurisdiction of the state apparatus. This movement can be seen as a direct response to the failure of the multistakeholder process to properly account for global interests in governing the internet.

6

Toward Information Sovereignty

The 21st century is a terrible time to be a control freak.

—Alec Ross, Senior Advisor for Innovation, U.S. State
Department, June 20, 2012

It's not the strongest of species that survive, nor the most
intelligent, but those most adaptable to change.

—Attributed to Charles Darwin, 1859

Globalization has not been good to the modern nation-state. Global trade requires transnational regimes of governance that make decisions that were previously the domain of sovereign states. Trade has increased global environmental degradation and enhanced its visibility, requiring states to again share decision-making responsibilities, at least if they hope to survive. Transnational media challenge the state's ability to control information flows, a critical means through which the nation has connected to the state, providing it legitimacy to govern. Alec Ross, the State Department's senior advisor for innovation, puts it another way: "The 21st century is a terrible time to be a control freak."[1]

Sovereignty—the authority to govern a particular geographic area—is the bedrock upon which social stability is built. It is also, however, an ephemeral social construct that exists in the eye of the beholder. Never absolute, always contested, conceptions of sovereignty have evolved over time as a means of enhancing legitimacy and easing social tensions. With continued expansion of global telecommunications pushing globalization to new heights, nation-state sovereignty is confronted by new challenges.[2]

From Benghazi, Tunisia, to the Occupy Wall Street movement, it is evident that governments are doing a poor job of governing, and citizens are eager and able to confront failing institutions. Given the state of the global communications ecosystem, this shouldn't be surprising. Increasingly, people have the technologies and education to demand better policy. What is surprising is that these demands almost always fall within the framework of the existing nation-state system; relatively few call for the end of state sovereignty or for the creation of regional or global governance structures. The most advanced experiment in shared sovereignty, the European Union, faces substantial challenges as a result of the ongoing economic and fiscal crises facing Greece, Spain, Portugal, Italy, and others. Although connective technologies allow for the creation of new and nontraditional communities and governance structures, nationalism is alive and well. Confronted with the complexities of an interconnected world, citizens clamor for more and better governance. Egypt's post-Mubarak transition is instructive. With a citizenry eager for a more democratic and accountable government, a relatively small number of candidates ran for president. Governing is hard work; it's getting to be more difficult, and people know it. In short, globalization may have been bad for the modern nation-state, but it has been good to sovereignty.

The history of technological modernization indicates a relationship between the specificities of popular communication technologies and successful governance in any given era.[3] The printing press facilitated the rise of nation-states through the growth and perfection of local languages, knowledge, and history. But these nation-states did not emerge out of thin air. Rather, they were formed from existing institutions and political actors eager to exploit new technologies. In the early twentieth century, pirate radio emerged, challenging state control over information flows. It was quickly regulated and become a critical tool of statecraft during World War II and again during the Cold War. States may fail to properly manage emerging media technologies and lose legitimacy, but they don't go away altogether. More able and savvy domestic political actors replace older ones.

This chapter explores the relationship between sovereignty, the nation-state, and connective technologies. Continuously challenged, states naturally seek means of legitimating their authority, a process that increasingly requires providing a citizenry with some level of freedom of expression. At the same time, technologies are evolving quickly and changing the ways communities are formed and authority is legitimized. For many states, allowing too much freedom of expression risks a loss of legitimacy by another sword: the rise of political challengers more able to engage the masses and offer alternative visions for the future. It is within this continuum—with absolute freedom of expression on one end and total information control on the other—that we explore four case studies wherein states restrict access to a singular internet and develop more malleable *intranets*[4] capable of creating a balance between freedom and control.

The Origins and Evolution of Sovereignty

Throughout history the concept of sovereignty adapted to meet the needs of society in times of transition. Specifically, as communities or nations became more complex, sovereignty evolved to reflect the changing needs for stronger, more legitimate governance. In the Middle Ages, as expanding economic activity required greater administrative regulation, sovereign authority evolved, allowing for greater delegation of decision-making to local governments. The Treaty of Westphalia did not create sovereignty; rather, it merely clarified who were the rightful sovereigns and when and where their authority could be exercised absolutely.

Max Weber defined sovereignty as the ability to maintain successfully a "monopoly of legitimate violence," meaning that a state could enforce absolute rule within its boundaries by physical power.[5] Weber, mesmerized by power, presents a functional commentary that does not give credence to sources of authority other than power. A better definition incorporates an understanding that as a result of acknowledged legitimacy, a sovereign possesses authority to issue commands that are expected to be obeyed.[6] Sovereignty has different meanings for disparate disciplines. Traditional political scientists use the term to denote supreme political power within a community in the absence of authority exercised by another political actor.[7] International relations scholarship uses the term polysemously to refer to concepts such as control of borders, supremacy of a political actor within a state, supremacy of the state itself, and legal independence.[8]

Sovereignty embraces two concepts in both sets of definitions. The first acknowledges a geographical limitation to the legitimate use of power, as embodied in concepts of territorial integrity and the sanctity of borders. The second affirms that the state constitutes the supreme authority to make laws within the confines of the country.

While the ability to project power on citizenry may be one way to acquire sovereignty—think autocratic regimes or the occupation of territories by foreign armies—a multitude of other factors may inculcate an expression of legitimacy for the sovereign. Cultural similarities, tradition, shared beliefs, and economic necessities are among the motivating factors. Political actors embrace sovereignty through their articulation of claims to legitimate or natural authority. Historian James Sheehan explains, "Sovereignty is best understood as a set of claims made by those seeking or wielding power, claims about the superiority and autonomy of their authority."[9]

Sovereignty is fundamentally a social construct.[10] Historically, it evolved as a consequence of the realization that increasingly complex societies required actors to coordinate tasks designed to enhance the public good. Coordination required a unitary system of making decisions, administering policies embodying those decisions, and evaluating outcomes. The absolute power of the state emanated from a belief that the sovereign—whether an individual or a committee—incorporated a social contract with subjects that provided, for the common good, absolute power to make laws, to enforce laws, to judge adherence to laws, to reward and punish, and to make war. These are among the twelve principal rights granted to sovereigns by subjects as delineated by Hobbes.[11]

Societal complexity drives the evolution of sovereignty. Isolated communities merged into larger polities to reap advantages from improved communication and transportation. Opportunities, such as new markets, impelled specialization. A region favorable to the production of grapes, for example, could devote a disproportionate amount of resources to the creation of a wine industry if the available transportation infrastructure allowed it to export wine and import other products. Innovation mandated an additional level of administrative coordination to manage the network of roads and the communication necessary for a market to function.

Inhabitants of "proto-urban" settlements concentrated geographically starting in the eighth century because of commerce "that does not appear to have transcended a strictly local horizon, nor does their differentiation of economic specialization appear to have led to the formation of new social structures."[12] Medieval villages, and later cities, formed because long-distance trade developed that linked cult centers, religious sites, and resources to centers of economic activity. Technology enabled changes in the structure of society that "called for the creation of centers of political, military, and economic administration."[13] Counties and duchies were larger than cities, which administratively amalgamated into still-larger kingdoms. These medieval entities in Europe submitted to an overall emperor, originally called the Emperor of Rome when Pope Leo III crowned Charles I in 800 CE, and later called the Holy Roman Emperor after 962 CE. The formation of larger states made economic sense because increased size reduced transaction costs and facilitated commerce.[14]

The imperative for sovereignty was based on the need for social structures that would both empower commerce and incorporate the influx of new ideas made possible by increased communication. "[T]he ores, the people and the ideas drawn from the south and the east made possible the construction of state organizations, above all the Carolingian Empire."[15] The modern conceptualization of sovereignty developed as a consequence of war—the organized, sanctioned application of violence against another group or groups—and in particular war motivated by doctrinal dissension within the Christian religion, culminating in a formulation at the Peace of Westphalia. Westphalia established nation-states as entities with equal status and rights and absolute monopolistic power within specific, agreed-upon geographic delineations (borders).

Global communication and transportation empower global commerce; governance of the new economy must also be on a global scale. To the extent that these changes transform societies, the citizens demand new, legitimate structures of governance to help navigate emerging complexities. The communication infrastructure itself must be governed; since the infrastructure exists on a global level, then its governance requires international coordination. Thus, the development and diffusion of global telecommunications technology represents a moment of transformation where effective global governance connects to effective governance at the local level, across nation-states. It was exactly this process that led to the creation of the International Telecommunications Union (ITU) in 1865, the world's first permanent secretariat tasked to administer a treaty whose purpose was precisely to facilitate international telecommunications.

However, these new structures and citizen demands do not imperil the existence of the state. Power exercised by an international organization—the ITU, for example—exists as an adjunct to state sovereignty. Organizations such as the ITU are deemed necessary because they promise to coordinate and maximize the benefits of a worldwide communication ecosystem. Effective administration by an international organization increases the viability of its member nations, thereby insuring both the continued vitality of the state and of its sovereignty. New transnational governance structures *enhance* the vitality of existing states by insuring the viability of debate within democracies while limiting the influence of special interests.[16]

ICT proliferation challenges institutionalized social systems in novel ways, resulting in greater social complexity. More choice—the hallmark of the Web—also means greater confusion. Movement toward ubiquitous, speedy communication networks and de-territorialized economic activity on a global scale clearly challenges *certain* powers of *certain* sovereign states. But it also strengthens the fundamental need for sovereignty: globalization increases the complexity of any given society, resulting in increased demand for legitimate governance.

The state system that serves as the bedrock of modern international relations depends on the perceived legitimacy of sovereign authority, which is essential for maintaining the rule of law and generating tax revenue. While the legitimacy of governing authority is often contested, and with state borders occasionally porous and changing, the concept of sovereignty remains relevant to the information age. Some states will certainly fail to adjust and will be broken up into smaller units or absorbed into larger entities. Most will evolve and exploit the opportunities created by extraordinarily complex social structures of the 21st century.

Technology and the Nation-State

Francis Bacon proposed: *"Scientia potentia est"*—"Knowledge is power."[17] Technological advances that create new opportunities for communication necessarily change how knowledge—collective belief in a set of truths—is constituted and shared, and thus affect power relations.[18] Analyzing the rise and fall of ancient Egyptian, Babylonian, Greek, and Roman Empires, Harold Innis found that every major communication technology contained intrinsic biases toward a particular organization and control of information, and thus shaped how authority was constituted. For example, Latin script written on parchment, the medium of the church in the high and late Middle Ages, allowed priests to maintain control over access to the word of God. The church's monopoly over "divine knowledge" imbued it with the authority to prescribe social policy, holding sway over kings and citizens alike.[19]

Benedict Anderson identified the widespread adoption of the printing press in Europe as critical for the emergence of the modern nation-state.[20] Arguing that no person could ever know every other member of his or her nation, Anderson found that as the printing press became more ubiquitous in the fifteenth and sixteenth centuries, entrepreneurs started printing books and media in local vernaculars rather than using the exclusive script languages, such as Latin, in order to maximize circulation. As a result, communication in various local dialects grew, facilitating the emergence and codification of independent communities, each with a common discourse. Shared discourses helped constitute community values and norms that were then documented, disseminated, and taught, via the printing press, for generations.

> The very possibility of imagining the nation only arose historically [with the emergence of] print-capitalism, which made it possible for rapidly growing numbers of people to think about themselves, and to relate themselves to others, in profoundly new ways. The first European nation-states were thus formed around their "national print-languages."[21]

A technology's physical traits are not the sole determinants of its particular communicative biases. Rather, the protocols and norms that govern how ideas are shared and how the technology is ultimately utilized dictate precisely how it will influence knowledge generation and the legitimation (or delegitimation) of authority. For example, different alphabets—shared protocols for the exchange of ideas via text—necessarily have biases too. Innis found that "a flexible alphabet favoured the growth of trade, development of the trading cities of the Phoenicians, and the emergence of smaller nations dependent on distinct languages."[22] The printing press itself did not cause a transition from tribes and empires to Westphalian sovereignty; rather, the use of the printing press to produce locally authored books in indigenous languages fostered a shift in consciousness as to what constituted legitimate authority in Europe. Similarly, had the U.S. Defense Advanced Research Projects Agency (DARPA) retained control over the internet rather than sharing it with universities and the private sector, then the modern proliferation of social media, along with the challenges they've presented for existing institutions, would not have occurred. Similarly, the U.S. decision to allow private use of the Global Positioning System (GPS)—originally developed and deployed at great cost as a military system—opened the way for numerous new applications and services, many integrated with the internet. It is not simply the technologies themselves but also the specific sociocultural and legal contexts that dictate emerging media's influence.

Just as the printing press reshaped the constitution of authority in the sixteenth century, the invention of wireless telegraphy reshaped geopolitical power relations in the twentieth century. Scholars have documented the role that propaganda—"a one-way communication system designed to influence belief"—played in the conduct of twentieth-century foreign affairs, especially in times of conflict.[23] Disseminated via radio, state-financed and state-operated international broadcasting was a critical tool of statecraft during World War II. Radio was so important to the Nazi war effort that foreign radio transmitters were often the first targets of any invasion. According to Oigen Hadamowski, director for Germany's radio operations during the war, "We spell radio with three exclamation marks because we are possessed in it of a miraculous power—the strongest weapon ever given to the human spirit—that opens hearts and does not stop at borders."[24] Every government involved in World War II utilized propaganda to influence foreign opinions, with British broadcasting (the BBC Empire Service, for example) holding particularly significant sway over European and American public opinions.[25] Some argue that British propaganda efforts were critical for propelling the United States to enter into both world wars.[26]

Studying the relationship between ICTs and democracy, Phillip Howard analyzed indicators of technology diffusion and democratic governance in seventy-five Muslim nations between 1994 and 2010 and found a generalizable, positive relationship between emerging media technologies and democracy.[27] There are caveats, though, and examples where the infusion of advanced communications technologies did not translate into improved governance. According to Howard, in order to become more democratic, technology must affect political actors. This is not always the case, especially in highly controlled, economically strong countries like Saudi Arabia and Bahrain, where there is little relationship between the diffusion of technologies and democratic governance. At the same time, e-government, wired political parties, digital journalism, and online civic groups all helped usher in democratic transitions or entrenchment. Just as historical analysis indicates, the context within which technologies are introduced is a critical variable in determining how they shape the structure of power relations in a given society.

Ongoing advances in communication technologies will continue to challenge institutions. Ulrich Beck suggests that one consequence of the rapid globalization witnessed in the past twenty-five years is the shattering of traditional means by which community is formed and maintained, both in the hyperlocal (family) and the societal (nation) contexts.[28] Just as the family served as the primary means through which children connected to their local community, the nation-state was the principle means through which citizens engaged with the international community. This, of course, is changing, given the nature of modern communication networks. Before commercial satellites, 99 percent of communication occurred within the boundaries of the nation-state.[29] Anderson's conception of the nation as an "imagined community" worked because nation-based media were shared among diverse groups, constituting shared histories, stories, and knowledge. As communication technologies become more mobile, affordable, and globally connected, people may form their own imagined communities, not based on the established, traditional strictures of authority but rather on their own ideas and passions.[30]

In 1999, Thomas Friedman predicted, "The days when governments could isolate their people from understanding what life was like beyond their borders or even beyond their village are over."[31] Such optimistic, cyber-utopian predictions have been rampant, including among State Department diplomats.[32] Philip Taylor summed up such optimism when he wrote: "Together with the internal combustion engine, penicillin and the splitting of the atom, [mass media] have served to transform the very nature not only of how human beings live their lives but of how they perceive the world around them."[33] Beneath Taylor's platitude is an argument with realpolitik resonance: controlling information flows has become increasingly difficult yet crucial for state actors, and efforts at managing information flows are metonymic for globalization's broader challenges to state sovereignty.

Information Sovereignty and the Rise of the Intranets

Many have suggested that the internet's growth means (or should mean)[34] the end of state sovereignty altogether. The logic behind such arguments is compelling. Technology has enabled citizens to create and join communities based not on geography but instead on shared interests and ideologies, thus threatening the rationale for state-based nationalism altogether. Why would a citizen pledge loyalty to a state-based nation when a cornucopia of alternative nations that speak to specific interests beckon via the World Wide Web? While states will certainly try to slow the transition and reassert their authority and legitimacy, for many scholars and pundits globalization inevitably means the end of the nation-state as we know it.[35]

At the same time, states control the telecommunications infrastructure that enables global connectivity. At a basic level, the physical nature of network connections allows any government to control information flow within its territory in a number of ways, including simply disconnecting its national communications infrastructure from all or part of the global network. Given the natural proclivity toward state control, what is stopping governments from restricting access to the internet? After all, even the father of international liberalism—Immanuel Kant—agreed that states are motivated first and foremost by self-preservation.[36]

Ethan Zuckerman added a level of sophistication to the debate, proposing his "cute cat theory" of internet activism. Its name stems from the fact that, around the world, one of the most popular uses of social media is for sharing videos and photos of cute cats.[37] According to the cute cat theory, governments cannot sustain widespread restrictions on internet content because activists and citizens communicate over the same central internet portals, like YouTube, Flickr, Facebook, Twitter, Pinterest, and the like. Access restrictions applied to any one central portal used by activists would block all access to the portal, limiting the sharing of apolitical but highly popular content (like cute cat videos), thereby engendering widespread citizen anger and increasing the likelihood of greater unrest. Zuckerman explains, "Cute cats are collateral damage when governments block websites. And citizens who could care less about politics are made aware that their government fears online speech so much that they're willing to censor the millions of banal videos on YouTube to block a few political ones."[38] Governmental efforts to restrict internet content will fail and in fact speed their loss of legitimacy and ultimate decline, or so the theory goes.

Cute cat theory builds on what Asa Briggs and Peter Burke describe as the "Conservative Dilemma."[39] When a conservative government—typically non-democratic regimes, but also some ruling governments in quasi-democratic systems—is confronted with widespread social protest, it has four options for restoring control: propaganda, censorship, total information control, and violent repression. Each choice entails risks—thus the dilemma. Inasmuch as propaganda and censorship are typically inexpensive and the least economically disruptive, they have also been the least effective, potentially leaving the regime vulnerable to further social fragmentation. Total information control and violent repression are highly effective at quieting public dissent and restoring social stability, at least on the surface, but risk a loss of regime legitimacy, pushing those uninterested in the initial protests to join fellow citizenry in calling for reform or regime change. Applying this model to state efforts to curtail social media, Clay Shirky found that total information control presented a dire threat to a state's economic vitality in light of the growing interdependence between information systems, national economies, and global trade. More than ever, total information control is an extraordinarily risky endeavor for states.[40]

Both cute cat theory and the conservative dilemma assume the existence of global connectivity. For Briggs and Burke, domestic propaganda and censorship often fail because citizens have access to information from actors unconstrained by a domestic censorship regime, thus exposing state efforts as manipulative. For example, during the Cold War, the BBC and Radio Free Europe/Radio Liberty (RFE/RL) circumvented Soviet censorship regimes using shortwave radio signals capable of reaching audiences behind the Iron Curtain. But without the comparative element—in this case the BBC and RFE/RL—propaganda and censorship are not as easily exposed, making them more potent tools of social control.

Similarly, Zuckerman did not foresee a world where governments would effectively transcend dependence on the global internet by creating their own *intranets*, based on localized content, connecting only to sanctioned parts of the World Wide Web. In place of cute cats on YouTube, for example, each intranet might have its own localized version of YouTube, with videos of local cats or, in some cases, copies of *selected* YouTube cute cats. Citizens eager to generate their own Web content contribute material to the state-based intranet, thus creating a series of smaller networks more easily controlled and monitored by the government while simultaneously providing locally created content and applications.

Information sovereignty refers to a state's attempt to control information flows within its territory. But control does not necessarily require a government to shut down access to the internet. It is asserted in a variety of ways, including filtering, monitoring, and structuring industry-government relations in order to maximize state preferences in privately operated communications systems (see chapter 2). A 2010 study by the OpenNet Initiative concluded that more than half a billion users—more than one-third of all users on the internet at that time—experienced some form of filtering.[41] This does not include various measures to enforce copyright or to prohibit hate speech, extremist propaganda, child pornography/exploitation, sales of controlled substances, and online gambling, all of which are enforced by a range of democratically oriented governments.

There is also the concern over the level of monitoring allowed for by internet-based communication. As more and more communication moves into the realm of the digital, government capacity to monitor private communication of all types increases. The digitization of information that is central to the internet's functionality similarly eases government efforts to access, record, and share data from around the world. Drawing on Jeremy Bentham's articulation of the panopticon, Michel Foucault argues that the mere possibility of ubiquitous yet unconfirmed monitoring of a population is among the most effective ways of controlling behaviors.[42] As users in Iran and China are well aware, internet browsing and communication changes drastically when one thinks the government is watching.

Increasingly, both democratic and nondemocratic governments are exploring ways to control access to the internet without losing legitimacy and, ultimately, power.[43] We explore these efforts through the idea of the intranet, whereby states implement hardware and software firewalls restricting access to their local networks, and local access to global networks, based on perceived need for social control and security. For some states, access is restricted only in times of emergency, as was the case in Egypt in 2011. For others, access is systematically restricted, as is the case in Iran. China adopts a multifaceted approach, which includes draconian regulation as well as encouraging local, indigenous content creation. The United States is concerned about the consequences of depending on a shared, unsecured internet and is thus exploring a variety of public-private partnerships in an effort to find the right balance between free speech and security.

Of course, governments don't describe their efforts to control access to the internet as the equivalent of creating an intranet. In fact, a true intranet, with no access to external networks, is a rare specimen. Nearly all secured networks have some connection to the broader internet. The closest statewide and comprehensive intranet is in North Korea, which has severed nearly all ties with the World Wide Web and built its own Kwangmyong (*bright* in Korean).[44]

Short of permanently cutting off all access to the internet, governments around the world are exploring the different options for exerting control over domestic information flows. In some cases these mechanisms allow for greater control over digital communications than was previously asserted over the analog and interpersonal. Exploring a small sample of strategies, we begin to map how some states adapt to meet the challenges presented by twenty-first-century connective technologies, and how others do not.

Egypt

On January 27, 2011 the Mubarak government isolated the country by severing its connections to the internet and shutting down all cell-phone services.[45] Cute cat theory and the conservative dilemma explain how Egypt's restrictions on telecommunications services failed to quell social revolt during the 2011 uprisings. Despite eight major undersea fiber links, dozens of internet providers, and a diversity of paths (satellite, microwave, and fiber links, for example) connecting Egypt to the global communications infrastructure, 93 percent of its connections to the internet were cut, with only government institutions remaining online.[46] Prior to this, Egypt's telecommunications sector was considered among the most sophisticated and privatized in the region; the majority of internet connectivity between Europe and Asia physically passes through Egyptian territory. However, dependent on state licenses to operate in Egypt, each ISP (including those that are foreign owned) agreed to the government's request without hesitation.[47]

There is some relevant, historical precedent worthy of note. While Egypt is the first state to intentionally pull the plug on all internet connectivity, it is not the first time it has confronted seemingly chaotic media use with extreme measures. On May 29, 1934, Egypt's private radio stations abruptly fell silent, replaced by government broadcasts two days later. Private radio broadcasts, which were unregulated at the time, posed a threat of social unrest through

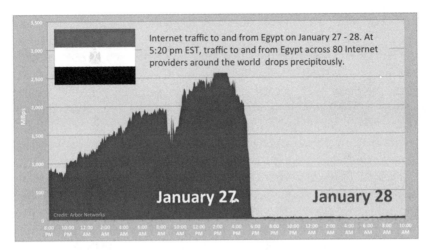

Internet traffic to and from Egypt on January 27 - 28. At 5:20 pm EST, traffic to and from Egypt across 80 Internet providers around the world drops precipitously.

Figure 6.1: Internet Traffic to and from Egypt, January 27–28

the spread of gossip and news. Deemed pirates—the twentieth century's hackers—private broadcasters were silenced as the Kingdom of Egypt exerted its right to information sovereignty and restored its control of the airwaves. By all accounts, the stringent measure was effective: not only did the private radio stations go off the air, but, primed for radio news, Egyptians tuned into government propaganda in the years that followed. Egypt went on to become the leading Arab radio broadcaster under President Nasser's Voice of the Arabs, a force that drove the Pan-Arab movement for two decades.

The Mubarak government's abrupt end to nongovernment Web access demonstrates the capability for modern states to control information flows within their borders. Even more worrisome is the relative ease and speed with which control was asserted, especially for those digital natives whose communications were entirely routed through internet and cell-phone services. While landlines remained operational, most Egyptian families do not have landlines, relying on mobile telephones and internet applications to reach family and friends. In 2006, fixed-line density stood at just fourteen per one hundred persons, or 10.8 million fixed telephones total.[48] For a large segment of the Egyptian population, mediated, multidirectional communications was made impossible in a matter of minutes.[49]

Isolating Egyptians from the internet came at great economic cost. The country lost $18 million per day of shutdown, according to the Organization for Economic Cooperation and Development (OECD).[50] It also didn't last very long. Five days after shutting down access to the internet, ISPs reestablished their services, allowing users to surf the Web, use VoIP applications, and access popular social-networking sites like Twitter and Facebook. At the same time, the decision to restore access to the internet does not appear to have been driven by economic factors or international pressure. Rather, access was restored just as the protests in Cairo turned violent. According to Hussein Amin, former advisor to the Mubarak government, "The government reestablished internet connections, simultaneously launching a bloody campaign against the protesters in Tahrir. The hope was for images of the crackdown to spread quickly, discouraging others from leaving their homes to join the movement."[51]

The case of Egypt's internet shutdown is instructive in two important ways. First, shutting down the internet signaled just how scared the Egyptian government was of having lost control, encouraging protesters to keep on pushing for Mubarak's removal. It also pushed nonprotesters and "fence-sitters" into the streets to seek information, thus building additional levels of trust and cohesion among the citizenry.[52] Just as the conservative dilemma model predicted, total information control furthered social unrest. In terms of preserving regime stability, the shutdown was counterproductive. Second, it demonstrated how easy it is for a government to assert control over its information flows quickly and decisively, despite a modern, multidimensional, and privatized information sector. While context made the decision disastrous, the mere fact that such disconnection was possible demonstrates that the Clinton-Gore global information infrastructure (GII, see chapter 4 for details) does little to prevent states from asserting sovereignty over digital information flows, albeit at great cost. According to telematics expert Iljitsch van Beijnum, Egypt is not an outlier; rather, its telecommunications infrastructure is similar to that of many other states: "Like in Egypt, in Europe almost all interconnection happens in the capitals of the countries involved . . . [so] killing the connections between ISPs wouldn't be too hard."[53]

China

China's multifaceted approach of government regulation, censorship, monitoring, self-regulation, encouragement of national industry, and protectionism has been highly effective at keeping Chinese netizens away from foreign applications and content. This effort coincides with a concerted campaign to reframe access to the internet as a privilege rather than a right, for those citizens able to use the Web in ways fit for China's harmonious society. Despite Western predictions of its inevitable failure, China's approach has worked. According to Harvard University's Berkman Center, 96 percent of all page views in China are of Web sites hosted within China.[54]

Although China adopted the concept of a Westphalian state later than most, it did so with ferocity, resulting in a "passionate belief in national sovereignty and territorial integrity"[55] that also motivates China's relationship with information technology. In 2010, just months after Hillary Clinton called for global recognition of a universal freedom to connect, China countered, arguing that access to the internet was not an international concern but rather a state issue. Issuing its first ever State Council White Paper in English, *The Internet in China* was unequivocal on the question of creating an international freedom to connect to the internet: "Within Chinese territory the internet is under the jurisdiction of Chinese sovereignty. The internet sovereignty of China should be respected and protected."[56] For China, restrictions on freedom of expression are justified by the need for state interests and power: "Laws and regulations clearly prohibit the spread of information that contains content subverting state power, undermining national unity [or] infringing upon national honor and interests."[57] Of course, China is not unique in that respect: all states, including Western democracies, place limits on the spread of some types of information; but the limits are stricter and more pervasively enforced in China than in many other countries. Chinese authorities deploy a variety of regulations (law), censorship filters (technology), private citizen content creators (subsidy), and intimidation (force) to maintain its information sovereignty.[58]

China is well on its way to having a popular and robust de facto intranet system. While technically connected to providers and content from around the world, the government uses variations of IP blocking, DNS filtering and redirection, URL filtering, packet filtering, connection reset, and network enumeration to control Web access throughout China. The architecture of its system allows the government to monitor and constrain every aspect of the system, from the deployment of technology to the operation of ISPs and the creation of regulatory agencies capable of enforcing censorship through a dedicated internet police force.[59] The government blocks Web sites that discuss the Dalai Lama, the 1989 crackdown on Tiananmen Square protesters, the banned spiritual movement Falun Gong, and others. According to Google, which closely tracks search queries that trigger government filtering, the word "freedom" has been censored since 2010. Microblogging sites (called weibos) are also tightly controlled. New users are required to verify their identity, matched against police data, with the service before they are allowed to post. Any user found disturbing social order or undermining social stability, including by "spreading rumors, calling for protests, promoting cults or superstitions and impugning China's honor," is punished, often without trial.[60]

Regulators also require ISPs to self-monitor their Web services and delete any objectionable content. The government employs more than two million paid "internet opinion analysts" who pose as ordinary Web users to monitor criticism of the government. Sometimes called the "50 Cent Party" members, the internet opinion analysts are paid 50 Chinese cents per posting.[61] Members of the government are increasingly encouraged to embrace social media to monitor public opinion (and anger) and "actively spread the core values of the socialist system, disseminate socialist advanced culture and build a socialist harmonious society."[62]

Despite these controls, the Chinese intranet connects to the world's internet in strategically advantageous ways, allowing connections to the global financial sector and many Western cultural exports. For example, the USITC estimated that in 2009, unauthorized Chinese downloading of copyrighted material cost the U.S. creative industries $48 billion per year.[63]

Most popular Western Web sites (such as Facebook and YouTube) are either heavily censored or, at times, banned altogether, leaving them unreliable and unpopular among Chinese netizens. As a result, a robust Chinese copycat internet industry has emerged, developing local variations of Google (Baidu), Twitter (Sina Weibo), Facebook (Renren), Ebay (TaoBao), MS Messenger (QQ), and YouTube (Youku). These local copies of popular Web services are hugely popular, sometimes providing more functionality than the Western counterparts. For example, Baidu, the Chinese version of Google, includes search results from sites that allow users to freely download copyrighted content, like music, movies, and television shows. Google, meanwhile, filters similar results due to its compliance with U.S. intellectual property law. Needless to say, Baidu is vastly more popular than Google among Chinese Web users.

Restricting foreign Web content and applications serve a protectionist agenda as well. The local variations of Western internet services are all owned and operated by Chinese nationals, creating flourishing internet industry that contributes to China's job growth and GDP. Tencent (better known as QQ) has annual revenue of $1 billion and a current market capitalization of $24 billion, making it as big as eBay and bigger than Yahoo! Baidu earns $1 billion in annual revenue. Overall, China's internet industry generated $42.1 billion in total revenue 2011. This is in addition to $10.8 trillion in total turnover from e-commerce and $118.7 billion in revenue from internet-based auctions.[64] Of course, Chinese-owned companies are also the least resistant to the government's myriad intrusive regulations.

At the same time, similar to their Iranian counterparts (see below), Chinese authorities seem cognizant of a need for the appearance of restraint in their efforts at controlling the Web. For example, in 2009, the government pushed (and ultimately backed off from) a rule that would have required the installation of a new software program called "Green Dam Youth Escort" on all computers sold in China. The software would effectively monitor a user's every move. After strong resistance at home and abroad, however, China indefinitely delayed enforcement of the requirement. The manufactures of Green Dam have since faced substantial financial difficulties and are on the brink of bankruptcy.

The decision to pull back from Green Dam suggests a careful balancing act between control and individual rights. The government has also slowly scaled back its blocking of Western content, allowing selective access to certain portals while still blocking particular Web pages with objectionable content. Such an approach allows users to feel as though they are not restricted from connecting to the outside world—yet unable to detect that their freedoms are more acutely controlled.[65]

While many Chinese activists use the internet to express criticism of government officials and policies,[66] these criticisms are increasingly contained within a system that allows criticism, but not public protest. Han Han, China's most popular blogger, recently soured on the potential for the internet to transform China, noting, "You feel everyone's really angry, you feel like you could go open the window and you would see protesters on the street. But once you open the window, you realize that there's nothing there at all."[67] The Economist suggests that the internet has helped Chinese leaders better manage public opinion, noting, "The internet may well turn out to have been an agent not of political upheaval in China but of authoritarian adaptation."[68]

China has served as a trendsetter for other governments. Russia, Nigeria, and Vietnam each launched its own versions of the 50 Cent Party. Using hardware bought from China's Huawei and ZTE, Belarus, Ethiopia, Iran, and many others use deep packet inspection technology to monitor for subversive messaging and content.[69]

Despite seemingly draconian controls—by Western standards—on the Web, 85 percent of Chinese citizens support government control and management of internet content.[70] A 2013 study by David Herold interviewed seventy university students in China and similarly found a remarkable consensus supporting government restrictions and controls online.[71] In terms of protecting its information sovereignty, China has adopted a multifaceted, flexible model that, thus far, has been quite effective.

Iran

With more than forty-six million Iranians surfing the Web, approximately 62 percent of the country is online, far surpassing the percentage that have access to a fixed-line telephone (34 percent).[72] The internet is a critical tool for communication among Iranians. It is also heavily regulated and controlled by the Iranian government, though the scope and means of control continue to evolve as Iran tries to balances its citizens' need for information with its own need for legitimacy and security. Responding to social unrest following the contested 2009 presidential elections, the Iranian government stepped up restrictions to "tens of thousands" of foreign Web sites and limited the amount of bandwidth available in country.[73] Approximately 27 percent of all internet sites are blocked in Iran, including *BBC News*, *The Guardian*, Fox News, *Huffington Post*, and the *New York Post*.[74]

Iran's desire to develop its own internally operated, governed, and monitored intranet is driven, in part, by Western efforts to use its connectivity to plant viruses on government and industrial computer systems in Iran. Stuxnet, a U.S.-Israeli virus targeting Iran's domestic nuclear infrastructure,[75] and Flame malware fueled urgent movements by Iranian policymakers toward disconnecting the country's information systems from the Web. Nearly all foreign-based internet technologies and Web sites are treated with suspicion, if not banned entirely. Google, Yahoo! and Twitter have each been identified as "threats to national security" and are treated as enemies of the Iranian state by government officials. Even Wikipedia is treated with suspicion, deemed a tool by the West "to spy on people around the world."[76]

The government deploys a wide variety of policy mechanisms to decrease Iranian use and dependence on foreign internet sites and services. Self-sufficiency is the goal of Iran's internet policies: according to the commander of the Iranian civil defense organization, Gholam Reza Jalali, "The final solution to problems of [cyberdefense and the] formation of Jihad, is to achieve economic self-sufficiency in the production of basic software such as operating systems and software."[77] For example, Iran's telecommunications ministry restricts local banks, insurance firms, and telephone operators from using foreign-based email systems, requiring the use of domain names ending with .ir. All government employees and educators are also required to use an Iranian e-mail service rather than Yahoo! Gmail, Hotmail, or other services based outside of Iran.[78] Gmail and Yahoo! Mail are routinely blocked, as are HTTPS Web sites and VPN services, leaving Iranians unable to surf the Web with any level of encryption. In June 2013, the IT Union Iran announced a new policy requiring all Web hosts to register their services, including the names, addresses, and contact details of their clients, threatening to shut down any company that fails to comply.[79] According to Chief of National Police Esmail Ahmadi Moghadam, "Why should we use services, including email, which are based in countries such as the [United States]," adding, "the relationship with the outside [world] should be as needed."[80]

Security software developed outside of Iran is also banned. According to Iran's communications minister Taghipour Anvari, "Domestic security programs have been improving, and Iran will use them, instead of foreign security software, which cannot be trusted."[81] This is in addition to robust surveillance apparatus and regulations, requiring anyone who logs on to the Web to provide authenticated identification information to the service provider overseeing the connection. By removing any means of anonymous surfing, Iranians have no expectation of privacy regarding data coming to and going from their personal computers.

Iran has also launched its own "halal network, aimed at attracting Muslims on an ethical and moral level."[82] Its National Information Network (NIN) replaced the internet in the daily management of the administration of state entities, the banking system, and public enterprises. According to Neal Ungerleider, "Iran's national intranet is specifically designed not to allow users to access websites outside of the country. There will be extensive built-in logging capabilities, with control of top-level network infrastructure lying in the hands of the government. The government and affiliated institutions will serve as primary content providers, and content creation by individual users will be heavily monitored."[83] While still in development, the NIN will reportedly provide connection speeds sixty times faster than are currently available, aiming to lure users away from trying to access restricted or foreign content.[84]

Restrictions and censorship skyrocketed in the run-up to the 2013 elections. In addition to restrictions to foreign content, access to the *Bahar* and *Mardom Salari* newspapers were blocked without explanation, as were polling sites (Good News Election) and official campaign sites for political opponents. Even Mehr News, typically considered a mouthpiece of the government, was blocked for publishing an interview critical of Iran's Web filters. According to a report by Small Media, "Iran's internet progressed from its relative sense of normality, to a nearly unusable network, whitelisted and throttling, and then overnight back to a routine set of restrictions internet." According to the *Ghanoon Daily*, "The Internet was in a coma."[85]

Yet Iran seems cognizant of the need to not go too far in its efforts to control Web access. A week after Western media outlets reported on Iran's plans to launch its "clean" internet, the Ministry of Communications and Information Technology issued a statement denying any such intentions and calling the interview with Communications Minister Taghipour a "hoax" perpetrated by a "propaganda wing of the West."[86] Yet the denial was published on www. ict.gov.ir, the ministry's own Web site. The target of the announcement was domestic news media and audiences. Since issuing the denial, in June 2013 Iran's state news agency broadcast a documentary heralding the accomplishments of the Ahmadinejad presidency, including the development of the national internet, scheduled for completion by 2016.

Opposition continues to grow to the government's cumbersome filtering, throttling, and restrictions online. In June 2013 a group of several thousand activists signed an open letter to President-elect Rouhani, demanding reforms. The letter appealed to Rouhani specifically, noting his use of Twitter during the campaign, arguing that social networking sites were crucial to encouraging the public to participate in the elections. Unlike China, Iran's domestic alternatives to Google, Facebook, YouTube, and Twitter have failed to gain popular support, and they lack the revenue to compete. With internet speeds randomly crawling to a halt, Iranian users are frustrated and eager for change. Whether or not Iran's halal intranet will provide that change remains to be seen.

The United States

Western governments, too, are actively pursuing their own intranets, though rarely are they mentioned in the same breath as those pursued by China and Iran. Yet from an analytical perspective, the efforts are similar: governments are pursuing policies that enable greater control over the flow of information. They are deploying law, technology, subsidy, and force in order to maintain and strengthen information sovereignty—control over the flow of information within a given physical territory. This section will explore how the U.S. government aims to secure the domestic internet from foreign attack or intrusion. The NSA's foreign surveillance programs are broader than the scope of this chapter and are addressed separately in chapter 7.

The United States is pursuing various means of controlling access to the internet under the auspices of maintaining security, preserving the integrity of confidential information, and protecting intellectual property. For the most part, new and secure technologies are tested in military networks and eventually deployed on civilian, federal Web sites and networks. Once implemented throughout the government, policymakers are interested in extending secure systems infrastructure, enabling a high level of monitoring and control, to private networks deemed important for national security. Precisely which private networks are considered critical for national security is evolving, but at a minimum this would include systems "essential to the minimum operations of the economy and government," including telecommunications, energy, banking and finance, transportation, water systems, and emergency services.[87]

From a technological perspective, the United States is ahead of many other governments in utilizing an intranet. Launched in the 1980s, the Department of Defense (DOD) operates the largest intranet in the world: the Nonsecure Internet Protocol Router Network (NIPRNET), created to exchange sensitive but unclassified information between internal users as well as providing users access to the internet. It is owned and managed by the Defense Information Systems Agency (DISA) and has since grown so large that the DOD is struggling to control the network. In 2012 the Pentagon requested $2.3 billion to bolster network security within the DOD as well as between it and the Department of Homeland Security (DHS). The intelligence community uses several intranets for a variety of purposes, including JWICS, SIPRNET, and Intelink-U. According to the Army Foreign Military Studies Office, "Intelink-U is a virtual private network—a government intranet." Most of the intelligence-related intranets are linked via Intelipedia, an online system for collaborative information sharing that Google helped establish in 2006.[88]

Outside the DOD and intelligence communities, the government is moving quickly to enhance the efficacy of government communication networks. As part of its efforts to boost cybersecurity, in 2010 the United States established Cyber Command (CYBERCOM) to defend the military's electronic networks, support military and counterterrorism missions, and assist civil authorities and industry planners. It is led by the director of the NSA, General Keith Alexander, and housed within NSA's headquarters at Fort Meade, Maryland. CYBERCOM's facilities cost $3.2 billion to construct, with $400 million spent on telecommunications and electrical costs alone.[89] CYBERCOM consists of a team of between five hundred and one thousand troops recruited from Marine Forces Cyber Command, the 24th Air Force, the 10th Fleet, and Army Forces Cyber Command and has developed advanced threat-monitoring systems for government networks, including Einstein 2 and Einstein 3. Einstein 2 has been widely implemented in most government agencies and allows for data inspection upon entry into a federal network. Einstein 3 goes a step further, more thoroughly inspecting all communication for threat risks and alerting DHS and the NSA of suspicious communication in real time.

Cybersecurity experts argue that Einstein 3 may "offer no intrinsic security value."[90] It functions differently from Einstein 2, which is considered highly effective at protecting federal networks. Rather than looking for malicious attack patterns directed at government sites, Einstein 3 collects, processes, and analyzes all person-to-person communications content using real-time, deep packet inspection technology and connects data with signatures based on personally identifiable information. According to cybersecurity expert Babak Pasdar, "The program is implemented where servers exchange traffic between one another—in the heart of a network system rather than at the perimeter, which interfaces with the outside world. This is similar to a home security system that only monitors the central interior of a house, rather than keeping an eye on the actual doors."[91] Decisions to monitor and share communications are determined by internal standards and protocols, but at a minimum this includes all federal employee communication from government computers (including private e-mails sent by government employees), as well as all content produced by any private foreign citizen communicating with government employees electronically or when signed on to a .gov website.

Similar to the role the military services played in assisting domestic recovery efforts after Hurricane Katrina and the 2010 Gulf Oil spill, CYBERCOM envisions its task as helping secure domestic and civilian electronic networks that are currently at risk. Once tested, the NSA and DHS plan on extending their cybersecurity systems to key private networks deemed critical to national security.[92] According to Deputy Defense Secretary William Lynn in 2010, "We are already using our technical capabilities . . . to protect government networks. We need to think imaginatively about how this technology can also help secure a space on the internet for critical government and commercial applications." Lynn is pushing to establish a hacker-free, online space for both government and civilian purposes. Faced with growing risks inherent in using the internet, Lynn suggests that private companies and citizens will jump at the opportunity to opt into secure government networks in the face of the "'wild, wild West' of the unprotected internet."[93]

DHS is moving quickly to help secure the commercial networks, too. Jason Healey, director of the Atlantic Council's cyber statecraft initiative explains that the DHS plans to place the "government at the center of the Web," adding, "If we're going to make progress . . . we have to treat the private sector as the supported command, not as the supporting command."[94] The DHS is rolling out Einstein 3 with civilian federal agencies now but is also planning to target industries outside the federal government considered critical to the nation's infrastructure.[95]

According to Deputy Assistant Secretary of Defense for Cyber Policy Robert J. Butler, collaborating with the private telecommunications sector is crucial for maintaining any semblance of cybersecurity: "You can't just do it with the federal sector. You have to have the ISPs and others who really understand the networks involved."[96] CYBERCOM and NSA Director Alexander clarified that securing private networks could not be achieved through voluntary mechanisms alone: "Recent events have shown that a purely voluntary and market-driven system is not sufficient. Some minimum security requirements will be necessary to ensure that the core infrastructure is taking appropriate measures to harden its networks."[97] Precisely what minimum security requirements will be imposed on which industries remains to be seen.

Industries considered critical to national security continue to expand, given the effect that an attack on almost any industry would have on the economy, thus providing rationale for governments securing large parts of the internet. Telecommunications is already considered a critical industry, but increasingly so is the intellectual-property sector. According to Deputy Secretary of Defense Lynn: "The threat to intellectual property . . . may over the long term be the most significant cyber threat our nation faces."[98] Americans are not necessarily opposed to securing networks from intellectual property theft, with a majority supporting penalties for downloading copyrighted music and movies.[99] Yet securing telecommunications and intellectual property sectors with military-grade technology would allow for the vast majority, if not all, of the internet connections in the United States to be monitored, analyzed, and their data archived in real time. Such an effort could also be described as, using Briggs and Burke's term, "total information control."[100]

Conclusion

Some suggest that internet governance emerged in a similar fashion as *lex mercatoria* during the medieval period.[101] Lex mercatoria—a reference to a body of trader-made and -enforced commercial law used by merchants—was distinct from government-made law. Local authorities typically had little to do with the enforcement of lex mercatoria, except for the purpose of collecting taxes on the exchange of goods. The laws emerged because traders, operating in distinct legal jurisdictions, needed a clear and efficient way of handling transactions with their counterparts around the world. Distrustful of the inefficient and biased local legal systems, traders developed and collectively imposed their own codes. As a result of this self-regulatory regime, trade flourished, and substantial wealth was generated and shared.

Today's international commercial law is the direct descendent of some of the fundamental principles of the lex mercatoria, including the choice of arbitrators, arbitration institutions, procedures, applicable laws, and the goal to reflect customs, usage, and good practice among the parties.

In many ways, the early history of states' efforts to control the internet follows the path of medieval merchant law. As transnational commerce grew, local institutions were slow to adapt, and so traders created their own rules and regulations that satisfied their collective needs and allowed for a self-sufficient and sustainable system of exchange. The internet's early history is rife with examples of self-made rules and regulations that were collectively adopted across national borders in order to allow for growth of prosperity on and use of the internet.

But eventually the merchant legal system broke down. As national commercial codes caught up with the times, local authorities enacted protections to ensure local businesses could compete against international businesses. Nationally enacted codes replaced lex mercatoria, and merchants lost authority to state institutions. State interests drove the need to develop sophisticated, nation-based legal institutions, and the cosmopolitan system of governance quickly collapsed. The nationalization of merchant law did not erase the codes and institutions the merchants had developed. Rather, it co-opted them. As Trakman argues, "In effect, the nation-states reconstituted the lex mercatoria in their image."[102]

Charles Darwin is credited with the idea that it is not the strongest of species that survive, nor the most intelligent, but those most adaptable to change. We have explored four case studies wherein governments endeavor to better control domestic information flows for self-preservation. The results indicate that it is not only species that need to adapt to survive, but states too. Egypt failed miserably with its poorly timed and overly stringent measures, pushing citizens into, rather than away from, Tahrir Square. Iran, too, struggles with this balance, though it has developed a more sophisticated strategy than Egypt's. Slowly implementing incremental restrictions, often framed as service improvements, Iran connects its control efforts to the collective memory of foreign efforts to infiltrate Iran. At the same time, its citizens are clamoring for more access and for privacy online, making the status quo unsustainable.

Despite substantial variations in policy, China and the United States are developing culturally specific, incremental, and advanced strategies for controlling internet access. Both acknowledge citizen demands for some privacy and free speech protections while arguing for a need for some level of government control. Both also connect to culturally resonant, compelling narratives. In China, 85 percent of those surveyed support government control and management of internet content.[103] In the United States as well, a majority of Americans support penalties for downloading copyrighted music and movies.[104] While the level of control exerted is drastically different, the strategies are analytically quite similar. Despite predictions that both governments would fail at taming the internet, they have achieved an impressive level of success thus far.[105]

Moving forward, continued adaptation and balancing of citizen demands and state security will determine the ultimate success or failure of state efforts and, in some cases, regime survival. As states develop different strategies for information control, ISPs adapt too, working with governments to provide specific services that comply with different legal systems. Google's continued compliance with China's censorship laws, and Research in Motion's acquiescence to monitoring requests from the UAE, Saudi Arabia, China, and others indicate momentum toward a world of intranets rather than a single, shared internet. This tension is explored further in chapter 7, which analyzes the significance of the NSA-led, globally robust surveillance apparatus and suggests a possible path forward that bridges the gap between "internet freedom" and "information sovereignty" approaches to international communication.

7

Internet Freedom in a Surveillance Society

May the Atlantic Telegraph, under the blessing of
Heaven, prove to be a bond of perpetual peace and
friendship between the kindred nations, and an instrument of Divine Providence to diffuse religion, civilization,
liberty, and law throughout the world. In this view, will
not all nations of Christendom spontaneously unite in
the declaration that it shall be for ever neutral, and that
its communication shall be held sacred in passing to their
places of destination, even in the midst of hostilities?

—President James Buchanan, Letter to Her Majesty
Victoria, Queen of England, 1858

The secrecy of correspondence, telephony, and other
confidential communications is inviolable.
—Section 10 of the Finnish Constitution, 2000

This chapter explores the tension between the internet-freedom movement and cybersecurity policy. Central to this tension is the question of anonymity, whether or not it is possible to connect behaviors or material online to the responsible person. On the one hand, anonymity is central to freedom online, for online speech in particular. Political dissidents depend on anonymous browsing and posting capabilities to express oppositional views free from government repression. On the other hand, anonymity en-ables criminal behavior online, ranging from intellectual property theft to whole-scale cyber warfare.

We begin by tracing the specific vision of internet freedom proposed by Secretary of State Clinton to the revelations of a NSA-led, robust, global surveillance apparatus. Specifically, we explore how the U.S. espousal of a freedom to connect deviates from traditional protections for freedom of expression because it does not incorporate protections for anonymous speech. This deviation is not merely the result of the NSA's surveillance programs; it is also the result of a specific legal vision proposed by internet-freedom advocates. After a review of the different ways anonymous speech online is eviscerated in the current political, economic, and legal environment, we offer a brief legal history to explain the centrality of anonymous speech to freedom-of-expression doctrine.

President Buchanan's message to Queen Victoria that introduced this chapter comes from the first transatlantic telegraph cable ever sent. It reflects an inherent optimism surrounding the emergence of new technologies facilitating international communication. But it also provides a helpful reminder of the importance of shared rules—"communication shall be held sacred in passing to their places"—for communication technologies to be a "bond of perpetual peace and friendship." The final two sections of this chapter explore the practical consequences of a global communications infrastructure that lacks any guarantee of confidentiality, a necessary consequence of the loss of anonymous messaging. It underscores how protecting the secrecy of correspondence is central to the foundations of modern-day international cooperation and governance. Connecting to arguments forwarded in each of the previous chapters, in this chapter we seek to challenge the relentless "internet freedom" versus "information sovereignty" approach to navigating questions of rights and security online, offering an alternative, historically grounded, and globally aware framing of this ongoing debate.

Internet Freedom 2.0

In 2011, thirteen months after her remarks at The Newseum (discussed in detail in chapter 1), Secretary Clinton issued a second speech on internet freedom. Sarah Labowitz, a State Department policy advisor, described this second speech as "the more careful, detailed articulation of what internet freedom means, from a legal and policy perspective."[1] Citing the power of the internet and other digital media with regard to the overthrow of Egyptian president Hosni Mubarak, Clinton suggested that greater precision and transparency is needed as countries embrace the internet and negotiate appropriate regulatory controls. Illustrative of the U.S. vision of internet freedom, Clinton noted, "The internet has become the public space of the twenty-first century. . . . The goal is not to tell people how to use the internet any more than we ought to tell people how to use any public square, whether it's Tahrir Square or Times Square."[2] It is in this speech that Clinton clarified her vision for what constitutes internet freedom; "Together, the freedoms of expression, assembly, and association online comprise what I've called the freedom to connect."[3]

Clinton's assertion that the internet be treated as a public space is interesting in part because it is definitely *not* a public space. It is a series of privately owned and operated computer networks and servers accessible to internet users around the world.[4] These varied networks and servers are each governed by the laws of the host state and the interests of the individual or corporate proprietor. So why would Clinton suggest otherwise? To describe these privately held distributed networks as collectively constituting a "public sphere" asserts that the internet contains certain expectations and norms of proper and improper behaviors. Public utilities are often treated as natural monopolies, a legal construct that is used to justify additional government regulation and control in a particular sector of the economy. Moreover, from a legal perspective, a public space is a publicly owned area that must be accessible to all. Freedom of assembly and expression in public spaces are treated differently, legally, from private and anonymous speech. There are, for example, no expectations of privacy in a public space and no protections for anonymous speech in a public square.

So how do anonymous speech and privacy fit into Clinton's freedom-to-connect doctrine? How about broader U.S. internet policy? Central to balancing the internet's democratic potential with the risk of enhanced criminal behavior is whether internet users are anonymous. Are they free to browse and post without fear of punishment, or can governments trace a post or an e-mail directly back to a user? The question is especially tricky because the answer seems to depend on end-user behaviors. For example, according to Clinton, "Those who use the internet to recruit terrorists or distribute stolen intellectual property cannot divorce their online actions from their real-world identities."[5] Clinton goes on to call for tools capable of helping "law enforcement agencies cooperate across jurisdictions," presumably acknowledging a need for the government's ability to de-anonymize user identity in certain situations.

At The Newseum, University of Utah professor Robert Gehl asked Clinton to clarify exactly how she would strike the balance between protecting anonymous speech when it concerns legal behavior and being able to de-anonymize users involved in illegal behavior, such as copyright theft. Clinton acknowledged the challenge of balancing the two and suggested that technology was central to managing the tension: "So how we go after this, I think, is now what we're requesting many of you who are experts in this area to lend your help to us in doing. We need the guidance of technology experts."[6]

Growing concern over cybersecurity and government's ability to ensure the security and stability of internet-based communication has elevated the significance of online anonymity. As businesses and governments move more and of their work online, Clinton acknowledged that people "must have confidence that the networks at the core of their national security and economic prosperity are safe and resilient. . . . Our ability to bank online, use electronic commerce, and safeguard billions of dollars in intellectual property are all at stake if we cannot rely on the security of our information networks."[7]

Cybersecurity thus requires some mechanism for de-anonymization. If cybersecurity efforts are largely the responsibility of governments, however, then allowing them to de-anonymize internet use raises substantial concerns over freedom of expression. In a post– 9/11 world, what is to stop a government from tracking down cyberdissidents using the same technological capacity used to maintain cybersecurity? Or, as Clinton cautions, "These challenges must not become an excuse for governments to systematically violate the rights and privacy of those who use the internet for peaceful political purposes."[8]

Currently, the structure of the internet allows for anonymous browsing by default. At the application layer, this changes fairly quickly, with content and service providers and, in some cases, governments requiring identity verification before certain content or services can be accessed. But from a technical perspective the internet allows for anonymous browsing. At the same time, one's online activities, from online shopping to engaging in political dissent, are fairly easy to monitor by service providers and governments. And the data collected from tracking one's online activities can easily, in the vast majority of cases, be used to de-anonymize the user.

At the center of this debate are two organizations, Google and the NSA. There are important differences between the two, but as a result of Google's centrality to all things online, and the NSA's zealous interest in using cyberspace for intelligence gathering, their fates seem increasingly intertwined. Moreover, while they are typically not thought of as similar, both entities share a common goal: gathering as much information about users' online activities as possible.

NSA to the Rescue

Google entered China's market in 2006 after a long debate regarding the limitations of operating in compliance with China's censorship and social-stability laws. In order to operate in China, Google had to agree to the government's extensive censorship protocols for searches queried through its google.cn search portal. Upon entering the world's largest market of internet users, Google struggled. Despite its lead in search markets around the world, Google trailed the Chinese-based Baidu search portal. It was, however, the second-most-popular search engine in China, gaining users with the rollout of Google maps, translation, and mobile services targeting Chinese users. As a result, by the end of 2009 Google was gaining user trust and starting to chip away at Baidu's user base.

Google's initial hesitance to enter the Chinese market was based, in part, on the company's fierce commitment to the internet-freedom agenda. From the beginning, Google's code of conduct was simple: "Don't be evil." Brin and Page elaborated in their 2004 IPO prospectus, adding: "We believe strongly that in the long term, we will be better served—as shareholders and in all other ways—by a company that does good things for the world even if we forgo some short term gains." This mission statement was in tension with Google's economic interest in competing in the world's largest and fastest-growing market for online services, China. How could it reconcile its mission statement—"Don't be evil"—while at the same time plan for the company's long-term future? Google decided to enter the Chinese market based on the idea that it would help open up China, and eventually be able to operate uninhibited by government censorship and regulations. Give us an inch, and we'll take a mile, or so the thinking went.

Four years later, on January 12, 2010, Google announced that it had identified an ultra-sophisticated attempt to hack into its corporate infrastructure originating from China, uncovering a large-scale effort to access secure user information and proprietary corporate information, as well as a broader campaign to hack into dozens of major Western corporations. As a result of the attacks, Google announced that, in addition to having its source code and other intellectual property stolen, the Gmail accounts for a number of Chinese human-rights activists were compromised.[9] Due to the sophistication and scope of the hacking effort, dubbed Operation Aurora, Google announced it was reconsidering its presence in China altogether. David Drummond, Google's Chief Legal Officer, wrote: "We have decided we are no longer willing to continue censoring our results on Google.cn. . . . We recognize that this may well mean having to shut down Google.cn, and potentially our offices in China."[10]

The Obama administration was especially concerned by Google's announcement that, in addition to compromising Google's security, Chinese-based hackers had broken into "at least twenty other large companies from a wide range of businesses—including the Internet, finance, technology, media and chemical sectors."[11] A government investigation later revealed that thirty-four companies were attacked, including Adobe Systems, Intel, Juniper Networks, Morgan Stanley, Northrop Grumman, Symantec, and Yahoo! Secretary of State Clinton announced the State Department's newborn internet-freedom doctrine, discussed in detail in chapter 1, just eleven days after Google's decision to shut down its China-based operations. Google emerged as a champion of free speech. Praising the company's decision to challenge Chinese censorship laws, Congressman Christopher H. Smith (R-New Jersey) proclaimed: "This is a remarkable, historic, and welcomed action. . . . [We] are greatly heartened by what Google has done."[12]

While raking in praise for taking such a clear stand in favor of Western values, Google turned to the NSA for help in patching its network and in tracking down the culprit.[13] Within twenty-four hours of Google's announcement regarding the attack, the two organizations signed a cooperative research-and-development agreement.[14] While the details of the agreement remain secret, press reports indicate that Google granted the NSA access to some of its data to study the intrusion, to better understand how the attack had happened, and to create defense mechanisms able to combat similar attacks in the future. In announcing the agreement, Google was keen to reassure customers that their privacy was protected, promising that it would not divulge information protected by Google's user agreement and privacy policy.

NSA, whose primary mandate is intelligence gathering, was an unusual partner for Google. It was the first time the two had cooperated, according to Google. Many considered the agreement as a sign of the significant nature of the threat presented by Operation Aurora. According to NSA spokeswoman Judi Emmel, "As part of its information-assurance mission, NSA works with a broad range of commercial partners and research associates to ensure the availability of secure tailored solutions for Department of Defense and national security systems customers."[15] Director of National Intelligence Admiral Dennis Blair defended the NSA's cooperative role with the private sector, noting, "The National Security Agency has the greatest repository of cybertalent."[16]

Two important details have emerged since the initial announcement of Operation Aurora. First, the hackers were Chinese, likely operating under the instruction of a government agency. A State Department cable outlines how the upper echelons of the Chinese Communist Party ordered the attack. The memo specifically identified China's State Council Information Office as coordinating the attack, indicating it was primarily politically motivated, and even included the location of the building where the attacks originated.[17] This information was confirmed by Verisign iDefense, a government contractor.

Second, the attackers used several tactics to access Google's system and compromise user privacy, including exploiting back doors mandated by the U.S. government to access user accounts suspected of criminal or terrorist behavior. According to Bruce Schneier, chief security technology officer of British Telecommunications, "In order to comply with government search warrants on user data, Google created a backdoor access system into Gmail accounts. This feature is what the Chinese hackers exploited to gain access."[18] Cybersecurity researchers also found that the attacks used a previously unknown zero-day vulnerability in Microsoft's Internet Explorer and Adobe's Reader and Acrobat applications.

The Google-NSA agreement was part of a broader NSA program to assist the private sector in protecting against cyberattacks from foreign agents. In July 2010 the *Wall Street Journal* reported a new NSA program called Operation Perfect Citizen. The purpose of the program was to detect cyberassaults on private companies running parts of the domestic critical infrastructure, including the electricity grid and nuclear power plants.[19] Government officials indicated that the NSA would even leverage existing contracts with the private sector as "incentives to urge them to cooperate."[20] According to Director Blair, internet and telecommunications companies are at the center of America's critical infrastructure: "Our information infrastructure is becoming both indispensable to the functioning of our society and vulnerable to catastrophic disruption in a way that the previous, analog, decentralized systems were not."[21] While the initial phase of Perfect Citizen targets the critical infrastructure sector, officials indicated that the initiative would eventually expand to help any part of the private sector unable to adequately protect itself from a foreign cyberattack.[22]

Of course, the critical nature of the today's information infrastructure also creates opportunities for abuse by powerful state and nonstate actors. Despite the outrage over allegations of China's hacking into major American companies, as it turns out, the NSA, in cooperation with intelligence agencies in Europe, was doing similar things, and more.

NSA and the End of Anonymity

Three years later, in June 2013, the *Guardian* and the *Washington Post* began publishing a series of top-secret NSA documents leaked to them by former NSA contractor Edward Snowden. The documents outlined the existence of a global, pervasive, NSA-operated electronic-surveillance system aiming to access, track, and often store online communication, including the content of e-mails, VoIP information, and even encrypted data exchange. Even a year after the revelations, it is unclear if any online material is secure from the NSA's surveillance systems. While the full extent of the surveillance operation would require its own book, there are several elements worth detailing here.

One program, PRISM, allows for the NSA, along with the FBI, to access user information through a Foreign Intelligence Surveillance Act (FISA) warrant. Figure 7.1 shows a slide from NSA's "Introduction to PRISM" PowerPoint presentation. NSA materials listed a number of high-profile American technology companies as partners, including Facebook, Google, and Microsoft. (See Table 7.1 for a complete list of U.S. companies participating in the PRISM program.) The program also allowed for the collection of huge quantities of raw internet-traffic data at major network exchange points, enabling the agency to perform real-time keyword searches of data moving online. There were, however, limits to PRISM. The FISA warrant process, while highly secretive and susceptible to abuse, provided a check on how many users the intelligence organization could track. Tapping into exchange points allowed access to data flows, but much of that data was encrypted, making it almost useless for real-time intelligence gathering.

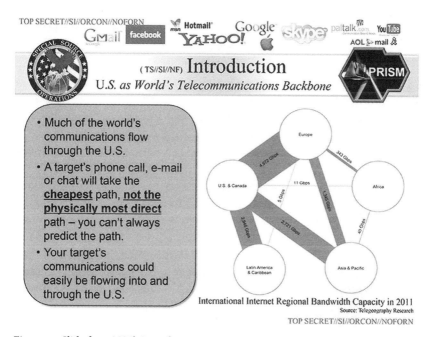

Figure 7.1: Slide from NSA's Introduction to PRISM Presentation (April 2013)

Table 7.1: List of Companies Enrolled in the PRISM Program

Company	Cooperation began
Microsoft	September 11, 2007
Yahoo, Inc.	March 12, 2008
Google	January 14, 2009
Facebook	June 3, 2009
PalTalk	December 7, 2009
YouTube	September 24, 2010
Skype	February 6, 2011
AOL	March 31, 2011
Apple	October 2012

"NSA Slides Explain the PRISM Data-Collection Program," *Washington Post*, June 29, 2013, available at http://www.washingtonpost.com/wp-srv/special/politics/prism-collection-documents (accessed July 31, 2014).

In an effort to work beyond these constraints, the NSA launched MUSCU-LAR, a complimentary program that partnered with the UK's Government Communications Headquarters (GCHQ). While most internet traffic is encrypted as it travels from a service provider to the end user, that same data is unencrypted while it is processed, archived and stored within a provider's own network. In order to access user information before it was encrypted, MUSCULAR tapped directly into Google and Yahoo!'s internal networks as they passed through international borders. Figure 7.2 shows a sketch of how the NSA's MUSCULAR physically exploits Google's cloud infrastructure. The program gave the agency unfettered access to content passing through the network, including e-mails, online chats, cloud storage, and search queries. Because cloud service providers replicate user data onto multiple servers to facilitate ease of access, nearly all user personal information is passed along internal networks on a routine basis. According to industry analyst Sean Gallagher, "The NSA had access to millions of messages and Web transactions per day without having to use its FISA warrant power to compel Google or Yahoo! to provide the data through PRISM. And it gained access to complete mailboxes of e-mail."[23] As of 2012, the agency had established a "defeat fingerprint" application that allowed it to scan Google's and Yahoo!'s internal networks for individual users as well as particular search terms (and who was using them).

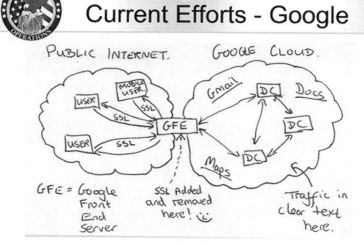

Figure 7.2: NSA's "Google Cloud Exploitation" PowerPoint (MUSCULAR)

Gallagher estimates that the MUSCULAR program provided the NSA access to nearly all of Google's user data, which is approximately a third of all the data the agency collects on a routine basis.[24] By the agency's own admission, it "touches" 29.21 petabytes of data a day. To put this figure in context, Google processes an average of 20 petabytes of data per day.[25] So, the NSA's daily reach is larger than all of Google's search queries, Gmail services, and mapping applications combined.

GCHQ's Tempora program, also detailed in Snowden's leaked documents, is similar to MUSCULAR. Tempora operates under British law and allows for the wholesale collection of data traffic passing through transatlantic fiber-optic cables, including e-mail, Facebook posts, messaging, internet search histories, and calls, all of which are shared directly with the NSA.[26] In all, GCHQ installed intercept probes in the British landing points of more than two hundred transatlantic fiber-optic cables, many of which carry data to and from Western Europe and North America. These intercepts were placed with the permission of the companies that own the cables; however, according to the leaked documents, the private companies "have no choice." "Should they decline, we can compel them to [cooperate]."[27] Additional leaked documents, seen by Germany's *Süddeutsche* newspaper, reveal that BT, Vodafone, Verizon, Global Crossing, Level 3, Viatel, and Interoute are among the companies that agreed to install GCHQ intercepts on their cables.[28]

According to the *Guardian*, "The sheer scale of the agency's ambition is reflected in the titles of its two principal components: Mastering the Internet and Global Telecoms Exploitation, aimed at scooping up as much online and telephone traffic as possible." In another leaked document, GCHQ attorneys advise against trying to list the total number of people targeted under Tempora because "this would be an infinite list which we couldn't manage."[29] In 2010 U.K. officials internally boasted that the program had greater access to internet data streams and produced far more metadata than any of the NSA's programs. As many as 850,000 NSA employees and defense contractors had access to CGHQ's database and could thus download and query extensive information about the internet browsing and use habits of American citizens.[30]

Despite pronouncements of outrage over the NSA surveillance programs, the leaked documents also demonstrate how German, French, Spanish, and Swedish intelligence services have each developed methods of mass surveillance of internet and phone traffic in close partnership with the UK's GCHQ.[31]

In a move to reassure users, Google is working toward encrypting all user data, even while it resides within Google's own servers and network. Yet documents leaked by Snowden indicate that the NSA has already found workarounds to commercial encryption technologies, including VPNs, TLS/SSL, https, SSH, IPSEC, encrypted chat, and the protective layer used in 4G smartphones. According a 2010 memo outlining the accomplishments of NSA's BULLRUN program, "In recent years there has been an aggressive effort, led by the NSA, to make major improvements in defeating network security and privacy involving multiple sources and methods. . . . Cryptanalytic capabilities are now coming online. Vast amounts of encrypted Internet data which have up till now been discarded are now exploitable."[32]

Efforts to defeat encryption go beyond breaking into major service-provider systems and de-encrypting known security protocols. They also include "actively engag[ing] the U.S. and foreign IT industries to covertly influence and/or overtly leverage their commercial products' designs" to make them more exploitable, including working with chipmakers to build back doors into their hardware. According to a 2013 budget request, the NSA's SIGINT Enabling Project, which has an annual budget of $250 million, leverages industry relationships, conducts clandestine operations, and lobbies professional and government organizations to "covertly influence" encryption technologies around the world.[33] In one case the NSA persuaded a leading technology manufacturer to insert a back door into its hardware before it was shipped for use by a foreign government.[34] A 2013 internal report bragged about the NSA's accomplishments, highlighting successes in "deliberately weakening the international encryption standards adopted by developers."[35] The classified documents confirm that the agency deliberately engineered a fatal weakness of modern encryption standards, discovered by Microsoft researchers in 2007. According to Heninger and Halderman, "There is now credible evidence that the NSA has pushed NIST, in at least one case, to canonize an inferior algorithm designed with a back door for NSA use. Dozens of companies implemented the standardized algorithm in their software, which means that the NSA could potentially get around security software on millions of computers worldwide."[36]

One of the most notorious and popular anonymization tools is an internet browser named Tor. Tor—short for The Onion Router—is an open-source project that bounces its users' internet traffic through several other computers to keep it anonymous. Funded in large part by the State Department, Tor was established as a means to help political activists in countries take their activism and planning online, anonymously, and thus safe from local surveillance. It is popular in China and Iran for exactly these purposes.

As a result of its ability to protect user identities, the Tor network has also become a hotbed for criminal activity. Thus, the NSA and GCHQ target users under the auspices of cybersecurity. The agency's efforts to crack Tor's protections include: exploiting software bugs in the Firefox browser and other software applications used by individual Tor users; staining a user as he or she enters the Tor network, making it possible to then follow his or her activities; and efforts to shape future software developments on the Tor network.[37] In many cases, the NSA was able to gain full control over a target's computer, accessing all files, keystrokes, and online activity. The *Washington Post* reported that these vulnerabilities allowed the NSA to successfully unmask twenty-four Tor users in a single weekend. The 2013 budget proposal included a specific request for additional funding to "reach an initial operating capability for SIGINT access to data flowing through a commercial Arabic-language /Middle East-oriented anonymous internet service."[38]

Responding to a media query regarding its efforts to break Tor's security, the NSA issued the following statement: "It should hardly be surprising that our intelligence agencies seek ways to counteract targets' use of technologies to hide their communications. Throughout history, nations have used various methods to protect their secrets, and today terrorists, cybercriminals, human traffickers and others use technology to hide their activities. Our intelligence community would not be doing its job if we did not try to counter that."[39]

The Value of Anonymity and the Re-emergent State

While there is much to be said about the legality and efficacy of these and other surveillance programs, for the purposes of this book there are two important takeaways. The first relates to anonymity. The Snowden revelations demonstrate that, from a technical perspective, complete online anonymity is nearly impossible. They also demonstrate that current laws do not adequately protect netizens' privacy rights and that the dominant norms guiding the intelligence operations favor near-ubiquitous surveillance of cyberspace. Between PRISM, MUSCULAR, BULLRUN, Tempora, and the NSA's attacks on encryption technology and the anonymizing Tor network, the collective effort represents a widely effective attack on anonymous speech.

So what? It is simple to equate anonymity online with a cover for criminal behavior. The vast majority of people would prefer it if individuals were connected to and held accountable for the things they said and did online. Accountability and transparency are critical to a healthy democracy, both of which can be complicated by systems that allow for anonymous speech. What is the value of anonymity?

There is a long history of defending anonymous speech as central to protecting freedom of expression. In prerevolutionary England, anonymous writing was the primary means by which citizens criticized the British government. American revolutionary-era colonial authors like Thomas Paine (*Common Sense*) depended on anonymity to publish critiques of the British government without fear of retribution. Both the *Federalist Papers* and the *Anti-Federalist Papers* were published under pseudonyms to protect the authors from social stigmatization or prosecution. The First Amendment itself was, in part, a reaction to English licensing laws that aimed to stifle criticism of government by requiring authors to verify their identity with the state prior to publication. Internet co-founder and Google vice president Vint Cerf made this point, arguing: "The reason we are sitting here in this bastion of freedom is because anonymously authored tracts agitated for revolution and independence. Part of the rationale for the First Amendment was to codify this right to anonymous speech, which the founders saw as the key to a public being able to organize and rebel. It guaranteed free expression without harm to the citizen."[40]

The value of anonymous speech goes beyond political speech. Many renowned literary and artistic figures have published using pseudonyms, including notable figures like Samuel Langhorne Clemens (Mark Twain), François-Marie Arouet (Voltaire) and Benjamin Franklin (Silence Dogood, Polly Baker, and Richard Saunders). Female authors of the nineteenth century, including Amandine Aurore Lucie Dupin (George Sand) and Mary Ann Evans (George Eliot) relied on pseudonyms in an effort to avoid social isolation and bypass sexist dismissals of their work. Put simply, anonymous speech allows the dissenting, the disenfranchised, and the disempowered to air their views while protecting them from retaliation and persecution.

The U.S. Supreme Court recognized the right to speak anonymously in its 1960 decision, *Talley v. California*,[41] wherein the court struck down a Los Angeles ordinance making it illegal to distribute handbills without clearly marking the person or persons responsible for the pamphlet. Recognizing the rich history of anonymous speech in American history, the court held that the ordinance constituted an unwarranted restriction on the freedom of expression and risked stifling controversial opinions and discussions of public importance. Again, in *McIntyre v. Ohio Elections Commission* (1995), the court struck down an Ohio statute prohibiting the distribution of anonymous campaign literature; the court ruled that regardless of the motivation for seeking anonymity, the interest in having anonymous works enter the marketplace of ideas outweighed the public's interest in knowing authors' identities. Supreme Court decisions in 1999 (*Buckley v. American Constitutional Law Foundation*)[42] and in 2002 (*Watchtower Bible and Tract Society v. Village of Stratton*)[43] also upheld the right to anonymous speech. It is, by all accounts, central to the modern conception of freedom of expression.

In *McIntyre*, the court specifically addressed the question of the possibility of abusing the right to anonymity, arguing the value of free speech outweighed these concerns. The court also argued that other criminal penalties unrelated to speech typically were in place to deter the people from engaging in illegal behavior: "The State may, and does, punish fraud directly. But it cannot seek to punish fraud indirectly by indiscriminately outlawing a category of speech, based on its content, with no necessary relationship to the danger sought to be prevented."[44] The court also addressed the question of the importance of an author's identity to the content of a message, noting: "People are intelligent enough to evaluate the source of an anonymous writing. They can see it is anonymous. They know it is anonymous. They can evaluate its anonymity along with its message, as long as they are permitted, as they must be, to read that message. And then, once they have done so, it is for them to decide what is responsible, what is valuable, and what is truth."[45]

The second important takeaway relates to the reemergence of the state. Despite the fact that private companies own and operate the vast majority of the internet, governments around the world seem to have little trouble in asserting authority and compelling private-sector cooperation under the guise of national security. Leaked documents illustrate that the vast majority of American technology and telecommunications companies cooperate with the NSA on a routine basis. They also demonstrate that British and European private sectors are similarly compelled into cooperation with their respective national intelligence authorities. According to the classified NSA documents, "the agency's success depends on working with internet companies—by getting their voluntary collaboration, forcing their cooperation with court orders or surreptitiously stealing their encryption keys or altering their software or hardware."[46]

In the United States, the one e-mail provider that tried to refuse cooperation with the authorities—Lavabit—was forced to close and destroy its users' data in order to prevent the federal government from accessing all of its users' private e-mails.[47] Lavabit's founder wrote a public letter to his disappointed customers warning "against anyone trusting their private data to a company with physical ties to the United States."[48] Silent Circle also shut down its e-mail services, expressing similar concerns.

Despite widespread anger over revelations that the government hacked into its system to access private user data, even Google acknowledges that state interests will inevitably dictate the future of the internet. According to Google's CEO, Eric Schmidt, "In a world of asynchronous threats it is too dangerous for there not to be some way to identify you. We need a [verified] name service for people. Governments will demand it."[49]

This trend challenges the prevailing logic of globalization, which champions the rise of transnational actors and corporations at the expense of the nation-state. Chapter 6 outlined how states are reasserting authority and using new technologies to enhance their legitimacy, while this chapter highlights how vulnerable the private sector is to government intervention on matters relating to national security. Some of the largest and most powerful corporations in the world, including Google, Microsoft, Verizon, and AT&T, were unwilling (or, in certain cases, unable) to challenge the various government efforts to access their proprietary systems, even when allowing that access clearly hurts their long-term economic interests. Chapter 2 highlighted the risks involved in high-level cooperation between the private sector and government; several of those risks are becoming increasingly clear in the aftermath of the Snowden revelations.

For General Keith Alexander, it is precisely because these technology companies are so powerful, operating in transnational contexts, that greater governmental control is required. Just as Secretary Clinton's description of the internet as a public good also provides a rationale for a certain level of governmental regulation to ensure its safety and security, Alexander's fear of the disruption that could result from destabilizing the nation-state helps to justify the intelligence community's surveillance tactics:

> You see Google acting in some ways as nation-states used to act, exercising to the best of their ability some attributes traditionally associated with sovereign states. . . . The last time we had such a powerful discontinuity is probably the European discovery of the Western Hemisphere. At that point, we had some big, multi-national corporations—East India Company and Hudson's Bay—that acted as states. And I see elements of that with the big Microsofts and Googles of the world. Because of their size, they actually are making decisions that have the impact of the kinds of decisions made in the halls of government.[50]

Alexander's reference to two private-sector trendsetters, the East India Company and Hudson's Bay, is telling. While both companies were champions of transnational trade and powerful political actors in their own right, eventually, due to regulatory, political, and economic changes, their influence declined. While Alexander calls attention to the power of technology companies, something detailed in chapters 2 and 4, he simultaneously reminds us of their inevitable decline.

A 2007 leaked document revealed why the NSA was devoting billions of dollars to be able to de-anonymize the internet; "In the future, superpowers will be made or broken based on the strength of their cryptanalytic programs. It is the price of admission for the US to maintain unrestricted access to and use of cyberspace."[51] Such an approach to cyber security necessarily has consequences for the future of internet freedom. According to encryption specialist Bruce Schneier, "Cryptography forms the basis for trust online. By deliberately undermining online security in a short-sighted effort to eavesdrop, the NSA is undermining the very fabric of the Internet."[52]

Theories of globalization and dependency alike argued that these transnational actors tied the world together, eroding the power of the nation-state, in an irreversible and profound way. Yet global suspicion of American-based information technology and service companies is inherent in the visceral

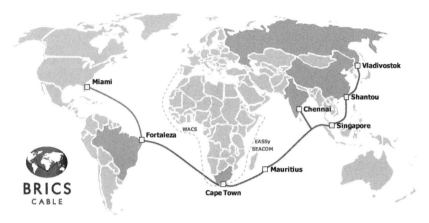

Figure 7.3: Proposed BRICS Cable

and widespread reaction to the Snowden leaks. Increasingly, governments are calling for the renationalization (or regionalization) of these industries in order to avoid using U.S. technology and services. One example is the BRICS Cable (see Figure 7.3), a 21,000-mile fiber-optic connection stretching from Brazil to South Africa, China, India. and Russia, connecting dozens of countries in-between. The purpose of the project, according to the *Voice of Russia*, is to "create a network inaccessible to the NSA"—though, the report cautioned, it will also require "constant checking and patrolling of the cable . . . in order to protect it from U.S. intelligence agencies or from the American military."[53] According to the developer, the BRICS Cable will be online and operational by 2015.

The BRICS cable is just one in a series of measures, ordered by Brazilian President Rousseff, designed to achieve greater Brazilian online independence and security. Rousseff has also called for laws requiring international internet service providers, such as Facebook, Google, and Skype, to store all data generated by Brazilian citizens on servers located inside Brazil in order to better shield it from NSA and European surveillance. Speaking at the UN General Assembly, Rousseff described the U.S. intelligence program as "a grave violation of human rights and civil liberties; invasion and capture of sensitive information relating to business activities and, *above all, disregard for national sovereignty*" (emphasis added).[54] Rousseff also hosted a 2014 summit, NETmundial, to discuss "proposals for the establishment of a landmark civil multilateral governance and use of internet and measures to ensure effective protection of data that travels through it."[55]

Germany, too, is taking a leadership role in exploring ways to limit the reach of American surveillance programs. According to Interior Minister Hans-Peter Friedrich, "Why should an e-mail from Munich to Berlin run through the USA? We need an autonomous European Internet infrastructure."[56] Deutsche Telekom, Germany's primary telecommunications provider, is building "a purely German Internet, with data packets only sent via German pathways if the sender and recipient are both within the country."[57] GMX, one of Germany's leading e-mail providers, is teaming up with Deutsche Telekom to offer a service called "E-Mail made in Germany," whereby data would remain in Germany and thus be protected by Germany's robust privacy regulations. Yet these initiatives also underscore the importance of governmental action, and thus the state. According to Deutsche Telekom, they can only proceed if the German government passes laws to establish a legal framework for such data protectionism. Without the framework, there is a risk that American and British competitors will file lawsuits claiming discrimination.

Germany has also proposed expanding the service to include the entirety of the Schengen zone, allowing all twenty-six countries to securely exchange data. However, the United Kingdom, due to their close ties with NSA, would not be part of the network. Separately, the European Union (EU) is considering funding the development of cloud storage infrastructure that operates independently of the United States. And, in December 2014, the UN General Assembly adopted its Resolution A/RES/68/167, "the right to privacy in the digital age," which is a thinly disguised condemnation of the NSA's surveillance programs and a call for actions to rein in such programs.

How will German and Brazilian initiatives to localize certain services affect the broader internet infrastructure? What effect will the UN resolution have? Do Edward Snowden's revelations doom the internet-freedom movement? What does the future hold for internet governance and civil liberties online? In this final section, we suggest one possible way forward by looking much further back.

Looking Backward before Moving Forward

There is widespread outrage over the revelations of the scale of internet surveillance by the intelligence community. Technology companies implicated in the scandal are pushing back, denouncing the NSA's hacking programs and appealing to the Justice Department for the right to disclose the full extent of their cooperation with the federal government.[58] Foreign governments are outraged too, calling for a new regime of internet governance that shifts the center of decision-making power away from the United States. Leading technologists are perhaps the most outraged and in many cases are vowing to defeat the intelligence community's attempts to surveil the entirety of the Web.[59]

Despite the fury, the private sector and technologists still depend on state actions for long-term solutions to privacy online. While AOL, Apple, Facebook, Google, LinkedIn, Microsoft, Twitter, Yahoo! and others condemn undue surveillance activities, their solution is to call for *policy* reform.[60] Technologists have promised to try and beat the government's invasive techniques, but even the best cryptographers in the world agree that it will take a tremendous amount of human effort, and years of work, to combat the NSA's surveillance programs. As Twitter's former head of cybersecurity Moxie Marlinspike explains, "We all have a long ways to go," adding, "[and] it's going to take all of us."[61] Outraged governments—fueled by their outraged publics—are calling for greater control over the international information flows, not less.

While it is easy for many in the United States and in parts of Europe to decry such perspectives as government censorship, or a power grab by international institutions (see chapters 4 and 5), the reality is that accepting some level of shared internet regulation is a far superior option to an internet splintered along geographical and national boundaries. This is exactly what will happen if current policies remain unchanged. Amid an onslaught of rhetoric that highlights how new technologies are changing societies and institutions around the world, it may be helpful to look back to how states navigated similar technological revolutions in the past, assess if and how those approaches worked, and determine their relevance to the challenges today's ICTs present.

The history of interstate cooperation and rulemaking is, actually, neatly intertwined with developments in international communication. The first two intergovernmental organizations were created in order to coordinate the rules by which information flowed across national borders. The International Telegraph Convention established the first organization in 1865. After the invention and widespread adoption of radio technology, it was renamed the International Telecommunications Union (ITU) to encompass all types of transnational telecommunication issues.

The second was the General Postal Union, established in Berne in 1875. The name was changed to the Universal Postal Union (UPU) in 1878 due to rapid increases in membership. According to the UPU, the Treaty of Bern "succeeded in unifying a confusing international maze of postal services and regulations into a single postal territory for the reciprocal exchange of letters. The barriers and frontiers that had impeded the free flow and growth of international mail had finally been pulled down." According to Arthur Deerin Call, in the first half of the nineteenth century, many were calling for post to be managed "in a cosmopolitan spirit."[62]

By the beginning of the twentieth century, the UPU's success was well known, at least among elites. In 1900 Josef Zemp, the head of Switzerland's railway and post operations, described the intergovernmental organization as "the most powerful work for peace which history has ever seen."[63] In fact, the UPU was so integral to international communication that adherence to its provisions was often among the first commitments made by newly established governments (and today adherence to the ITU is often among the first priorities of newly established states).[64] According to Brigadier-General F. H. Williamson, director of Britain's Postal Services, the UPU was, by 1897, "the first union in history including all the nations of the world."[65]

The UPU aimed to address only the technical and financial aspects of international post, focusing on facilitating a robust system for the exchange of letters, books, postcards, newspapers, and other printed materials. It established uniform rates for the transmission of materials, guaranteed the right of transmission throughout the territory of the union, and allowed for each government to keep the postage collected. Because of the UPU's standardization and coordination, "classification of mails means the same thing throughout the world, rates are more nearly uniform, and transportation is far more expeditious."[66]

While international post may seem seamless today, it is only a result of the coordination and standardization procedures established in the nineteenth century. At the time, there were substantial disagreements over a range of issues, as international information flows were as politicized as they are today. According to Call, "There were difficulties of nearly every description. The post office departments of many nations had large numbers of contracts covering postal regulations. There were problems of transit, a variety of interests and of opinions. Joining the Postal Union meant heavy financial losses for some of the larger powers."[67] Before standardization, rates varied from service to service, and from day to day. There was no agreement on how shipments were to be weighed, and prepayment was allowed only for certain types of letters (and never for newspapers). Size limits also varied, occasionally resulting in a package being shipped and then refused by another service along the way, well before it reached its intended destination.

In the nineteenth and early twentieth centuries, descriptions of the international post mirrored those of the internet today. Speaking in 1924 at the fiftieth anniversary of the UPU, Director General of Swedish Posts Claes Juhlin noted:

> The post is a means of communication on which everybody depends; for this reason all eyes are turned towards us. The post is especially important for the extension of intellectual culture and of civilization, for the encouragement of co-operation among nations, for the development of industry and commerce. It is consequently expedient for us to make it, to the very utmost, accessible to everybody, to cheapen it, and to simplify its use.[68]

Yet, according to Juhlin, such a system required states to "have the will to subordinate special interests to general interests. It is in possessing these great qualities that we shall best and most thoroughly serve both our own interests and those of the world."[69]

Concern regarding the confidentiality of messages crossing international borders played a central role in driving governments to agree to set their national interests aside to allow for a stable, secure system of international communication. In order to preserve the security of telegraph messages, in 1865 the European governments agreed to take the necessary steps to ensure confidentiality and safe transmission of messages through their government-operated telegraph systems. In 1875, in St. Petersburg, the agreement was included verbatim as Article 2 of the International Telegraph Convention. American telegraph companies, via state and contract law, were also barred from divulging the content of the messages they transmitted. These protections were also codified into U.S. law by *Ex parte Jackson* (1878), where the Supreme Court ruled that the Fourth Amendment protected copies of telegrams retained at telegraph offices "with the same sanctity as now protects letters by mail."[70] The 9th Circuit Court extended such expectations of privacy for wired-telephone communication in the *United States v. Hall* (1973).[71]

The European pledge of confidentiality in state-run telegraph systems was extended to wireless radio in the International Radiotelegraph Convention in 1906, a convention that the United States ratified in 1912. The Radio Act of 1912 extended protections for the confidentiality of radio communications, prohibiting disclosure not only by the employees of radio and telegraph companies but also by outsiders, persons "having knowledge of the operation of any station or stations."[72] Today, many countries have a constitutional right to privacy of correspondence, including Belgium, Brazil, Bulgaria, Chile, the Czech Republic, Denmark, Estonia, Finland, Greece, Hong Kong, Iceland,

Italy, Japan, and South Korea. Finland's constitution, for example, declares: "The secrecy of correspondence, telephony and other confidential communications is inviolable."[73] Even the Soviet Union's constitution listed the right to privacy of correspondence among the fundamental rights of its citizens.[74]

So, where did the principle of secrecy of correspondence go? Codified in international and domestic laws, how was the norm not considered parallel to, if not more important than, protections for free speech online? Looking back, Clinton's articulation of the internet-freedom paradigm—which inculcated the internet as a shared, public space—wasn't simply lofty neoliberal rhetoric. It was, as is alluded to in the beginning of this chapter, a deliberate framing of human rights online that protects free speech but not the anonymity of that speech or the secrecy of one's communications. According to Western legal doctrine, once one enters a shared, public space, their individual rights are curtailed in order to preserve the security and integrity of that space. For example, in a public park, it is perfectly legitimate for a government to monitor your behavior and listen to your conversations.

Mail, on the other hand, is considered a specific transmission of information between two or more people, and is afforded robust protections from government intrusions on the content of the messages. The content of telephone calls, too, is typically considered private, unless they take place in a public place. International treaties and organizations were founded and continue to provide oversight to ensure the secrecy of correspondence, as long as that correspondence takes place via traditional, twentieth-century means of communicating. So why wouldn't analogous attempts to communicate, when taking place via the internet, be afforded similar types of protections?

The answer, as is outlined in careful detail in the preceding chapters, comes down to economics and geopolitics. By exempting information exchanged online from the privacy protections afforded to other types of communication, the modern internet economy was born. Targeted advertising accounts for the vast majority of internet revenue. It is a technique incompatible with the principle of secrecy of correspondence. If correspondence (and browsing) remained secret, internet companies couldn't promise advertisers that their ads will be effective. Advertisers would thus revert to traditional mass communication platforms to reach their potential consumers. The modern internet economy is dependent on gathering and analyzing individual user behavior and benefits a handful of Western countries and companies (chapter 4).

As a result of the Snowden revelations, however, the dynamics of today's internet economy are changing fast. Some experts estimate the economic fallout will cost American technology companies $35 billion in business from 2013 to 2016 alone.[75] Policymakers and consumers alike are demanding changes, and the underlying business model that has thrived will have to change. Internet giants will have to decide if they want to go the way of the East India Company or adapt to the emerging dynamics of the post-Snowden internet economy.

Protecting anonymity online would similarly disrupt governments' abilities to surveil for criminal behavior, likely allowing for enhanced criminal activities and coordination. This would also represent a challenge to the various ways governments maintain control in democratic and nondemocratic societies alike. Governments, however, have weathered allowing such privacy protections for centuries. Indeed, these protections were crucial to the rise in international communications, commerce, and trade. They allowed for trust between people and governments, trust which governments leveraged to establish broader agreements, treaties, and norms. When the UPU was formed, statesman understood that establishing shared standards and rules for communication across national borders, including protecting the confidentiality of messages, was critical. Their commitments became integral to the emergence of today's international institutions, the bedrock of modern international relations. As was declared at the 1897 Universal Postal Congress:

> The Postal Union is one of the first ripe fruits of the new internationalism of our time, which is ultimately to bring all the nations of the world into a regular and harmonious cooperation in the promotion of the highest interests of each and all. Such a Union establishes, so far, the peace of the world, and must prove a powerful antidote, in its way, in preventing the periodic outbreak of war with its disturbances and destructions.[76]

Shared protocols and rules of international communication are the foundation for international cooperation between states. With this in mind, acknowledging the necessary fallout from the Snowden revelations and the real possibility of the emergence of walled-off, nationally based intranets, perhaps it is time to consider expanding our definition of internet freedom to include a guarantee of secrecy of correspondence. Such a move may, at a minimum, provide a path forward for a shared, global, and thriving internet.

Conclusion

Few dispute the centrality of information to modern economies and governance. What is contested, however, is the legitimacy of institutions governing global information flows and the appropriate scope of state authority in managing information within its sovereign borders. The real cyber war is thus a competition among different political economies of the information society.

Discourses of "internet freedom," most prominently articulated by former Secretary of State Hillary Clinton, serve to legitimize a particular political economy of globalism. America's "free flow" doctrine is a strategic vision to legitimize a specific geopolitical agenda of networking the world in ways that disproportionally benefit Western governments and economies. Similarly, the increasingly vocal call for information sovereignty serves a legitimating function for state efforts to govern highly complex societies in a world wired for globally instantaneous communications.

If information and data are the new oil (chapter 3), research on comparative and competing information policies requires a method of inquiry that spans beyond a particular disciplinary focus. Taken alone, neither economics, political science, law, nor environmental studies were sufficient to understand and explain the powerful role natural resources played in twentieth-century geopolitics. Similarly, a more historical and holistic account is required to place the current battle for control over the world's information flows into focus. By emphasizing four lines of conceptual inquiry—history, social totality, moral philosophy, and praxis—a political-economy framework places the internet-freedom movement in the broader geopolitical and economic context within which strategic actors are competing for resources and power. It joins case studies that may otherwise not be seen as connected, draws on historical comparison, and goes beyond documenting what is by emphasizing what ought be.

Historical analysis is woven throughout each chapter because such context is crucial to a proper understanding of current debates over information freedom and sovereignty. The introduction outlined the historical legacy and competing visions of international communications, including the related theoretical trends connecting to visions of a world governed by the free flow of information or one committed to overcoming the structural challenges of colonialism and imperialism. Chapters 1 and 2 offer historical analysis of the importance of information policy to U.S. geo-strategic interests and present a detailed account of the role of the U.S. government in the emergence of an information-industrial complex during the second half of the twentieth century. Historical comparisons to information governance regimes overseeing global telecommunications and post are raised in the discussion of the economics of internet connectivity (chapter 4) and in our discussion of the consequences of a globally robust surveillance regime (chapter 7). Combined, these historical elements provide crucial context for thinking through alternative approaches to managing a world defined by global instantaneous information flows and a rich canvas upon which the contemporary drive for internet freedom can be appropriately mapped.

Understanding the social totality of the implications of internet-freedom policy and norms is dealt with in the second half of the book. The rich description of Google's efforts to dominate each of the four distinct aspects of the information economy (chapter 3) offers an alternative and empirical explanation for what drives the company beyond its oft-cited yet under-interrogated mission, "Don't be evil." The economics of internet connectivity (chapter 4) and the myth of multistakeholderism (chapter 5) also contribute to an understanding of the various economic and political interests at stake in debates over internet governance, challenging the predominant media narrative characterizing these debates as being about protecting global rights to freedom of expression. Chapter 6 explores the resurgence of state control mechanisms through a series of case studies arguing that most, if not all, governments aim to preserve their information sovereignty to one extent or another. Combined, each chapter adds another layer to understanding the current debate over information freedom in order to come closer to the social totality of issues at stake in ongoing debates. We touch on other controversies that, with additional research and analysis, would assist in coming closer to addressing the social totality of these debates, including cybersecurity, e-waste, environmental change, and economic inequality.

While this book does not take a stance as to which approach to managing international information flows is most ethical, it does address the question of moral philosophy by way of challenging the prevailing narrative equating the U.S. doctrine of internet freedom with a virtuous defense of freedom of expression. Highlighting the underlying economic and geo-strategic motivations driving U.S. information policy is a crucial first step to delegitimizing the powerful and pervasive rhetoric surrounding its internet-freedom agenda. Moreover, by detailing the programmatic attack on anonymous speech (chapter 7), a bedrock principle that historically has been central to robust political debate, we highlight the sizeable gap between a moral imperative—the fundamental right to communicate—and America's "twenty-first-century statecraft." This analysis could also be developed further through an examination of the various ways democratic and nondemocratic states alike are restricting freedom of expression, including case studies on Wikileaks, restrictions to accessing social media, draconian treatment of government whistleblowers, as well as additional work on the long-term implications of robust surveillance regimes on self-censorship.

Finally, addressing the question of praxis, or "the fundamental unity of thinking and doing,"[1] the analysis offers several suggestions for policymakers and civil-society stakeholders. At the level of policy, the emergence of an information industrial complex (chapter 2) represents more than a blatant government intervention into a crucial economic sector. Historical analysis shows that such co-dependent relations between the private sector and government eventually leave both worse off. As corporations strive to meet the needs identified in government contracts, they become less competitive vis-à-vis foreign corporations focused on cutting-edge innovation and consumer needs. Worse, government dependence on private-sector expertise and operational capacity constrains and corrupts the decision-making process, leaving policymakers unable to enact laws contrary to the private sector's economic interests. The damaging nature of this co-dependence can be seen in the growing skepticism toward U.S. technology companies after Edward Snowden's revelations outlining the various ways the NSA compels private-sector cooperation (chapter 7).

The origins of the Universal Postal Union (UPU) and the specific historical conditions prompting its 1874 charter offer important guidance for policymakers. In addition to standardizing postal policies and costs across national borders, the UPU established norms favoring the secrecy of correspondence. These norms were considered crucial to maintaining confidence in the world's first coordinated system of global communication, confidence that is credited with facilitating the emergence of other forms of international cooperation and governance.[2] Given the clear historical importance of maintaining a trusted system of global communication, governments need to enact policies restoring confidence in the integrity of *certain* communications online. This is not to suggest that all information exchanged online need be absolutely confidential. Governments have legitimate interests in monitoring certain international communications. But, just as the UPU limits the scope of surveillance of international posts, governments need to agree to a similar set of transparent rules governing the scope of acceptable surveillance online. Creating a system that ensures a qualified guarantee of secrecy of correspondence, including mechanisms for accountability and oversight, is required for the Web to truly constitute, in the words of cyber-libertarian John Perry Barlow, "a world where anyone, anywhere may express his or her beliefs, no matter how singular, without fear of being coerced into silence or conformity."[3]

Turning to civil society, activists and academics alike need to be much more cautious in their use and defense of internet-freedom discourse. This is not to suggest that they should abandon the idea of internet freedom altogether; quite the contrary. Instead, this analysis shows how the internet-freedom narrative is used to legitimize a particular geo-strategic vision of the Web that has little to do with the foundational principles of internet freedom, including freedom of expression and net neutrality. Activists and defenders of the original vision of the Web as a "fair and humane" cyber-civilization need to avoid lofty "internet freedom" declarations and instead champion specific reforms required to protect the values and practices they hold dear. Additional research is also needed to identify how specific corporate policies undermine freedom online, and which institutional arrangements allow for governments and companies to weaken the integrity of the Web.

Civil-society groups need to be much more critical of the consensus-building processes upon which multistakeholder institutions base their legitimacy (chapter 5). While this book examined just three case studies—ICANN, IETF, and ISOC—the findings were especially troubling for civil-society groups aiming to influence policy change. Multistakeholder processes may actually be worse than the alternative from the perspective of certain aspects of civil society. Not only is legitimate dissent stifled, but discourses of inclusion and openness lend legitimacy to institutions that protect the interests of powerful corporations and governments. At the same time, the promise of multistakeholderism need not be abandoned in total. Clearer demarcations between commercial and political interests and internet governance decision-making bodies would be a first step in ensuring these institutions are not simply legitimizing the actions of powerful strategic actors.

The combination of these four lines of conceptual inquiry—history, social totality, moral philosophy, and praxis—offers clear insight into what we describe as the "real cyber war." At the center of debates over internet freedom, information sovereignty, global surveillance, and digital protectionism is a single question that, despite its significance, is too often overlooked: What authority (or responsibility) do states have to manage the flow of information into and within their sovereign borders? The ongoing competition of narratives offering visions for how global information flows should be governed is central to any discussion of cyber war, as its result will shape the use and scale of cyber weapons, espionage, piracy, and rights in the twenty-first century.

The outcome of this "war" is far from clear. Despite numerous international conventions guaranteeing citizens everywhere "the right to freedom of opinion and expression . . . regardless of frontiers,"[4] the multitude of perspectives, ranging from the absolute free flow of information to an absolute sovereignty approach, with many variations in between, indicate how far we remain from a establishing a consensus.

Rather, despite the existence of robust international law calling for a fundamental right to impart and receive information, numerous organizations have documented how governments around the world are increasingly restricting the flow of information, including the United States.[5] As we drift further and further from the ideal outlined in the Universal Declaration of Human Rights, international norms governing international communication will continue to break down. Yet, it is precisely these norms that established the bedrock for greater international cooperation and coordination among states. It is no coincidence that the first and second intergovernmental organizations were established specifically to create a stable system for coordinating and facilitating international communication. At the time, policymakers and businesses realized that greater cooperation and agreement in the areas of international communication were crucial to effectively managing the global economy as well as interstate relations.

To close, let's revisit the idea that data is the new oil. Imagine a world in which a state's capacity to control the flow of oil in and out of its sovereign territory is in flux. This is to say, not only is the government struggling to control its production, but it is also managing the distribution of oil to its citizenry. International institutions tasked with governing oil's global trade lack legitimacy, as do the means through which governments would typically have asserted regulatory authority. As a result, powerful states and corporations compete to control the production and distribution of this precious resource, especially in less stable, foreign territories. This might-is-right scenario would likely result, at a minimum, in international chaos, conflict, and increased wealth inequality.

Fortunately for us, the institutions charged with governing the global oil industry remain vibrant. But there is no equivalent with the legitimacy or the authority capable of managing global data flows. While the value of data today cannot be considered a true equivalent to the value of oil, it is, without question, an extremely valuable commodity, and its importance is increasing. Yet there is little consensus on crucial questions at the center of this geo-strategic sector, including: Who owns data gathered abroad? Is it appropriate for governments to tax companies generating revenue on data gathered within its sovereign territory? Do governments have the right to regulate local data economies to ensure companies are held accountable? Under what circumstances is it appropriate for another government to stage an "information intervention" into a foreign market? Last but not least, do governments have a responsibility to protect their citizens from foreign entities aiming to access local information for geopolitical gain?

If we were discussing oil or any other natural resource, there would be little question that governments not only have the authority but also the responsibility to exert a certain level of control to ensure consumer safety, environmental care, labor rights, as well as national security. As data and information are treated more and more as resources to be accumulated, processed, and traded, it becomes difficult to envision a world wherein governments will collectively agree on the need for their free flow across borders. This reasoning offers at least a partial explanation as to why information-control policies are becoming more prominent throughout the world today. At the same time, it offers an analytic framework for thinking through questions about the appropriate level of government intervention in specific areas or aspects of the global data economy. Most important, the analogy refocuses our attention to the central question of this book—and a remarkably stagnant area of academic inquiry: What legitimate authority do states have in managing information flows into and within their sovereign territories? We hope that this analysis of the real cyber war moves scholars, activists, and practitioners to revisit this crucial question at a time when the norms governing international information flows are malleable, states are assertive, and greater international cooperation is a necessity.

Notes

Preface

1. Dan Schiller, *How to Think about Information* (Urbana: University of Illinois Press, 2006).

Introduction

1. John Arquilla and David Ronfeldt, "Cyberwar is Coming!" *Comparative Strategy* 12 (1993): 141–65.

2. John Arquilla, "Cyberwar Is Already upon Us," *Foreign Policy*, February 27, 2012, available at http://www.foreignpolicy.com/articles/2012/02/27/cyberwar_is_already _upon_us (accessed June 24, 2014).

3. International information policy and infrastructure has historically been a critical site for geopolitical contestation (see chapter 2).

4. Metaphors matter and can affect policy discourse and decisions, as pointed out in Stefan Larsson, "Metaphors, Law and Digital Phenomena: The Swedish Pirate Bay Court Case," *International Journal of Law and Information Technology* 21 (2013): 1–26.

5. Jacques Ellul, *Propaganda: The Formation of Men's Attitudes*, translated by Konrad Kellen and Jean Lerner (New York: Vintage, 1973).

6. Rudolf Kjellén, *Studier öfver Sveriges politiska gränser* (Stockholm: 1899), 3.

7. Friedrich Ratzel, *Die Erde und das Leben: Eine vergleichende Erdkunde,* 2 vols. (Leipzig: Bibliographisches Institut, 1901).

8. These include: Dan Schiller, *Digital Depression: Information Technology and Economic Crisis* (Urbana: University of Illinois Press, 2014); Monroe Price, *Media and Sovereignty: The Global Information Revolution and Its Challenge to State Power* (Cambridge, Mass.: MIT Press, 2002); Jill Hills, *Telecommunications and Empire*

(Urbana: University of Illinois Press, 2007); Dan Schiller, *How to Think about Information* (Urbana: University of Illinois Press, 2006); Sandra Braman, *Change of State: Information, Policy, and Power* (Cambridge, Mass.: MIT Press, 2007); Ernest J. Wilson, *The Information Revolution and Developing Countries* (Cambridge, Mass.: MIT Press, 2006); Herbert I. Schiller, *Communication and Cultural Domination* (Armonk, N.Y.: Sharpe, 1976); Dan Schiller, *Digital Capitalism: Networking the Global Market System* (Cambridge, Mass.: MIT Press, 1999); Armand Mattelart, *Networking the World, 1794–2000* (Minneapolis: University of Minnesota Press, 2000); Armand Mattelart, *The Information Society: An Introduction* (London: Sage, 2003); Armand Mattelart, *The Invention of Communication* (Minneapolis: University of Minnesota Press, 1996); Paula Chakravartty and Katharine Sarikakis, *Media Policy and Globalization* (New York: Palgrave, 2006); Yuezhi Zhao, *Communication in China: Political Economy, Power, and Conflict* (Lanham, Md.: Rowman and Littlefield, 2008); and Robert McChesney and Dan Schiller, "The Political Economy of International Communications: Foundations for the Emerging Global Debate about Media Ownership and Regulation," United Nations Research Institute for Social Development, Technology, Business and Society Programme, paper number 11, October 2003.

9. For a discussion of the legitimacy of various information control mechanisms, see Milton L. Mueller, *Networks and States: The Global Politics of Internet Governance* (Cambridge, Mass.: MIT Press, 2010).

10. Text available at http://www.un.org/en/documents/udhr (accessed June 28, 2014).

11. Franklin Delano Roosevelt, "The Four Freedoms," speech, Mills Center for Public Affairs, January 6, 1941, available at http://www.fdrlibrary.marist.edu/pdfs/fftext.pdf (accessed June 30, 2014).

12. Hillary Rodham Clinton, "Remarks on Internet Freedom," speech delivered at The Newseum, Washington, D.C., January 21, 2010. Text available at http://www.state.gov/secretary/20092013clinton/rm/2010/01/135519.htm

13. See http://www.state.gov/statecraft/cs20/index.htm (accessed June 28, 2014).

14. Alec Ross, "Briefing on Internet Freedom and 21st Century Statecraft," Department of State, January 22, 2010, available at http://www.state.gov/j/drl/rls/rm/2010/134306.htm (accessed June 28, 2014).

15. Hillary Clinton, "Internet Rights and Wrongs: Choices and Challenges in a Networked World," speech, George Washington University, February 15, 2011, available at http://www.state.gov/secretary/20092013clinton/rm/2011/02/156619.htm (accessed June 30, 2014).

16. For a summary of U.S. legal protection of anonymous speech, see Anna Vamialis, "Online Defamation: Confronting Anonymity," *International Journal of Law and Information Technology* 21 (2012): 1–23. A more detailed discussion is given in chapter 7 herewith, which also discusses how pervasive surveillance defeats anonymity.

17. Ibid.

18. Vincent Mosco, *The Political Economy of Communication: Rethinking and Renewal* (London: Sage, 1996): 130.

19. Daniel Lerner, *The Passing of Traditional Society: Modernizing the Middle East* (New York: Free Press, 1958).

20. William Schramm, *Mass Media and National Development: The Role of Information in the Developing Countries* (Stanford, Calif.: Stanford University Press, 1964).

21. Everett Rogers, *The Diffusion of Innovations*, (Glencoe, Ill.: Free Press, 1962).

22. Ithiel de Sola Pool, "Development of Communication in the Future Perspective," UNESCO's Discoveries International Symposium, "Communication in Human Activity," October 23–27, 1978.

23. Kaarle Nordenstreng and Herbert Schiller, *National Sovereignty and International Communication: A Reader* (Norwood, N.J.: Ablex 1979), xiii.

24. Vincent Mosco, *The Political Economy of Communication: Rethinking and Renewal*, 2nd edition (London: Sage, 2009), 99–100.

25. World Bank, "World Development Indicators," 2011, available at http://data .worldbank.org/data-catalog/world-development-indicators/wdi-2011 (accessed July 1, 2014).

26. Jonathan D. Aronson and Peter F. Cowhey, *When Countries Talk: International Trade in Telecommunications Services*, (Cambridge, Mass.: Ballinger, 1988).

27. Nordenstreng and Schiller, *National Sovereignty*, xiv.

28. Ibid., 4.

29. Mosco, *Political Economy* (2009), 101.

30. A good account of the origins of WSIS and how it turned largely into a discussion on internet governance is given in Mueller, *Networks and States*.

31. *People's Daily* (Renmin Ribao), January 25, 2010, 4, via John Huntsman, "Media Reactions: Secretary Clinton's Speech, Haiti," E.O. 12958, available at http://www .wikileaks.org/plusd/cables/10BEIJING192_a.html (accessed July 1, 2014).

32. *Global Times* (Huanqiu Shibao), January 27, 2010, 14, via John Huntsman, "Media Reactions: Internet Freedom," E.O. 12958, available at http://www.wikileaks .org/plusd/cables/10BEIJING216_a.html (accessed July 1, 2014).

33. *International Herald Leader* (Guoji Xianqu Daobao), January 22, 2010, 4, via John Huntsman, "Media Reaction: Secretary Clinton's Speech, U.S.-Japan Relations," E.O. 12958, available at http://www.wikileaks.org/plusd/cables/10BEIJING167_a.html (accessed July 1, 2014).

34. *People's Daily* (Renmin Ribao), January 25, 2010, 4, via Huntsman, "Media Reactions: Secretary Clinton's Speech, Haiti."

35. *International Herald Leader* (Guoji Xianqu Daobao), January 22, 2010, via Huntsman, "Media Reaction: Secretary Clinton's Speech, U.S.-Japan Relations."

36. *People's Daily* (Renmin Ribao), January 25, 2010, 3, via Huntsman, "Media Reactions: Secretary Clinton's Speech, Haiti."

37. Ibid.

38. *Guangming Daily* (Guangming Ribao), January 27, 2010, 14, via Huntsman, "Media Reactions: Internet Freedom."

39. *Global Times* (Huanqiu Shibao), January 27, 2010, 14, via Huntsman, "Media Reactions: Internet Freedom."

40. *Global Times* (Huanqiu Shibao), January 25, 2010, 14, via Huntsman, "Media Reactions: Secretary Clinton's Speech, Haiti."

41. *Global Times* (Huanqiu Shibao), January 26, 2010, 14, via John Huntsman, "Media Reaction: Internet Freedom, U.S.-China Relations, U.S. Military," E.O. 12958, available at http://www.wikileaks.org/plusd/cables/10BEIJING204_a.html (accessed July 1, 2014).

42. *Global Times* (Huanqiu Shibao), January 25, 2010, 7, via Huntsman "Media Reactions: Secretary Clinton's Speech, Haiti."

43. John Huntsman, "Google Update: China Tech Business Community Speculates and Evaluates," January 29, 2010, E.O. 12958, available at http://www.wikileaks.org/plusd/cables/10BEIJING247_a.html (accessed July 1, 2014).

44. *Global Times* (Huanqiu Shibao), English edition, January 26, 2010, 7, via Huntsman, "Google Update: PRC Role in Attacks and Response Strategy," Secret Section Beijing 000207, E.O. 12958, available at http://www.wikileaks.org/plusd/cables/10BEIJING207_a.html (accessed July 1, 2014).

45. *China Youth Daily* (Zhongguo Qingnianbao), January 28, 2010, 2, via Huntsman, "Media Reaction: Internet Freedom, China Policy," E.O. 12958, available at http://wikileaks.org/plusd/cables/10BEIJING183_a.html.

46. Huntsman, "Media Reaction: Secretary Clinton's Speech, U.S.-Japan Relations."

47. John Arquilla and David Ronfeldt, *Networks and Netwars: The Future of Terror, Crime, and Militancy* (Rand Corporation, 2001), available at http://www.rand.org/pubs/monograph_reports/MR1382.html (accessed July 1, 2014).

48. John D. Negroponte, McLarty Associates, and Samuel J. Palmisano, "Defending an Open, Global, Secure, and Resilient Internet" Task Force Report No. 70, Council on Foreign Relations, June 2013, available at http://www.cfr.org/cybersecurity/defending-open-global-secure-resilient-internet/p30836 (accessed July 1, 2014).

49. Mueller, *Networks and States*; Milton Mueller, *Ruling the Root: Internet Governance and the Taming of Cyberspace* (Cambridge, Mass.: MIT Press, 2002).

50. Peter F. Cowhey and Jonathan Aronson, *Transforming Global Information and Communication Markets: The Political Economy of Innovation*, with Donald Abelson (Cambridge, Mass.: MIT Press, 2009).

51. Jack Goldsmith and Tim Wu, *Who Controls the Internet? Illusions of a Borderless World* (Oxford University Press, 2008).

52. Tim Wu, *The Master Switch: The Rise and Fall of Information Empires* (New York: Vintage Books, 2011).

53. Rebecca MacKinnon, *Consent of the Networked: The Worldwide Struggle for Internet Freedom* (New York: Basic, 2012).

54. Urs Gasser, Robert Faris, and Rebekah Heacock, "Internet Monitor 2013: Reflections on the Digital World." Berkman Center Research Publication No. 27 (2013).

55. Berkman Center for Internet and Society at Harvard University, Global Network Initiative, available at http://cyber.law.harvard.edu/research/principles (accessed April 29, 2014).

56. Ronald Deibert, *Access Denied: The Practice and Policy of Global Internet Filtering* (Cambridge, Mass.: MIT Press, 2008); Ronald Deibert, John G. Palfrey, Rafal Rohozinski, and Jonathan Zittrain, *Access Controlled: The Shaping of Power, Rights, and Rule in Cyberspace* (Cambridge, Mass.: MIT Press, 2010); Ronald Deibert, *Access Contested: Security, Identity, and Resistance in Asian Cyberspace Information Revolution and Global Politics* (Cambridge, Mass.: MIT Press, 2012).

57. Richard Fontaine and Will Rogers, *Internet Freedom: A Foreign Policy Imperative in the Digital Age* (Washington, D.C.: Center for a New American Security, 2011).

58. Eric Schmidt and Jared Cohen, *The New Digital Age: Reshaping the Future of People, Nations and Business* (New York: Knopf, 2013).

59. Ronald Deibert, *Black Code: Inside the Battle for Cyberspace* (Toronto: McClelland and Stewart, 2013).

60. Evgeny Morozov, *The Net Delusion: The Dark Side of Internet Freedom* (New York: PublicAffairs, 2011).

61. Mosco, *Political Economy* (2009), 2.

62. Victor J. Willi and Rico Oyola, "Personal Data: The "New Oil" of the 21st Century," presentation, World Economic Forum on Europe and Central Asia, Vienna, Austria, June 9, 2011, available at http://www.weforum.org/sessions/summary/personal-data-new-oil-21st-century (accessed July 1, 2014).

63. Mosco, *Political Economy* (2009), 11.

64. Ibid., 14.

65. Karl Marx, "The 18th Brumaire of Louis Bonaparte, 1852." *Karl Marx and Frederick Engels: Selected Works in One Volume* (Moscow: Progress, 1937).

66. Deborah Fallows, "Most Chinese Say They Approve of Government Internet Control," Pew Internet and American Life Project, March 26, 2008, available at http://www.pewinternet.org/files/old-media/Files/Reports/2008/PIP_China_Internet_2008.pdf.pdf (accessed July 1, 2014).

67. American Assembly at Columbia University, "Copyright Infringement and Enforcement in the U.S.," Research Note, November 2011, available at http://piracy.americanassembly.org/wp-content/uploads/2011/11/AA-Research-Note-Infringement-and-Enforcement-November-2011.pdf (accessed July 1, 2014).

Chapter 1. Information Freedom and U.S. Foreign Policy

1. Richard Hill, "Internet Governance: The Last Gasp of Colonialism, or Imperialism by Other Means?" in *The Evolution of Global Internet Governance: Principles and Policies in the Making*, edited by Roxana Radu, Jean-Marie Chenou, and Rolf H. Weber (Berlin: Springer, 2014), 79–94.

2. Joseph S. Nye, *Soft Power* (New York: PublicAffairs, 2004).

3. Charles More, *Understanding the Industrial Revolution* (London: Routledge, 2000).

4. Michele Boldrin and David K. Levine, *Against Intellectual Monopoly* (New York: Cambridge University Press, 2008).

5. More, *Understanding the Industrial Revolution*; Peter Andreas, *Smuggler Nation: How Illicit Trade Made America* (New York: Oxford University Press, 2013).

6. Alexander Hamilton, "Report on Manufactures" (Annals of Congress, December 5, 1791), 982–83, available at http://www.constitution.org/ah/rpt_manufactures.pdf.

7. Ibid., 992.

8. Andreas, *Smuggler Nation*.

9. Sandra Braman, "Defining Information Policy," *Journal of Information Policy* 1 (2011): 3.

10. Lawrence Lessig, "The New Chicago School," *Journal of Legal Studies* 27, no. 2 (1998): 661–91; Lawrence Lessig, *Code and Other Laws of Cyberspace* (New York: Basic, 2000); Lawrence Lessig, *Code 2.0* (New York: Basic, 2005), available at http://codev2.cc (accessed July 1, 2014).

11. Bruce Smith et al., "Federal Information Policy and Access to Web-Based Federal Information," *Journal of Academic Librarianship* 26, no. 4 (July 2000): 274.

12. David Jackson, "Obama: 'Violence Is Not the Answer' in Egypt," *USAToday. com*, January 28, 2011, available at http://content.usatoday.com/communities/theoval/post/2011/01/obama-violence-is-not-the-answer-in-egypt/1#.U7RRLI1dV7A (accessed July 1, 2014).

13. The White House, "National Security Strategy of the United States," May 2010, sec. 3, available at http://www.whitehouse.gov/sites/default/files/rss_viewer/national_security_strategy.pdf (accessed July 1, 2014).

14. Dwayne Winseck and Robert Pike, "Communication and Empire: Media Markets, Power and Globalization, 1860–1910," *Global Media and Communication* 4, no. 1 (2008): 7.

15. Jesse Ames Spencer, *History of the United States of America, from the Earliest Period to the Administration of President Johnson*, vol. 3 (New York: Johnson, Fry, 1866), 542, available at http://books.google.com/books?id=OopPAAAAYAAJ (accessed July 1, 2014).

16. Daniel R. Headrick and Pascal Griset, "Submarine Telegraph Cables: Business and Politics, 1838–1939," *Business History Review* 75, no. 3 (2001): 543–78.

17. Ibid.

18. Alfred T. Mahan, *The Influence of Sea Power upon History, 1660–1783* (New York: Dover, 1987).

19. Headrick and Griset, "Submarine Telegraph Cables."

20. Ibid., 559.

21. David Harvey, *The New Imperialism*, Clarendon Lectures in Geography and Environmental Studies (Oxford: Oxford University Press, 2005); Armand Mattelart, *The Information Society: An Introduction* (Thousand Oaks, Calif.: Sage, 2003).

22. Daya Kishan Thussu, *International Communication: Continuity and Change* (New York: Hodder Arnold, 2003).

23. "Overview of ITU's History," *ITU*, n.d., available at http://www.itu.int/en/history/Pages/ITUsHistory.aspx (accessed July 1, 2014).

24. Thussu, *International Communication*.

25. Robert Pike and Dwayne Winseck, "The Politics of Global Media Reform, 1907–23," *Media, Culture and Society* 26, no. 5 (2004): 643–75.

26. Peter J. Hugill, "The American Challenge to British Hegemony, 1861–1947," *Geographical Review* 99, no. 3 (July 2009): 403–25.

27. Elizabeth C. Hanson, *The Information Revolution and World Politics*, New Millennium Books in International Studies (Lanham. Md.: Rowman and Littlefield, 2008).

28. G. Stanley Shoup, "The Control of International Cable and Radio Communications," *Congressional Digest* 9, no. 4 (April 1930): 107.

29. Aitor Anduaga, *Wireless and Empire: Geopolitics, Radio Industry, and Ionosphere in the British Empire, 1918–1939* (Oxford: Oxford University Press, 2009).

30. Winseck and Pike, "Communication and Empire," 311.

31. Richard Collins, "The Reith Mission: Global Telecommunications and the Decline of the British Empire," *Historical Journal of Film, Radio and Television* 32, no. 2 (June 2012): 169, doi:10.1080/01439685.2012.669883.

32. Jill Hills, *Telecommunications and Empire*, The History of Communication (Urbana: University of Illinois Press, 2007), 224; Collins, "Reith Mission."

33. Winseck and Pike, "Communication and Empire," 14.

34. Woodrow Wilson, *The Papers of Woodrow Wilson, Volume 25: Aug.-Nov., 1912*, 25:502–3.

35. Ray S. Baker, *Woodrow Wilson and World Settlement: Written from His Unpublished and Personal Material*, vol. 1 (London: William Heinemann; New York: Doubleday, Page, 1923), 441.

36. Richard Hill, *The New International Telecommunication Regulations and the Internet: A Commentary and Legislative History* (New York: Schulthess/Springer, 2013).

37. Hugill, "American Challenge."

38. George Arthur Codding and Anthony M. Rutkowski, *The International Telecommunication Union in a Changing World* (Dedham, Mass.: Artech, 1982).

39. Ibid.; "Overview of ITU's History."

40. Hills, *Telecommunications and Empire*, 23.

41. Ibid., 172.

42. Ibid., 43.

43. Palmer Hoyt, "Last Chance: Mutual Unrestricted Freedom of News," *Vital Speeches of the Day*, September 18, 1945, 2.

44. Gary Madden, *World Telecommunications Markets* (Northampton, Mass.: Elgar, 2003).

45. USTR, "Final Text: U.S.-Colombia Trade Agreement," *Office of the U.S. Trade Representative*, November 22, 2006, available at http://www.ustr.gov/trade-agreements/free-trade-agreements/colombia-fta/final-text (accessed July 1, 2014).

46. USTR, "U.S.-Colombia Trade Agreement: Increasing U.S. Competitiveness," *Office of the U.S. Trade Representative*, n.d., available at http://www.ustr.gov/uscolombiatpa/facts (accessed July 1, 2014).

47. Robert C. Fonow, *The New Reality of International Telecommunications Strategy*, Defense and Technology Papers (Washington D.C.: Center for Technology and National Security Policy, National Defense University, 2006), available at http://oai .dtic.mil/oai/oai?verb=getRecord&metadataPrefix=html&identifier=ADA450141 (accessed July 1, 2014).

48. Hills, *Telecommunications and Empire*, 178.

49. W. Preston, E. Herman and H. I. Schiller, *Hope and Folly: The United States and UNESCO, 1945–1985* (Minneapolis: University of Minnesota Press, 1989).

50. V. Pickard, "Neoliberal Visions and Revisions in Global Communications Policy From NWICO to WSIS," *Journal of Communication Inquiry* 31, no. 2 (April 1, 2007): 118–39, doi:10.1177/0196859906298162.

51. Milton L. Mueller, *Networks and States: The Global Politics of Internet Governance*, Information Revolution and Global Politics (Cambridge, Mass.: MIT Press, 2010).

52. Ibid.

53. Hill, *New International*.

54. Hill, *New International*; Richard Hill, "WCIT: Failure or Success, Impasse or Way Forward?" *International Journal of Law and Information Technology* 21, no. 3 (September 2013): 313–28.

55. Richard Hawkins, "Prospects for a Global Communication Infrastructure in the 21st Century: Institutional Structuring and Network Development," in *Media in Global Context: A Reader*, edited by Annabelle Sreberny-Mohammadi, Dwayne Winseck, and Oliver Boyd-Barrett, Foundations in Media (London: Arnold; New York: St. Martin's Press, 1997), 177–93; Dwayne Winseck and Marlene Cuthbert, "From Communication to Democratic Norms: Reflections on the Normative Dimensions of International Communication Policy," in Sreberny-Mohammadi, Winseck, and Boyd-Barrett, *Media in Global Context*, 162–76.

56. Hills, *Telecommunications and Empire*, 54.

57. Ibid.

58. Ibid., 216, 221–22.

59. TWN, *Proposed Malaysia-United States Free Trade Agreement (MUFTA): Implications for Malaysian Economic and Social Development*, February 25, 2007 (Penang, Malaysia: Third World Network), available at www.twnside.org.sg/title2/par/MUFTA .doc (accessed July 1, 2014).

60. Hills, *Telecommunications and Empire*, 215.

61. John W. Berry, "The World Summit on the Information Society (WSIS): A Global Challenge in the New Millennium," *Libri* 56, no. 1 (2006): 1–15.

62. WGIG, *Report of the Working Group on Internet Governance* (Château de Bossey, 2005).

63. Mueller, *Networks and States*.

64. U.S. State Department, "U.S. Outlines Priorities for World Summit on the Information Society," December 3, 2003, available at http://iipdigital.usembassy.gov/ st/english/texttrans/2003/12/20031203194358retropco.2882501.html#axzz36LK8BLL2 (accessed July 1, 2014).

65. Department Of State, Office of Electronic Information, "Briefing on World Summit on the Information Society" December 3, 2003, available at http://2001-2009 .state.gov/e/eeb/rls/rm/2003/26862.htm (accessed July 30, 2014).

66. Lennard G. Kruger, "Internet Governance and the Domain Name System: Issues for Congress" (Washington D.C.: Congressional Research Service, Library of Congress, 2013), available at https://www.fas.org/sgp/crs/misc/R42351.pdf (accessed July 1, 2014).

67. Johnathan Weinberg, "Essay: Governments, Privatization, and 'Privatization': ICANN and the GAC," *Michigan Telecommunications and Technology Law Review* 18, no. 1 (Fall 2011): 189.

68. Milton L. Mueller, "Commerce Department: 'Foreign Devils Made Us Do It,'" *Internet Governance Project*, March 7, 2011, available at http://www.internetgovernance .org/2011/03/07/commerce-department-"foreign-devils-made-us-do-it" (accessed July 1, 2014).

69. Mueller, *Networks and States*; Kruger, "Internet Governance." In March 2014 the NTIA again announced its intention to relinquish control over the DNS. It remains unclear under what conditions such a transfer of authority would take place, given several explicit preconditions outlined in the NTIA's announcement. It is also unclear if the transfer would include the various functions performed by Verisign under contract with the U.S. Department of Commerce.

70. Thussu, *International Communication*.

Chapter 2. The Information-Industrial Complex

1. Daniel Guerin, *Fascism and Big Business*, 2nd ed. (Atlanta: Pathfinder, 1994).

2. Manuel Castells, *The Information Age: Economy, Society and Culture* (Malden, Mass.: Blackwell, 2000); Andrew Chadwick, *Internet Politics: States, Citizens, and New Communication Technologies* (Oxford: Oxford University Press, 2006).

3. C. Wright Mills, "Structure of Power in American Society," *British Journal of Sociology* 9 (1958): 29–41, 32.

4. Mills, "Structure of Power," 32.

5. Ibid., 33–34.

6. Jennifer Raab, "FDR & IBM SS Act: Public-Private Partnerships in U.S.," presentation, Roosevelt House Public Policy Institute at Hunter College, New York, N.Y., 2011. Incidentally, IBM continues to play a crucial role in the information-technology industry and in 2012 built one of the world's fastest supercomputers, Sequoia, for the National Nuclear Security Administration.

7. Mills, "Structure of Power," 33.

8. Dwight D. Eisenhower, "Final Address to the Nation," Dwight D. Eisenhower Presidential Library, box 38, Final TV Talk (1), Papers as President, Speech Series, 1961.

9. Adam Smith, *The Wealth of Nations*, edited by Edwin Cannan (New York: Modern Library, 1776), 364.

10. Eisenhower, "Final Address."

11. Sheldon S. Wolin, *Democracy Incorporated: Managed Democracy and the Specter of Inverted Totalitarianism*, (Princeton, N.J.: Princeton University Press, 2008): 284.

12. Walter Adams, "The Military-Industrial Complex and the New Industrial State," *American Economic Review* 58, no. 2 (May 1, 1968): 655.

13. Chalmers Johnson, "Tomgram: Chalmers Johnson, Warning: Mercenaries at Work," *TomDispatch.com*, July 7, 2008, available athttp://www.tomdispatch.com/post/174959/chalmers_johnson_warning_mercenaries_at_work (accessed July 7, 2014).

14. Gary Denman, "Statement by Dr. Gary L. Denman, Director, Advanced Research Projects Agency," Department of Defense, 1993, available at http://www.dod.mil/pubs/foi/Science_and_Technology/DARPA/586.pdf (accessed July 7, 2014).

15. Originally named Advanced Research Projects Agency, ARPA was renamed to "DARPA" (for Defense) in March 1972, then renamed "ARPA" again in February 1993, and once more renamed "DARPA" in March 1996.

16. Paul Baran, "Reliable Digital Communications Systems Using Unreliable Network Repeater Nodes," Product Page, RAND Corporation Paper Series (Santa Monica, Calif.: RAND, 1960), available at http://www.rand.org/pubs/papers/P1995.html.

17. The world's first operational packet-switching network was actually the telegraph network; the world's first widely commercially deployed modern packet-switching network was the ITU's connection-oriented X.25, extensively used from the mid 1970s through 1990.

18. Mitch Waldrop, "DARPA and the Internet Revolution," *DARPA: 50 Years of Bridging the Gap* (Washington, D.C.: Department of Defense, 2008), 78–85.

19. Cerf joined the board of ICANN in 1999 and served until the end of 2007; Cerf has worked for Google as a vice president and "chief internet evangelist" since September 2005.

20. ICANN, "Vinton G. Cerf, Vice President and Chief Internet Evangelist," *ICANN.org*, available at https://www.icann.org/resources/pages/vinton-cerf-2014-05-23-en (accessed July 7, 2014).

21. In 1993 Gore was awarded the First Annual Cisco Systems Circle Award "in recognition of his visionary leadership in building global awareness of computer networking through the National Information Highway Initiative." After leaving office, Gore went on to serve on Apple's board of directors and as a senior advisor to Google.

22. National High Performance Computer Technology Act of 1991, Public Law 102-194.

23. Ibid., section 3.

24. Keith Perine, "The Early Adopter—Al Gore and the Internet—Government Activity," *Industry Standard*, October 23, 2000.

25. Edmund Andrews, "Computer Executives Seek Broader Federal Support," *New York Times*, December 4, 1991.

26. HPCC, "High Performance Computing and Communications Panel Report," Viewpoints, President's Council of Advisors on Science and Technology, Office of

Science and Technology Policy, Executive Office of the President, December 1992, 2–3, available at http://www.eric.ed.gov/PDFS/ED354860.pdf, accessed July 1, 2014).

27. Daniel Burton Jr., "High-Tech Competitiveness." *Foreign Policy* 92 (1993): 125.

28. Ibid.

29. Albert Gore Jr., "Remarks by the Vice President at the National Press Club Newsmaker Luncheon," speech, National Press Club, Washington, D.C., December 21, 1993, available at http://clinton6.nara.gov/1993/12/1993-12-21-vp-gore-remarks-at -national-press-club.html (accessed July 1, 2014).

30. Reed Hundt, "Speech of Chairman Reed E. Hundt, Comnet 1995," Federal Communications Commission, Washington, D.C., January 26, 1995, available at http://transition.fcc.gov/Speeches/Hundt/spreh502.txt (accessed July 1, 2014).

31. Gore, "Newsmaker Luncheon."

32. The Advanced Technology Program at the Department of Commerce supports precompetitive, generic technologies in areas that lead to commercial applications. Established in 1990, its initial budget was $10 million. By 1997, its budget had increased to $750 million.

33. Gore, "Newsmaker Luncheon"; Brian Kahin, Ernest J Wilson, and Global Information Infrastructure Commission, *National Information Infrastructure Initiatives Vision and Policy Design* (Cambridge, Mass.: MIT Press, 1997); Clifford Holliday, "The National Information Infrastructure," *Telephony* 229, no. 4 (July 1995).

34. Gary Denman, *Statement by Dr. Gary L. Denman, Director, Advanced Research Projects Agency*, Washington, D.C. 1993, available at http://www.dod.mil/pubs/foi/ Science_and_Technology/DARPA/586.pd (accessed July 11, 2014); italics in original.

35. William Clinton, "Remarks at the Technology Reinvestment Project Conference," American Presidency Project, April 12, 1993, available at http://www.presidency.ucsb .edu/ws/?pid=46420 (accessed July 1, 2014).

36. Ibid.

37. In addition to the internet, ARPA grants and partnerships have been crucial to the commercialization of numerous consumer goods and technologies, including GPS, satellite technology, HDTV, precision guided weapons, stealth, battlefield sensors, unmanned aerial vehicles), unmanned underwater technology (submarines), space lasers, multiprocessor computer architectures, spintronics (a portmanteau meaning "spin transport electronics," which resulted in the development of the solid-state hard drive), and the like.

38. UCLA Center for Communication Policy, from the archive of Center for the Digital Future at digitalcenter.org (2006), available at http://archive.today/c1cU (accessed July 1, 2014).

39. Tim Jones, "Information Highway Hype Has Familiar Ring," *Chicago Tribune*, January 16, 1994, available at http://articles.chicagotribune.com/1994-01-16/business/ 9401160005_1_lotus-development-corp-information-superhighway-new-technology (accessed July 1, 2014).

40. Brian Lowry, "Changing Channels: Superhighway Arteries Merge at UCLA Summit," *Daily Variety*, January 5, 1994.

41. Albert Gore Jr., "Remarks as Delivered by Vice President Al Gore to the Superhighway Summit," Royce Hall, University of California—Los Angeles, January 11, 1994, available at http://clinton1.nara.gov/White_House/EOP/OVP/other/superhig. html (accessed July 1, 2014). Emphasis added.

42. Ibid.

43. Hundt, "Speech, Comnet 1995."

44. Alert Gore Jr., "Vice President Proposes National Telecommunications Reform," press release, The White House, Office of the Vice President, January 11, 1994, available at http://www.ibiblio.org/icky/release.txt (accessed July 1, 2014).

45. Albert Gore Jr., "Remarks Prepared for Delivery by Vice President Al Gore for the International Telecommunications Union," speech, World Telecommunication Development Conference, Buenos Aires, Argentina, March 21, 1994.

46. Ivan Sutherland, Committee to Study High Performance Computing and Communications, "Evolving the High Performance Computing and Communications Initiative to Support the Nation's Information Infrastructure: Status of a Major Initiative," National Research Council, National Academy Press, Washington, D.C., 1995.

47. Robert D. Atkinson, Stephen Ezell, Scott M. Andes, and Daniel Castro, *Internet Economy 25 Years after .com.* (Washington, D.C.: Information Technology and Innovation Foundation, 2010), available at http://www.itif.org/publications/internet -economy-25-years-after-com (accessed July 1, 2014). This measurement includes not just e-commerce and the activities of the commercial internet but also other IT manifestations, such as the use of electronic kiosks, more efficient IT-enabled machines in factories, and software systems in enterprises.

48. In-Q-It, "In-Q-It and CIA Partner to Find Leading-Edge Technology Solutions; New Entity Seeks to Partner with the IT Community to Solve Problems of Joint Interest," *CIA Press Releases and Statements*, September 29, 1999, available at https:// www.cia.gov/news-information/press-releases-statements/press-release-archive -1999/pr093099.html (accessed July 1, 2014).

49. Ryan Gallagher, "An In-Mouth Mic and Other Crazy Spy Techonologies Subsidized by The CIA's Investment Fund" (blogpost previously titled "In-Q-Tel's Funding for Spy and Surveillance Technologies") *Future Tense, Slate*, June 13, 2012, available at http://www.slate.com/blogs/future_tense/2012/06/13/in_q_tel_s_funding_for_spy _and_surveillance_technologies_.html (accessed July 1, 2014); Terence O'Hara, "In-Q-Tel, CIA's Venture Arm, Invests in Secrets," *Washington Post*, August 15, 2005, available at http://www.washingtonpost.com/wp-dyn/content/article/2005/08/14/ AR2005081401108.html (accessed July 1, 2014).

50. Rick Yannuzzi, "In-Q-Tel: A New Partnership between the CIA and the Private Sector," *Defense Intelligence Journal* 9, no. 1 (2000): 29–30.

51. Ibid.

52. Ibid.

53. Ibid.

54. Kevin Maney, "CIA Invests in Start-ups. The payoff? Technology," *USA Today*, March 3, 2004, available at http://usatoday30.usatoday.com/tech/news/2004-03-03 -cia-cover_x.htm (accessed July 1, 2014).

55. Yannuzzi, "New Partnership."

56. Gallagher, "In-Mouth Mic."

57. O'Hara, "In-Q-Tel."

58. David S. Hilzenrath, "Cyber Security Specialist Named to Lead In-Q-Tel," *Washington Post*, August 29, 2006, available at http://www.washingtonpost .com/wp-dyn/content/article/2006/08/28/AR2006082801180.html (accessed July 1, 2014).

59. Tim Oren, "Mission: In-Q-Tel," *Tim Oren's Due Diligence* (blog), January 27, 2005, available at http://due-diligence.typepad.com/blog/2005/01/mission_inqtel.html (accessed July 1, 2014).

60. Maney, "CIA Invests"

61. David Petraeus, "Remarks by Director David H. Petraeus at In-Q-Tel CEO Summit," speech, In-Q-Tel CEO Summit, March 1, 2012, available at https://www .cia.gov/news-information/speeches-testimony/2012-speeches-testimony/in-q-tel -summit-remarks.html (accessed July 1, 2014).

62. Tara O'Toole, "Testimony of the Honorable Dr. Tara O'Toole, Under Secretary for Science and Technology Directorate, before the House Committee on Science, Space, and Technology," Department of Homeland Security, March 14, 2011, available at http://www.dhs.gov/ynews/testimony/testimony_1300132944135.shtm (accessed July 1, 2014).

63. Marc Kaufman, "NASA Invests in Its Future with Venture Capital Firm," *Washington Post*, October 31, 2006.

64. Matt Richtel, "U.S. Military Recruits Investors to Scout Start-ups for Innovations." *International Herald Tribune*, May 8, 2007, available at http://www.highbeam .com/doc/1P1–139132912.html (accessed July 1, 2014).

65. O'Hara, "In-Q-Tel."

66. "In-Q-Tel Names New Chief Executive," *Homeland Security News Wire*, August 29, 2006, available at http://www.homelandsecuritynewswire.com/q-tel-names-new -chief-executive (accessed July 1, 2014); Robert Cyran, "Venture Capital's Sluggish Performance," *New York Times*, February 4, 2013, available at http://dealbook.nytimes .com/2013/02/04/venture-capitals-sluggish-performance (accessed July 28, 2014).

67. In-Q-Tel is distinct from IARPA, which was launched in 2008. It is the intelligence community's counterpoint to DARPA.

68. U.S. Insider Trading Database, 11/9 (4227), 11/9 (1409), 12/8 (197), 12/8 (592).

69. William Jackson, "In-Q-Tel Investment Proves Its Worth in Iraq," *Government Computer News*, June 27, 2003, available at http://gcn.com/articles/2003/06/27/inqtel -investment-proves-its-worth-in-iraq.aspx (accessed July 1, 2014).

70. Joe Panettieri, "Google Apps, Enterprise Cloud Revenues: $1B In 2013?" *Talkin' Cloud*, January 23, 2013, available at http://talkincloud.com/cloud-services-providers/

google-apps-enterprise-cloud-revenues-1b-2013 (accessed July 1, 2014); Julie Bort, "Google Generates $1 Billion on Five Enterprise Products: Can You Name Them?" *Business Insider*, June 12, 2012, available at http://www.businessinsider .com/google-generates-1-billion-on-five-enterprise-products-can-you-name-them -2012-6#ixzz20EprYLQy (accessed July 1, 2014).

71. Adam Fisher, "Google's Road Map to Global Domination," *New York Times*, December 11, 2013, available at http://www.nytimes.com/2013/12/15/magazine/googles -plan-for-global-domination-dont-ask-why-ask-where.html (access July 28, 2014).

72. Brian Deagon, "NetApp Takes On the Challenge in Data Storage World," *Investor's Business Daily*, November 12, 2013, available at http://news.investors.com/ technology-tech-exec-qanda/111213-678907-netapp-interview-with-nicholas-noviello .htm#ixzz38nSh5Ose (accessed July 28, 2014).

73. In 2011, NetApp was accused of selling software to Syria that enabled the country's crackdown against protestors and opposition groups.

74. Paul McDougall, "IBM Has the Tools for Digging Deeper into Data," *Information Week*, June 2, 2006, available at http://www.informationweek.com/ibm-has-the -tools-for-digging-deeper-into-data/d/d-id/1043888 (accessed July 1, 2014).

75. Steve Lohr, "New IBM Software Would Permit Anonymous Data Sharing," *New York Times*, May 25, 2005, available at http://www.nytimes.com/2005/05/24/ technology/24iht-blue.html (accessed July 1, 2014).

76. Sarah Novotny, "BuzzMetrics + Intelliseek = Neilsen BuzzMetrics," *Adotas*, January 7, 2006, available at http://www.adotas.com/2006/01/buzzmetrics-intelliseek -nielsen-buzzmetrics (accessed July 1, 2014); Nicholas Johnston, "Intelliseek Gains $1.4 Million from CIA-Backed Firm," *Washington Post*, June 25, 2001.

77. M. Baquiran and D. Wren, "2014 Consumer Security Products Performance Benchmarks," 2nd ed., PassMark Software (2013), available at http://www.passmark.com/ ftp/antivirusinternetsecuritysuites-dec2013.pdf (accessed August 4, 2014).

78. Lou Whiteman, "HP to Buy ArcSight," *Daily Deal*, September 13, 2010.

79. It is worth noting that pervasive surveillance programs were first proposed and implemented well before 2001. For example, see: Alfred McCoy, "Surveillance Blowback: The Making of the U.S. Surveillance State, 1898–2020," *Popular Resistance*, July 15, 2013.

80. See, for example, "The Memorandum and Order of 27 December 2013" in *American Civil Liberties Union et al. v. James R. Clapper et al.*, United States District Court, Southern District of New York, 13 Civ. 3994 (WHP).

81. Leslie Cauley, "NSA Has Massive Database of Americans' Phone Calls." *USA Today*, May 11, 2006, available at http://www.usatoday.com/news/washington/2006 -05-10-nsa_x.htm (accessed July 1, 2014).

82. Ibid.

83. Mark Klein, "Declaration of Mark Klein in Support of Plaintiffs' Motion for Preliminary Injunction," U.S. District Court, Northern District of California, No. C-06-0672-VRW, 2006.

84. Wired, "Whistle-Blower's Evidence, Uncut," *Wired*, May 22, 2006, available at http://archive.wired.com/science/discoveries/news/2006/05/70944 (accessed July 1, 2014).

85. Narus, one of several surveillance companies with links to Israeli military intelligence, has since provided its internet monitoring technologies to other governments, including Egypt. See: Michael Kelley, "The NSA's General Didn't Lie to Congress about Spying on Americans—They Hire It Out to the Israelis," *Business Insider*, April 4, 2012.

86. Kevin Poulsen, "Watergate Echoes in NSA Courtroom," *Wired*, June 6, 2006, available at http://archive.wired.com/science/discoveries/news/2006/06/71227?current Page=all (accessed July 1, 2014). AT&T's cooperation with NSA is reminiscent of Project Shamrock, a World War II–era project wherein NSA's predecessor, the Armed Forces Security Agency, worked with Western Union, RCA, and ITT to monitor all telegraphic traffic entering or leaving the United States. During the height of Project Shamrock, approximately 150,000 telegraph messages were analyzed by the NSA monthly.

87. Klein, "Declaration."

88. Peter D. Henig, "Can Uncle Sam Save Tech?" *Venture Capital Journal*, February 1, 2003; Peter D. Henig, "Uncle Sam Takes Center Stage in '03: IT Spending by the Federal Government Will Outpace Capital Expenditures by Private Enterprise This Year," *Venture Capital Journal*, February 1, 2003.

89. Jeffrey Rosen, "Silicon Valley's Spy Game," *New York Times*, April 4, 2004.

90. Victoria Murphy Barret, "The Extraordinary Life of Oracle CEO Larry Ellison," *Forbes*, August 11, 2006, available at http://in.rediff.com/money/2006/aug/11oracle.htm (accessed July 1, 2014); Todd Wallack, "Oracle's Coziness with Government Goes Back to Its Founding: Firm's Growth Sustained as Niche Established with Federal, State Agencies," *San Francisco Chronicle*, May 20, 2002.

91. See also: Cisco Systems, "FY2013 Revenue by Product Category & Service," Cisco, Annual Financial Statements, http://investor.cisco.com/financialStatements.cfm.

92. Henig, "Uncle Sam"

93. Rosen, "Spy Game," 46.

94. Ibid.

95. Henig, "Uncle Sam."

96. Eric Schmidt and Jared Cohen, *The New Digital Age: Reshaping the Future of People, Nations and Business* (New York: Knopf, 2013).

Chapter 3. Google, Information, and Power

1. Global Intelligence Files, "Re: GOOGLE & Iran ** internal use only—pls do not forward," email ID 1121800, February 27, 2011, available at http://search.wikileaks.org/gifiles/?viewemailid=1121800 (accessed July 1, 2014).

2. Julian Assange, "Google and the NSA: Who's Holding the 'Shit-bag' Now?" *The Stringer*, August 24, 2013, available at http://thestringer.com.au/google-and-the-nsa-whos-holding-the-shit-bag-now/#.UsIApWRDuUk (accessed July 1, 2014).

3. Open Secrets, "Top Spenders 2012," available at http://www.opensecrets.org/lobby/top.php?indexType=s&showYear=2012 (accessed July 1, 2014).

4. Tom Hamburger and Matea Gold, "Google, Once Disdainful of Lobbying, Now a Master of Washington Influence," *Washington Post*, April 12, 2014, available at http://www.washingtonpost.com/politics/how-google-is-transforming-power-and-politicsgoogle-once-disdainful-of-lobbying-now-a-master-of-washington-influence/2014/04/12/51648b92-b4d3-11e3-8cb6-284052554d74_story.html (accessed July 1, 2014).

5. Cited in Alvin Snyder, "U.S. Foreign Affairs in the New Information Age: Charting a Course for the 21st Century" (Washington, D.C.: Annenberg Washington Program in Communications Policy Studies of Northwestern University, 1994), available at http://www.annenberg.northwestern.edu/pubs/usfa (accessed July 1, 2014).

6. Meglena Kuneva, "Keynote Speech," Roundtable on Online Data Collection, Targeting and Profiling, Brussels, March 31, 2009, available at http://europa.eu/rapid/press-release_SPEECH-09-156_en.pdf (accessed July 1, 2014).

7. "Data, Data Everywhere," Special Report on Managing Information, *The Economist*, February 25, 2010, available at http://www.economist.com/node/15557443 (accessed July 1, 2014).

8. Michael Palmer, "Data Is the New Oil," ANA Marketing Maestros, November 3, 2011, available at http://ana.blogs.com/maestros/2006/11/data_is_the_new.html (accessed July 1, 2014).

9. For more on the analogy between information and oil, see: Ernest J. Wilson, *The Information Revolution and Developing Countries* (Cambridge, Mass.: MIT Press, 2006).

10. "About Google," available at http://www.google.com/about (accessed December 28, 2012).

11. Harold Borko, "Information Science: What Is It?" *American Documentation* 19 no. 1 (1968): 3–5.

12. Miguel Helft, "Fortune Exclusive: Larry Page on Google," *Fortune*, December 11, 2012, available at http://tech.fortune.cnn.com/2012/12/11/larry-page (accessed July 1, 2014).

13. Ibid.

14. Ibid.

15. Virginia Scott, *Google*, (Greenwich, Conn.: 2008), 38; Michael Pollick, "Google It," Sarasota Herald-Tribune, April 18, 2004, available at http://www.heraldtribune.com/article/20040418/BUSINESS/404180423 (Accessed July 30, 2014).

16. "Detailed Company Profile for Google Inc.," *Dow Jones Company Report*, 2012, Factiva.

17. Simon Tabor, "Google's Downtime Caused a 40% Drop in Global Traffic," Go-Squared Engineering, August 16, 2013, available at https://engineering.gosquared.com/googles-downtime-40-drop-in-traffic (accessed July 1, 2014).

18. Rob Pegoraro, "Google's Eric Schmidt Steps Down, Depriving Web of Future Quotes," *Washington Post*, January 21, 2011, available at http://www.washingtonpost .com/wp-dyn/content/article/2011/01/20/AR2011012006128.html (accessed July 1, 2014).

19. Holman W. Jenkins, "Google and the Search for the Future," *Wall Street Journal*, August 14, 2010, available at http://online.wsj.com/news/articles/SB10001424052748 704901104575423294099527212 (accessed July 1, 2014).

20. Mike Elgan, "Google Wants to Own the Future . . . by Predicting It!" *IT Business Edge/Datamation*, September 9, 2010, available at http://www.datamation.com/ entdev/article.php/3902526/Google-Wants-to-Own-the-Futureby-Predicting-It.htm (accessed July 1, 2014).

21. Latanya Sweeney, "Simple Demographics Often Identify People Uniquely," Data Privacy Working Paper 3, Data Privacy Lab, Carnegie Mellon University, Pittsburgh, 2000, available at http://impcenter.org/wp-content/uploads/2013/09/Simple-Demographics -Often-Identify-People-Uniquely.pdf (accessed July 1, 2014).

22. David E. Pozen, "Deep Secrecy," *Stanford Law Review* 62 no. 2, (2010): 257, 284.

23. See Orin Kerr, "The Mosaic Theory of the Fourth Amendment." *Michigan Law Review* 111 (2012): 311–54.

24. Paul Ohm, "Broken Promises of Privacy: Responding to the Surprising Failure of Anonymization," *UCLA Law Review* 57 (2009): 1701, 1748.

25. Jenkins, "Search for the Future."

26. Catherine Lui, Panagiotis T. Metaxas, and Eni Mustafaraj, "On the Predictability of the U.S. Elections through Search Volume Activity," unpublished research paper, Department of Computer Science, Wellesley College, Wellesley, Mass., 2011. For more on the significance of Palin's interview, see David Horsey, "Shameless and Clueless Sarah Palin," *David Horsey Cartoons and Commentary*, September 26, 2008, available at http://blog.seattlepi.com/davidhorsey/2008/09/26/shameless-and-clueless-sarah -palin (accessed July 1, 2014).

27. Seth Stephens-Davidowitz, "Google's Crystal Ball," *New York Times*, October 20, 2012, available at http://campaignstops.blogs.nytimes.com/2012/10/20/googles -crystal-ball (accessed July 1, 2014).

28. Seth I. Stephens-Davidowitz, "Using Google Data to Predict Who Will Vote," SSRN 2238863 (March 24, 2013), available at http://ssrn.com/abstract=2238863 or http://dx.doi.org/10.2139/ssrn.2238863 (accessed July 30, 2014).

29. Stephens-Davidowitz, "Google's Crystal Ball."

30. Rob Pegoraro, "Schmidt Steps Down."

31. "Ingress," game description, Google Play, available at https://play.google.com/ store/apps/details?id=com.nianticproject.ingress (accessed July 1, 2014).

32. Derek Gildea, "Very Clever: Google's Ingress Masks Data-Collection in Gaming," *Take Five* (blog), Institute for Public Diplomacy and Global Communication, December 9, 2012, available at http://takefiveblog.org/2012/12/09/ingress-gathering -data-through-gaming (accessed July 1, 2014); Hal Hodson, "Why Google's *Ingress*

Game is a Data Gold Mine," *New Scientist*, November 29, 2012, available at http://www.newscientist.com/article/mg21628936.200-why-googles-ingress-game-is-a-data-gold-mine.html (accessed July 1, 2014).

33. Jefferson Graham, "Google Units Include Social Networking, Photos, Maps," *USA Today*, December 20, 2005, available at http://usatoday30.usatoday.com/tech/news/2004-12-19-goodle-usat_x.htm (accessed July 1, 2014).

34. Stefanie Olsen, "Google Sees Profit in Product Images," *CNET*, December 19, 2001, available at http://news.cnet.com/2100-1023-277198.html (accessed July 1, 2014).

35. Kamal Ahmed, "Google's Eric Schmidt Predicts the Future of Computing—and He Plans to Be Involved," Daily *Telegraph*, February 5, 2011, available at http://www.telegraph.co.uk/technology/google/8303847/Googles-Eric-Schmidt-predicts-the-future-of-computing-and-he-plans-to-be-involved.html (accessed July 1, 2014).

36. Federal Communications Commission, "Notice of Apparent Liability for Forfeiture," file no. EB-10-IH-4055, DA 12-592, FCC, April 13, 2012.

37. Ibid.

38. Steve Lohr and David Streitfeld, "Data Engineer in Google Case Is Identified," *New York Times*, April 30, 2012.

39. Simon English, "Google Print to Challenge Amazon," *Daily Telegraph*, October 7, 2004, available at http://www.telegraph.co.uk/finance/2896598/Google-Print-to-challenge-Amazon.html (accessed July 1, 2014).

40. John Markoff and Edward Wyatt, "Google Is Adding Major Libraries to Its Database," *New York Times*, December 14, 2004, available at http://www.nytimes.com/2004/12/14/technology/14google.html (accessed July 1, 2014). "Each agreement with a library is slightly different. Google plans to digitize nearly all the eight million books in Stanford's collection and the seven million at Michigan. The Harvard project will initially be limited to only about 40,000 volumes. The scanning at Bodleian Library at Oxford will be limited to an unspecified number of books published before 1900, while the New York Public Library project will involve fragile material not under copyright that library officials said would be of interest primarily to scholars."

41. Ibid.

42. Ibid.

43. Jonathan Band, "The Google Library Project: Both Sides of the Story" (Ann Arbor: MPublishing, University of Michigan Library, 2006), available at http://hdl.handle.net/2027/spo.5240451.0001.002 (accessed July 30, 2014).

44. Joab Jackson, "Google: 129 Million Different Books Have Been Published," *PCWorld*, August 6, 2010. Available at http://www.pcworld.com/article/202803/google_129_million_different_books_have_been_published.html (accessed August 1, 2014).

45. Jefferson Graham, "Google's Library Plan 'A Huge Help,'" *USA Today*, December 15, 2004, available at http://usatoday30.usatoday.com/tech/news/2004-12-14-google-usat_x.htm (accessed July 1, 2014).

46. Markoff and Wyatt, "Adding Major Libraries."

47. Stephanie Kirchgaessner and Chris Nutall, "Google Writes Its Place in the World's History Books," *Financial Times*, December 16, 2004, available at http://www.ft.com/cms/s/0/cef45036-4f09-11d9-9488-00000e2511c8.html#axzz375S2D2Gc (accessed July 1, 2014).

48. Ibid.

49. Google Cultural Institute, "Art Project," Google, available at http://www.google.com/culturalinstitute/about/artproject (accessed July 1, 2014). "Google Partners with SCAD Museum of Art and Gibbes Museum of Art," *Savannah Morning News*, April 11, 2012 (newspaper source, EBSCOhost [accessed July 30, 2014]); Donna Doherty, "Yale British Art Center Works 'Hang' in Google Art Project Gallery," *New Haven Register*, June 2, 2012 (newspaper source, EBSCOhost [accessed July 30, 2014]).

50. Sergey Brin and Lawrence Page, "The Anatomy of a Large-Scale Hypertextual Web Search Engine," *Computer Networks and ISDN Systems* 30 (April 1998): 107–17.

51. Ibid.

52. It should be noted that doubts have been raised regarding the neutrality of Google's search results. For example, see Uta Kohl, "Google: The Rise and Rise of Online Intermediaries in the Governance of the Internet and Beyond (Part 2)." *International Journal of Law and Information Technology* 21, no. 2 (2013): 222–28.

53. Google Search Features, available at http://www.google.com/intl/en/help/features.html (accessed July 31, 2014).

54. Kohl, "Google," 211–20.

55. Eric Schmidt, "Response of Eric Schmidt, Executive Chairman, Google Inc., Before the Senate Committee on the Judiciary Subcommittee on Antitrust, Competition Policy, and Consumer Rights, Hearing on 'The Power of Google: Serving Consumers or Threatening Competition?'" September 21, 2011.

56. Ibid.

57. "SEO Case Study: Sites See More Pages Indexed by Google Than Bing—Even Post Panda," *Brafton News*, June 9, 2011, http://www.brafton.com/news/seo-case-study-sites-see-more-pages-indexed-by-googlethan-bing-even-post-panda-800527170 (accessed July 1, 2014).

58. Schmidt, "Response."

59. Sean F., "Congress Wants Google to Do More to Stop Online Piracy, Including Filtering Results," *Digital Digest*, April 8, 2011, available at http://www.digital-digest.com/news-62962-Congress-Wants-Google-To-Do-More-To-Stop-Online-Piracy-Including-Filtering-Results.html (accessed July 1, 2014).

60. Eric Schmidt, "Statement," Senate Judiciary Subcommittee, "The Power of Google: Serving Consumers or Threatening Competition?" Committee on the Judiciary Subcommittee on Antitrust, Competition Policy, and Consumer Rights, 112th Congress, 1st session., September 21, 2011.

61. Chris Sherman and Gary Price. "The Invisible Web: Uncovering Sources Search Engines Can't See," *Library Trends* 52, no. 2 (2003): 282–98.

62. Stephen Levy, "Google Throws Open Doors to Its Top-Secret Data Center," *Wired*, October 17, 2012, available at http://www.wired.com/2012/10/ff-inside-google -data-center/all (accessed July 1, 2014).

63. James Pearn, "AI Research at Google [Google X Lab]." Artificial Brains, August 10, 2012, available at http://www.artificialbrains.com/google (accessed July 1, 2014).

64. Ibid.

65. Steven Levy, "Going with the Flow: Google's Secret Switch to the Next Wave of Networking," *Wired*, April 17, 2012, available at http://www.wired.com/wiredenterprise/ 2012/04/going-with-the-flow-google/all (accessed July 1, 2014).

66. Jeff Dean, "Designs, Lessons, and Advice from Building Large Distributed Systems," keynote presentation, 3rd ACM International Workshop on Large Scale Distributed Systems and Middleware, Big Sky, Montana, October 11, 2009, available at http://www.cs.cornell.edu/projects/ladis2009/talks/dean-keynote-ladis2009.pdf (accessed July 1, 2014).

67. Levy, "Google Throws Open Doors."

68. Ibid.

69. Jenkins, "Search for the Future."

70. Cade Metz, "Meet the Man Who's Rewiring Google from the Inside Out," *Wired*, September 5, 2012, available at http://www.wired.com/wiredenterprise/2012/09/meet -the-man-whos-rewiring-google-from-the-inside-out/all (accessed July 1, 2014).

71. Ryan Singel, "Google to Build Ultra-Fast, Consumer Broadband Networks in U.S.," *Wired*, February 10, 2010, available at http://www.wired.com/business/2010/02/ google-isp (accessed July 1, 2014). Google, "Think Big with a Gig: Our Experimental Fiber Network," *Official Blog*, February 10, 2010, available at http://googleblog .blogspot.com/2010/02/think-big-with-gig-our-experimental.html (accessed July 1, 2014).

72. "Google.org Awards Grant to Internet Society to Advance Internet Exchange Points in Emerging Markets," CircleID, February 25, 2013, available at http://www.circleid .com/posts/20130225_google_awards_grant_internet_society_to_advance_ixps (accessed July 1, 2014).

73. Google, "Introducing Project Loon: Balloon-Powered Internet Access," *Official Blog*, June 14, 2013, available at http://googleblog.blogspot.com/2013/06/introducing -project-loon.html (accessed July 1, 2014).

74. Steven Norris, "Google Tests White Spaces as Rural Educational Broadband Solution," *Memeburn*, March 25, 2013, available at http://memeburn.com/2013/03/ google-tests-white-spaces-the-rural-broadband-solution (accessed July 1, 2014).

75. Fortune Mgwili-Sibanda, "Announcing a New TV White Spaces Trial in South Africa," *Google Africa Blog*, March 25, 2013, available at http://google-africa.blogspot. com/2013/03/announcing-new-tv-white-spaces-trial-in.html (accessed July 1, 2014).

76. Arthur Suermondt, "The Impact of Googlenomics," class paper, INFO231– Economics of Information, University of California—Berkeley School of Information, Spring 2011, 11.

77. Ibid., 13.

78. Google also offers site-targeted advertising for text, banner, and rich-media ads. The AdWords program includes local, national, and international distribution. Google's text advertisements are short, consisting of one headline of twenty-five characters and two additional text lines of thirty-five characters each. Image ads can be one of several different Interactive Advertising Bureau (IAB) standard sizes.

79. Google, "Financial Tables," *Google Investor Relations*, archived from the original on February 13, 2008.

80. "Revealed: Google's Biggest Advertiser Is the University of Phoenix Spending Nearly $200,000 Every Day," *Daily Mail*, October 30, 2012, available at http://www.dailymail.co.uk/news/article-2225459/Revealed-Googles-biggest-advertiser-University-Phoenix-spending-nearly-200-000-day.html (accessed July 1, 2014).

81. Google, "Google Builds World's Largest Advertising and Search Monetization Program," *News From Google* (blog), March 4, 2003, available at http://googlepress.blogspot.com/2003/03/google-builds-worlds-largest.html (accessed July 1, 2014).

82. Brian Womack, "Google Is Projected to Expand Lead in Online-Ad Market," *Bloomberg*, June 13, 2013, available at http://www.bloomberg.com/news/2013-06-13/google-is-projected-to-expand-lead-in-online-ad-market.html (accessed August 1, 2014); "Mobile Growth Pushes Facebook to Become No. 2 US Digital Ad Seller," *eMarketer*, December 19, 2014, available at http://www.emarketer.com/Article/Mobile-Growth-Pushes-Facebook-Become-No-2-US-Digital-Ad-Seller/1010469 (accessed July 30, 2014); Clark Fredricksen, "U.S. Digital Ad Spending to Top $37 Billion in 2012 as Market Consolidates," *eMarketer Newsroom*, September 20, 2012, available at http://www.emarketer.com/newsroom/index.php/digital-ad-spending-top-37-billion-2012-market-consolidates/#vVIEm58HMx3PdlMx.99 (accessed July 1, 2014). Derek Thompson, "Facebook and Google Own the Future of Advertising—in 2 Charts," *The Atlantic*, March 24, 2014, available at http://www.theatlantic.com/business/archive/2014/03/facebook-and-google-own-the-future-of-advertising-in-2-charts/359568 (accessed July 30, 2014).

83. Statista, "Google Ad Revenue Surpasses All of Print Media," in Covestar's *Smarter Investing*, November 12, 2012, available at
http://investing.covestor.com/2012/11/google-ad-revenue-surpasses-all-of-print-media (accessed July 1, 2014).

84. ZenithOptimedia, "Google Takes Top Position in Global Media Owner Rankings," May 28, 2013, available at http://www.zenithoptimedia.com/wp-content/uploads/2013/05/Top-30-Global-Media-Owners-2013-press-release.pdf (accessed July 30, 2014).

85. Marketing Charts, "The World's 10 Largest Global Media Owners," May 6, 2014, available at http://www.marketingcharts.com/wp/traditional/the-worlds-10-largest-global-media-owners-42481 (accessed July 30, 2014).

86. Sam Thielman, "Digital Media Is Now Bigger than National TV Advertising, Will Surpass Total TV by 2018," *Adweek*, June 16, 2014, available at http://www

.adweek.com/news/television/digital-media-now-bigger-national-tv-advertising
-will-surpass-total-tv-2018-158360 (accessed July 30, 2014).

87. "2013 Financial Tables," Google Investor Relations, available at https://investor
.google.com/financial/2013/tables.html (accessed July 30, 2014.)

88. Google, "Google's Economic Impact, United States," 2012, available at http://
www.google.com/economicimpact (accessed July 1, 2014).

89. Eric Schmidt, interview by Richard Haass at the Council on Foreign Relations,
New York, N.Y., November 29, 2010, video available at https://www.youtube.com/
watch?v=eJAMD5p5tQo (accessed July 1, 2014).

90. Conversation quoted in James Bladel, "RE: What Is the Intervention for Deleting the Resolution?" email message to Iren Borissova, Audrey L. Plonk, Marilyn Cade;
Vernita D. Harris and members@uswcitdel.org, December 12, 2012. Correspondence
was accessed via FOIA request.

Chapter 4. The Economics of Internet Connectivity

1. Albert Gore Jr., "Remarks Prepared for Delivery by Vice President Al Gore for
the International Telecommunications Union," World Telecommunication Development Conference in Buenos Aires, Argentina, March 21, 1994.

2. Ibid.

3. Ibid.

4. Ibid.

5. United States Telecommunications Training Institute (USTTI), "About USTTI,"
available at http://ustti.org/about/index.php (accessed on August 29, 2013); NTIA,
"Speaker: Michael Garder," Technology Opportunities Program, Networks for People 2000, available at http://www.ntia.doc.gov/legacy/otiahome/top/conference
workshops/NFP2000/nfp2000_gardner.html (accessed July 1, 2014).

6. "USTTI Family of Volunteer Trainers and Supporters in 2010–2011," USTTI,
available at http://ustti.org/about/sponsors.php (accessed July 1, 2014).

7. Dave Burnstein, "The Right Question: What Should We Do, Internationally,
for the Billions Not Online," *Net Policy News*, October 7, 2012, available at http://
netpolicynews.com/index.php/reporting/33-the-right-question-what-should-we
-do-internationally-for-the-billions-not-online (accessed July 1, 2014).

8. "ITU Formalizes Training to Developing Countries in Agreement with USTTI,"
press release, ITU, June 1, 2004, available at http://www.itu.int/newsarchive/press
_releases/2002/28.html (accessed July 1, 2014).

9. According to a 2013 report regarding the annual USTTI course on ICT Policymaking in a Global Environment, "Using the multistakeholder theme as the centerpiece,
each presentation conveyed to the attendees throughout the day why it was important
and valuable to discuss Internet Governance and Internet policymaking issues in a
multi-stakeholder environment." Vernita D. Harris, "USTTI Readout and Road to PP-
14 Outreach Idea," email message to Larry Strickling, Fiona Alexander, John Morris,
and Jade Nester, April 23, 2013. Email obtained via a FOIA request to the NTIA.

10. Digital Freedom Initiative, "Fact Sheet," March 2008.

11. Digital Freedom Initiative Annual Report, March 2004–March 2005, USAID.

12. Tim Receveur, "U.S. Promotes Information Technology in Developing World," Department of State, IIP Digital, November 10, 2005, available at http://iipdigital .usembassy.gov/st/english/article/2005/11/20051110155428btruevecer0.7696802 .html#ixzz2Wbjqfe3 (accessed July 1, 2014).

13. "The Leland Initiative," oAfrica, September 21, 2010, available at http://www .oafrica.com/ict-policy/the-leland-initiative (accessed July 1, 2014).

14. Gary Locke, "Secretary of Commerce Gary Locke Remarks at National Export Initiative Event," Department of Commerce, May 11, 2010, available at http:// www.commerce.gov/news/secretary-speeches/2010/05/11/remarks-national-export -initiative-event-leesburg-virginia (accessed July 1, 2014).

15. Atkinson, Ezell, Andes, Castro, and Bennett, "Internet Economy 25 Years after .COM: Transforming Commerce and Life," ITIF, 2010, available at http://www.itif .org/files/2010-25-years.pdf (accessed July 28, 2014).

16. McKinsey Global Institute (MGI), "Internet Matters: The Net's Sweeping Impact on Growth, Jobs and Prosperity," May 2011, v.

17. MGI, "Internet Matters," 2. "Internet-related activities as we define them correspond to the totality of internet activities (for example, e-commerce) and to a portion of the information and communication technologies (ICT) sector delineated by activities, technologies and services linked to the Web" (8). This definition likely underestimates the impact of the internet and connectivity on economies in that it does not account for improved productivity, savings from increased Web-based competition, and so on.

18. OECD, "Broadband and the Economy," Ministerial Background Report, Future of the Internet Economy, June 17–18, 2008, available at http://www.oecd.org/internet/ ieconomy/40781696.pdf (accessed July 1, 2014).

19. Internet maturity refers to "the depth of a country's maturity in access infrastructure and internet usage by individuals, companies and governments." MGI, "Internet Matters," 19.

20. MGI, "Internet Matters," 3.

21. David F. Fisher, "International Telecommunication Union Constitution and Convention," Committee on Foreign Relations, U.S. Senate, Senate Executive Report 105-3, October 20, 1997, http://www.gpo.gov/fdsys/pkg/CRPT-105erpt3/html/CRPT -105erpt3.htm (accessed July 1, 2014).

22. Ibid.

23. MGI, "Internet Matters," 4. These figures do not include revenue generated by traditional content producers, such as the Walt Disney Corporation, Time Warner, News-Corp, or Viacom.

24. MGI, "Internet Matters," 4.

25. Daniel J. Weitzner, "Testimony of Associate Administrator Daniel Weitzner on Do Not Track Legislation," NTIA, December 2, 2010, available at http://www.ntia .doc.gov/speechtestimony/2010/testimony-associate-administrator-daniel-weitzner -do-not-track-legislation (accessed July 1, 2014).

26. Atkinson, et al., "25 Years after .COM." This measurement includes not just e-commerce and the activities of the commercial internet but also other IT effects, such as the use of electronic kiosks, more efficient IT-enabled machines in factories, and software systems in enterprises.

27. Maria Borga and Jennifer Koncz-Bruner "Trends in Digitally-Enabled Trade in Services, BEA, U.S. Department of Commerce, 1998–2010, available at http://www .bea.gov/international/pdf/Trends%20in%20Digitally%20Enabled%20Services.pdf (accessed July 1, 2014).

28. ICT-enabled services include those in the following IMF Balance of Payments categories: communications services, insurance, financial services, computer and information services, royalties and license fees, other business services, and personal, cultural, and recreational services. See United Nations Conference on Trade and Development (UNCTAD) Information Economy Report 2007–2008: Science and Technology for Development; The New Paradigm of ICT, 2007, 120.

29. Google Investor, "2013 Financial Tables," Google, available at http://investor .google.com/financial/tables.html (accessed July 1, 2014).

30. "FY2011 Revenue by Geographic Segment," Cisco Systems Annual Financial Statements, available at http://investor.cisco.com/financialStatements.cfm (accessed July 1, 2014).

31. "The U.S. Hosts 43% of the World's Top 1 Million Websites," *Royal Pingdom* [blog], July 2, 2012, available at http://royal.pingdom.com/2012/07/02/united-states -hosts-43-percent-worlds-top-1-million-websites (accessed July 1, 2014).

32. MGI, "Internet Matters," 43.

33. Cameron Kerry, "Remarks of Cameron Kerry, General Counsel, Commerce Department," State of the Net Conference, Washington, D.C., January 18, 2011, available at https://docs.google.com/viewer?url=http%3A%2F%2Fwww.ntia.doc.gov%2Ffiles %2Fntia%2Fpublications%2Fkerry_stateofthenet_01182011.pdf (accessed July 1, 2014).

34. Gary Locke, "Remarks at U.S. Chamber of Commerce on Global Flow of Information on the Internet," Department of Commerce, June 16, 2011, available at http:// www.commerce.gov/news/secretary-speeches/2011/06/16/remarks-us-chamber -commerce-global-flow-information-internet (accessed July 1, 2014).

35. MGI, "Internet Matters," 5.

36. MGI, "China's Digital Transformation: The Internet's Impact on Productivity and Growth," July 2014, 6.

37. Jake Calvin, "Economics of Internet Freedom," Internet @ Liberty 2012 Conference, The Newseum, Washington, D.C., May 22–24, 2012.

38. Locke, "Remarks on Global Flow."

39. Yahoo! Inc.'s credibility was tarnished in 2006 after news broke of its sharing of private information with the Chinese government that resulted in the jailing of a Chinese human rights activist, Shi Tao. Responding to the news, Congressman Christopher H. Smith (R-New Jersey) called a congressional hearing to investigate

the incident, inviting Shi Tao's mother to attend and sit in the front row of the Rayburn House Office Building.

40. Daniel J. Weitzner, "Testimony of Associate Administrator Daniel Weitzner on Human Rights Challenges Facing the Technology Industry," U.S. Senate Subcommittee on Human Rights and the Law, Committee on the Judiciary, Washington, D.C., NTIA, March 2, 2010, available at http://www.ntia.doc.gov/speechtestimony/2010/testimony-associate-administrator-daniel-weitzner-human-rights-challenges-facin (accessed July 1, 2014).

41. Eli Noam, "Overcoming the Three Digital Divides," in *International Communication: A Reader*, edited by Daya Thussu (London: Routledge, 2011), 50.

42. Kenneth E. Train, *Optimal Regulation: The Economic Theory of Natural Monopoly* (Cambridge, Mass.: MIT Press, 1991).

43. Noam, "Three Digital Divides," 50.

44. Ibid., 48–55.

45. Ibid., 52.

46. Ibid., 51.

47. Reuben Abraham, "Mobile Phones and Economic Development: Evidence from the Fishing Industry in India," *Information Technologies and International Development* 4 (Fall 2007): 5–17; Kevin Sullivan, "For India's Traditional Fishermen, Cellphones Deliver a Sea Change," *Washington Post*, October 15, 2006.

48. *The Mobile Money Revolution*, ITU-T Technology Watch Report (2013), available at http://www.itu.int/en/ITU-T/techwatch/Pages/mobile-money-standards.aspx (accessed July 1, 2014).

49. Wikipedia, "List of Mergers and Acquisitions by Google," available at http://en.wikipedia.org/wiki/List_of_mergers_and_acquisitions_by_Google (accessed July 18, 2014); Leena Rao, "Eric Schmidt: Google Is Buying One Company a Week," *Techcrunch*, December 7, 2011, available at http://techcrunch.com/2011/12/07/eric-schmidt-google-is-buying-one-company-a-week (accessed July 18, 2014); Victoria Stunt, "Why Google Is Buying a Seemingly Crazy Collection of Companies," *CBC News*, February 19, 2014, available at http://www.cbc.ca/news/technology/why-google-is-buying-a-seemingly-crazy-collection-of-companies-1.2537110 (accessed July 18, 2014).

50. UNCTAD (2012); UNCTAD statistics show China is now the world's largest exporter and importer of ICT products. UNCTAD press release, March 29, 2012, available at: http://unctad.org/en/pages/PressRelease.aspx?OriginalVersionID=72&Sitemap_x0020_Taxonomy=20 (accessed July 28, 2014).

51. Abossé Akue-Kpakpo, "Study on International Internet Connectivity in Sub-Saharan Africa," ITU Telecommunication Development Sector, March 2013.

52. Funded by a soft loan from the Chinese government, the National Information and Communication Technology Broadband Backbone (NICTBB) was built by the Tanzanian government and is operated by the Tanzanian Telecommunications Company (TTCL).

53. S. M. Pazi and C. R. Chatwin, "Assessing the Economic Benefits and Challenges of Tanzania's National ICT Broadband Backbone," *International Journal of Information and Computer Science* 2, no. 7 (2013): 117–26 (quote from p. 117).

54. August B. Kowero, "Exploiting the Potentials of the National Information and Communication Technology Broadband Backbone in Tanzania," *Tanzania Country Level Knowledge Network*, July 2012.

55. ITU, "Percentage of Individuals Using the Internet," 2013, available at https://docs.google.com/viewer?url=http%3A%2F%2Fwww.itu.int%2Fen%2FITU-D%2FStatistics%2FDocuments%2Fstatistics%2F2014%2FIndividuals_Internet_2000-2013.xls (accessed July 28, 2014).

56. Vernita Harris, "RE: USTTI Readout and Road to PP-14 Outreach Ideas," e-mail message to OIA, John Morris, and Aaron Burstein, April 25, 2013. Correspondence was accessed via Freedom of Information Act request.

57. Based on data collected from Bloomberg Market Research (2013), available at http://www.bloomberg.com/professional/news-research/research (accessed July 28, 2014), and the ITU's ICT Statistics (2013), available at http://www.itu.int/en/ITU-D/Statistics/Pages/stat (accessed July 28, 2014).

58. Ibid.

59. Eli Noam, "Interconnection Practices," *Handbook of Telecommunication Economics 1*, 2002, available at

http://www.citi.columbia.edu/elinoam/articles/interconnection_pricing.htm accessed July 1, 2014).

60. "History," ITU, 2013, available at http://www.itu.int/en/about/Pages/history.aspx (accessed July 1, 2014).

61. *From Semaphore to Satellite* (Geneva: ITU, 1965), 67.

62. ITU, "History."

63. "Biennial Budget of the ITU for 2012–2013 Resolution 1337," adopted at the Tenth Plenary Meeting, ITU, October 21, 2011.

64. "The ITU: A Link in the Chain of the Information Society," Swiss Federal Office of Communications, available at http://www.bakom.admin.ch/org/international/01011/index.html?lang=en (accessed July 1, 2014).

65. "Choice of Class Contribution for Defraying the Union's Expenses," ITU Secretary General, September 5, 2011, Document C11/41-E.

66. Leo Kelion, "U.S. Resists Control of Internet Passing to UN Agency," *BBC*, August 2, 2012, available at http://www.bbc.co.uk/news/technology-19106420 (accessed July 1, 2014).

67. "International Telecommunication Union Constitution and Convention," Committee on Foreign Relations, U.S. Senate, S. Rep. No. 105-3, October 20, 1997, statement of Vonya McCannn, available at http://www.gpo.gov/fdsys/pkg/CRPT-105erpt3/html/CRPT-105erpt3.htm (accessed July 1, 2014).

68. ITU, *Semaphore to Satellite*, 72.

69. "International Telecommunication Union Constitution and Convention," Committee on Foreign Relations, U.S. Senate, S. Rep. No. 105-3, October 20, 1997, statement of Lon C. Levin, Vice President, American Mobile Satellite Corporation and President, American Mobile Radio Corporation, available at http://www.gpo.gov/fdsys/pkg/CRPT-105erpt3/html/CRPT-105erpt3.htm.

70. Satellite Industry Association, "State of the Satellite Industry Report," Tauri Group, May 2014, p. 5.

71. Committee on Foreign Relations, "ITU Constitution and Convention."

72. Committee on Foreign Relations, "ITU Constitution and Convention," U.S. Senate, S. Rep. No. 105-3, October 20, 1997, (statement of David F. Fisher), available at http://www.gpo.gov/fdsys/pkg/CRPT-105erpt3/html/CRPT-105erpt3.htm (accessed July 1, 2014).

73. "The Role of U.S. Delegates to the ITU and Related Organizations," United States International Telecommunications Union Association (USITUA), December 2005, available at http://www.usitua.org/policy.htm (accessed July 1, 2014).

74. Audrey Allison, "Letter to President-Elect Barack Obama and the Obama-Biden Transition Team," USITUA, January 16, 2009.

75. Richard Hill, *The New International Telecommunication Regulations and the Internet.* (New York: Springer, 2014).

76. For example: Robert McDowell, "The U.N. Threat to Internet Freedom," *Wall Street Journal*, February 21, 2012; L. Gordon Crovitz, "The U.N.'s Internet Power Grab: Leaked Documents Show a Real Threat to the International Flow of Information," *Wall Street Journal*, June 17, 2012.

77. For a legal critique of such allegations, see Richard Hill, "WCIT: Failure or Success, Impasse or Way Forward?" *International Journal of Law and Information Technology* 21 (2013): 313–28.

78. Victoria Shannon, "UN Agency Wants to Nourish the Internet, Not Govern It," *New York Times*, December 3, 2006, available at http://www.nytimes.com/2006/12/04/technology/04telecom.html (accessed July 1, 2014).

79. Richard Hill, "The Internet, Its Governance, and the Multistakeholder Model," *Info* 16, no. 2 (2014).

80. "Resolution 1305: Role of the Dedicated Group in Identifying Internet-Related Public Policy Issues," ITU Council, Document C09/105-E, October 28, 2009.

81. Vernita D. Harris, "Summary of Activities related to Internet Resolutions," e-mail message to Larry Strickling, Fiona Alexander, and Jade Nester, April 22, 2013. Correspondence was accessed via Freedom of Information Act request.

82. Noam, "Three Digital Divides," 55.

83. "U.S. Releases List of Delegates for Global Telecom Conference in Dubai, UAE," Department of State, Bureau of Economic and Business Affairs, October 25, 2012, available at http://www.state.gov/e/eb/cip/rls/199738.htm (accessed July 1, 2014).

84. "Frequently Asked Questions about the World Conference on International Telecommunications (WCIT)," Department of State, Bureau of Economic and Business Affairs, December 6, 2012, available at http://www.state.gov/e/eb/cip/rls/201601.htm (accessed July 1, 2014).

85. For example, see e-mail from NTIA's head of international affairs Fiona Alexander to ARIN CEO John Curran and Google's Vint Cerf arguing against a proposed "compromise at a time when staying principled ... is more important." Alexander added: "You are setting yourself up with a working program that you can perhaps influence but the final outcome—recommendations—you will have no say on approval and are likely not to have any friendly governments in the room to help you out." Fiona Alexander, "RE: Time sensitive problem at WTSA on IP addressing," e-mail message to John Curran, Larry Strickling, Vint Cerf and Vernita D. Harris, November 27, 2012. Correspondence was accessed via Freedom of Information Act request.

86. "Take Action," *Google.com*, available at https://www.google.com/intl/en/takeaction (accessed July 1, 2014).

87. Ben Rooney, "U.N. Talks Threaten Open Web, Says Google Executive," *Wall Street Journal*, September 13, 2012, available at http://blogs.wsj.com/tech-europe/2012/09/13/u-n-talks-threaten-open-web-says-google (accessed July 1, 2014).

88. For historical context, see: Susan P. Crawford. *Captive Audience the Telecom Industry and Monopoly Power in the New Gilded Age* (New Haven, Conn.: Yale University Press, 2013).

89. See, for instance, the analysis in *Direction of Traffic: Trading Telecom Minutes* (ITU/TeleGeography, October 1999), available at http://www.itu.int/ITU-D/ict/publications/dot/1999/index.html (accessed July 1, 2014).

90. This is discussed in some detail in Hill, *New International Telecommunication Regulations*.

91. See Milton Mueller, "Threat Analysis of WCIT Part 3: Charging You, Charging Me," *Internet Governance Project*, June 9, 2012, available at http://www.internetgovernance.org/2012/06/09/threat-analysis-of-wcit-part-3-charging-you-charging-me (accessed July 1, 2014).

92. Dave Burstein, "Follow the Money from Africa to AT&T," *Net Policy News*, 2012, http://netpolicynews.com/index.php/reporting/46-follow-the-money-from-africa-to-at-t (accessed July 1, 2014).

93. Milton Mueller, "ITU Phobia: Why WCIT Was Derailed," *Internet Governance Project*, December 18, 2012, available at http://www.internetgovernance.org/2012/12/18/itu-phobia-why-wcit-was-derailed (accessed July 1, 2014).

94. Proposals for adjusting how internet interconnection rates are negotiated were forwarded to WCIT and formally supported by: the regional group for Africa (C-16), the regional group for Asia-Oceania (C-27), Egypt (C-60), Paraguay (C-84), Russia (C-60), the Arab States (C-68), Iran (C-48), CITEL (C-66), Brazil, Belarus, Costa Rica, Côte d'Ivoire, Dominican Republic, Moldova, Peru, Uruguay, and Venezuela. See: Amy Alvarez, "CWG/WCIT12 Position Paper No. 6.5: International Internet

Connectivity," April 12, 2012. Retrieved via Freedom of Information Act Request to the NTIA.

95. ITU Statistics, "Global ICT Developments, 2001–2014," 2014, available at https://docs.google.com/viewer?url=http%3A%2F%2Fwww.itu.int%2Fen%2FITU-D%2FStatistics%2FDocuments%2Fstatistics%2F2014%2Fstat_page_all_charts_2014.xls (accessed July 28, 2014).

96. Pauline Tsafak Djoumessi, "International Internet Connectivity: ITU Workshop on Apportionment of Revenues and International Internet Connectivity," presentation, Geneva, Switzerland, January 23–24, 2012. International connections costs are substantial elsewhere, too. In Indonesia, international link costs account for 33 percent to 35 percent of the overall cost of internet connectivity. Gunawan Hutagalung, "International Internet Connectivity Case: Indonesia; Apportionment of Revenues and International ITU Workshop on Internet Connectivity," presentation, Geneva, Switzerland, January 23–24, 2012.

97. Jérôme Bezzina, "Interconnection Challenges in a Converging Environment Policy Implications for African Telecommunications Regulators," World Bank, Global Information and Communication Technologies Department, June 2005.

98. Pedro Oliva Brunet, "ITU Workshop on Apportionment of Revenues and International Internet Connectivity," presentation, ITU Headquarters Geneva, Switzerland, January 23–24, 2012. See also Fernàndez González and Juan Alonso, "Economic Sustainability of International Telecommunication Networks," *Info* 13, no. 11 (2011): 6.

99. Tier 1 revenue data gathered from each company's 2012 annual report. Saudi Arabia's GDP is based on the World Bank's World Development Indicators, available at http://data.worldbank.org/indicator/NY.GDP.MKTP.CD (accessed July 1, 2014).

100. Hamadoun I. Touré, "UN: We Seek to Bring Internet to All," *Wired*, November 7, 2012, available at http://www.wired.com/opinion/2012/11/head-of-itu-un-should-internet-regulation-effort (accessed July 1, 2014).

101. Touré, "Internet to All."

102. Broadband Commission for Digital Development, "The State of Broadband 2013: Universalizing Broadband," ITU and UNESCO, September, 2013, available at https://docs.google.com/viewer?url=http%3A%2F%2Fwww.broadbandcommission.org%2FDocuments%2Fbb-annualreport2013.pdf (accessed July 28, 2014).

103. For more on network externalities, see Stanley M. Besen, "Innovation, Competition, and the Theory of Network Externalities," Panel 6: Innovation, Technological Progress and Competition, The World Economy in the 21st Century, Graduate School, Department of Economics Reunion, Yale University, April 18, 1999, available at http://www.econ.yale.edu/alumni/reunion99/besen.htm (accessed July 1, 2014).

104. Jeffrey Rohlfs, "A Theory of Interdependent Demand for a Communications Service," *Bell Journal of Economics and Management Science* (Spring 1974): 16.

105. Josephine Adou, "Network Externalities and Network Growth in Developing Countries," presentation, ITU Workshop on Apportionment of Revenues and International Internet Connectivity, Geneva, Switzerland, January 23–24, 2012.

106. William Godfrey, "Network Externalities and Termination Rates—The UK Experience," presentation, ITU Workshop on Apportionment of Revenues and International Internet Connectivity, Geneva, Switzerland, January 23–24, 2012.

107. European Telecommunications Network Operators, "Revision of the International Telecommunications Regulations—Proposals for High-Level Principles to Be Introduced in the ITRs," CWG-WCIT12 Contribution 109, Wikileaks, June 6, 2012, available at http://files.wcitleaks.org/public/ETNO%20C109.pdf (accessed July 1, 2014).

108. Ken Fisher, "SBC: Ain't No Way VoIP Uses Mah Pipes!" *Ars Technica*, October 31, 2005, available at http://arstechnica.com/uncategorized/2005/10/5498-2 (accessed July 1, 2014).

109. Telegeography, "Global Internet Geography," 2012.

110. Milton Mueller, "An Internet 'Free from Government Control': A Worthy Principle," *Internet Governance Project*, April 14, 2013, available at http://www.internet governance.org/2013/04/14/an-internet-free-from-government-control-a-worthy -principle (accessed July 1, 2014).

111. E-mails accessed via FOIA requests to the NTIA confirm that WCIT negotiators worked tirelessly to remove references to "discriminatory access," "network externalities," and other references of the economics of connectivity. For example, see Vernita D. Harris, "RE: 2012 WTSA Daily Report 1—November 20, 2012," email message to Fiona Alexander, Arthur Webster, BldrSRStaff, Ashley Heineman, Christopher Hemmerlein, and Diane Cooper, November 26, 2012. Correspondence was accessed via FOIA request.

112. Brian Patten, "RE: Meeting with Karl, Fiona and Staff re: ITU issues," email message to Darlene Drazenovich, May 10, 2013. Correspondence was accessed via FOIA request. Redacted version of "Review of U.S. Participation in the ITU" accessed via: Darlene Drazenovich, "FW: Staff Meeting," email message to Brian Patten, May 13, 2013. Correspondence was accessed via FOIA request.

113. Jonathan Williams, "RE: FYA: U.S. Policy and Strategy in the ITU SUSP: 20 May, 1:00 P.M.," email message to Darlene Drazenovich; ISP&PD and Edward M. Davison, May 20, 2013. Correspondence was accessed via FOIA request.

114. "ITU Development Sector (ITU-D)." No date. No Author. Policy paper retrieved via FOIA request to the NTIA.

115. Vernita D. Harris, Ashley Heineman, and Chris Hemmerlein, "Trip Report: World Telecommunication Standardization Assembly Dubai, United Arab Emirates," November 18–29, 2012. Policy paper retrieved via FOIA request to the NTIA.

Chapter 5. The Myth of Multistakeholder Governance

1. Lawrence E. Strickling, "Keynote Address," Conference on The Future of Internet Governance After Dubai, New York, NY, June 20, 2013), National Telecommunications and Information Administration, U.S. Department of Commerce, available at

http://www.ntia.doc.gov/speechtestimony/2013/keynote-address-assistant-secretary
-strickling-columbia-institute-tele-informat (accessed July 10, 2014).

2. See numerous Congressional Resolutions arguing against any change in the internet's fundamental governance structures, including, most recently, 112th Congress, 2nd Session, Concurrent Congressional Resolution 50, September 22, 2012.

3. "NTIA Announces Intent to Transition Key Internet Domain Name Functions," National Telecommunications and Information Administration, March 14, 2014, available at http://www.ntia.doc.gov/press-release/2014/ntia-announces-intent -transition-key-internet-domain-name-functions (accessed July 1, 2014). The shift is "conditional" in the sense that NTIA chose ICANN as the only organization it would allow to manage the DNS, explicitly rejecting any proposal that "replaces the NTIA role with a government-led or an inter-governmental organization solution."

4. Working Group on Internet Governance, "Report of the Working Group on Internet Governance," Chateau de Bossey, June 2005. This definition was noted in the WSIS Tunis Agenda for the Information Society, Document WSIS-05/TUNIS/ DOC[6(rev. 1)-E (November 18, 2005), paragraph 34, available at http://www.itu.int/ wsis/docs2/tunis/off/6rev1.html (accessed July 1, 2014).

5. "The DNS helps users find their way around the Internet. As stated, every computer on the Internet has a unique numerical address called its 'IP address' (Internet Protocol address). An example IP address is 207.142.131.236, which is an IP address under IPv4. [The] IPv6 numbers have and even more complex structure. Because IP addresses are hard to remember, the DNS allows a more mnemonic, familiar string of letters to be used instead, which is the domain name such as un.org. Domain names also provide a persistent address for some service when it is necessary to move to a different server, which would have a different IP address." Internet Governance Forum, "Draft WGIG Issue Paper on the Administration of Internet Names and IP Addresses," available at http://www.wgig.org/docs/WP-IPaddresses.pdf, p. 2 (accessed July 10, 2014).

6. Ibid., 1.

7. Ibid., 4.

8. Lawrence Lessig, *Code, and Other Laws of Cyberspace* (New York: Basic, 1999).

9. Joel R. Reidenberg, "Lex Informatica: The Formulation of Information Policy Rules through Technology," *Texas Law Review* 76 (1998): 588.

10. Lawrence E. Strickling, "Keynote Address by Assistant Secretary Strickling at Columbia Institute for Tele-Information," Conference on The Future of the of Internet Governance after Dubai, Columbia University, New York, N.Y., June 20, 2013, available at http://www.ntia.doc.gov/speechtestimony/2013/keynote-address-assistant-secretary-strickling-columbia-institute-tele-informat (accessed July 10, 2014).

11. Robert Boorstin, "Not a Choice between Anarchy and Ruin," at the Principles of Internet Governance: An Agenda for Economic Growth and Innovation, The Brookings Institution Falk Auditorium, 1775 Massachusetts Ave., N.W., January 11, 2012.

12. These arguments are dealt with in greater detail in chapter 6.

13. TCP/IP was developed in competition to an international standardization effort, OSI, which took place under the aegis of IEC, ISO, and ITU, and was, consequently, far more "multistakeholder" than the TCP/IP development.

14. "International Telecommunication Union Constitution and Convention," Committee on Foreign Relations, U.S. Senate, S. Rep. No. 105-3, October 20, 1997, statement of Lon C. Levin, vice president, American Mobile Satellite Corporation, and president, American Mobile Radio Corporation, available at http://www.gpo.gov/fdsys/pkg/CRPT-105erpt3/html/CRPT-105erpt3.htm (accessed July 10, 2014).

15. Terry Kramer, "U.S. Intervention at the World Conference on International Telecommunications," Media Note, Office of the Spokesperson, December 13, 2012. See also: Eli Dourado, "Behind Closed Doors at the UN's Attempted 'Takeover of the Internet,'" Ars Technica, December 20, 2012, available at http://arstechnica.com/tech-policy/2012/12/behind-closed-doors-at-the-uns-attempted-takeover-of-the-internet (accessed July 10, 2014).

16. For example, see Christopher Hemmerlein, "Subject: Weekly Input," email message to Diane Cooper and Ashley Heineman, May 16, 2013. Correspondence was accessed via FOIA request: "[The Office of International Affairs] accomplished its primary mission at the WTPF, which was the consensus adoption of 6 non-binding Opinions on topics that include broadband, Internet Exchange Points, two opinions on IP numbering, the multistakeholder model of Internet governance, and the concept of 'enhanced cooperation.' These opinions were sent to the WTPF from a multistakeholder Informal Experts Group convened by the ITU Secretary-General over the past year." See also Christopher Hemmerlein, "Subject: WTPF Day 3 Readout," e-mail message to Fiona Alexander, Ashley Heineman, Suzanne Radell, Vernita Harris, and Jade Nester, May 16, 2013. Correspondence was accessed via FOIA request. ITU Council Resolution 1336 (Council Working Group on Iinternational Internet-related Public Policy Issues, Document C11/99-E, 2011) also required the ITU's Council Working Group on international Internet-Related Public Policy Issues (CWG-IIRPPI) to become "open to all stakeholders," evidence that the ITU is clearly capable of fostering multistakeholder discussions.

17. "WCIT Final Acts," International Telecommunications Union, Dubai, 2012, available at http://www.itu.int/en/wcit-12/Documents/final-acts-wcit-12.pdf (accessed July 10, 2014); for a detailed analysis of the WCIT treaty, see Richard Hill, The New International Telecommunication Regulations and the Internet. (Berlin: Springer, 2014); Richard Hill, "WCIT: Failure or Success, Impasse or Way Forward?" International Journal of Law and Information Technology 21 (2013): 313–28.

18. Sally Shipman Wentworth, "WCIT Postmortem—The Lessons Learned," speech, North American Network Operators' Group Conference, Orlando, Florida, February 3, 2013, Internet Society, available at http://www.internetsociety.org/doc/wcit-postmortem-lessons-learned (accessed July 10, 2014).

19. Nathalie A. Steins and Victoria M. Edwards, "Platforms for Collective Action in Multiple-Uuse Common-Ppool resources," Agriculture and Human Values 16 (1999): 244.

20. Menu Hemmati, *Multistakeholder Processes for Governance and Sustainability: Beyond Deadlock and Conflict* (London: Earthscan, 2002), 2.

21. Eric Trist, "Referent Organizations and the Development of Interorganizational Domains," *Human Relations* 36, no. 3 (1932): 269–84.

22. Jürgen Habermas, *The Theory of Communicative Action*, vol. 1, (Boston: Beacon, 1984).

23. Ironically, in light of the internet governance debates, the ITU was actually an excellent instantiation of such a situation for much of its history and continues to be for issues less politicized than internet governance. See Booz Allen Hamilton, "The World's Most Enduring Institutions," 2004, available at http://www.boozallen.com/media/file/143411.pdf (accessed July 1, 2014).

24. David Edmunds and Eva Wollenberg, "A Strategic Approach to Multistakeholder Negotiations," *Development and Change* 32 (2001), 231–53, doi: 10.1111/1467-7660.00204.

25. Ibid., 237.

26. Steins and Edwards, "Platforms," 242.

27. See, for example: Robert D. Putnam, "Diplomacy and Domestic Politics: The Logic of Two-Level Games," *International Organization* 42, no. 3 (Summer 1988): 427–60; William Lafi Youmans, and Shawn Powers, "Remote Negotiations: International Broadcasting as Bargaining in the Information Age." *International Journal of Communication* 6 (2012): 2149–72.

28. James Ball, Julian Borger, and Glenn Greenwald, "Revealed: How U.S. and U.K. Spy Agencies Defeat Internet Privacy and Security," *Guardian*, September 6, 2013, available at http://www.theguardian.com/world/2013/sep/05/nsa-gchq-encryption-codes-security (accessed July 10, 2014); "Secret Documents Reveal N.S.A. Campaign against Encryption," *The New York Times*, September 5, 2013, available at http://www.nytimes.com/interactive/2013/09/05/us/documents-reveal-nsa-campaign-against-encryption.html (accessed July 1, 2014).

29. David Edmunds and Eva Wollenberg, "Disadvantaged Groups in Multistakeholder Negotiations," CIFOR Programme Report, June 2002, p. 2, available at http://www.cifor.org/publications/pdf_files/Strategic_Negotiation_report.pdf (accessed July 1, 2014).

30. Evelyn I. Légaré, "Canadian Multiculturalism and Aboriginal People: Negotiating a Place in the Nation," *Identities* 1, no. 4 (1995): 347–66.

31. "Working Group to Examine the Mandate of WSIS Regarding Enhanced Cooperation as Contained in the Tunis Agenda," United Nations Conference on Trade and Development, Working Group on Enhanced Cooperation (WGEC), 2013, available at http://unctad.org/en/Pages/CSTD/WGEC.aspx (accessed July 10, 2014).

32. Jon Postel, who as a graduate student at UCLA maintained the list of host names and addresses of ARPANET, oversaw the ISI, which continued to maintain a list of addresses under contract with DARPA. IANA, also under contract with DARPA, was responsible for allocating blocks of numerical addresses to regional IP registries (ARIN in North America, RIPE in Europe, and APNIC in the Asia/Pacific region).

IANA was also responsible for researching, publishing, and maintaining the technical parameters for use by protocol developers and the broader internet community. NSI, under contracts with the NSF, oversaw the registration of domain names in the generic top-level domains (gTLDs) on a first-come, first-served basis and also maintains a directory linking domain names with the IP numbers of domain name servers. Today, NSI manages registration, coordination, and maintenance functions of the internet domain name system.

33. "Statement of Policy on the Management of Internet Names and Addresses," National Telecommunications & Information Administration, U.S. Department of Commerce, docket no. 980212036-8146-02, June 05, 1998, available at http://www.ntia.doc.gov/federal-register-notice/1998/statement-policy-management-internet-names-and-addresses (accessed July 10, 2014).

34. International Ad Hoc Committee Charter, 1996, available at http://web.archive.org/web/19980415072030/http://www.gtld-mou.org/docs/iahc-charter.html (accessed July 10, 2014).

35. Milton Mueller, "ICANN and Internet Governance," *Info: The Journal of Policy, Regulation and Strategy for Telecommunications, Information and Media* 1, no. 6 (1999): 506.

36. NTIA, "Statement of Policy."

37. "Memorandum of Understanding between the U.S. Department of Commerce and the Internet Corporation for Assigned Names and Numbers," NTIA, November 25, 1998, available at http://www.ntia.doc.gov/page/1998/memorandum-understanding-between-us-department-commerce-and-internet-corporation-assigned- (accessed July 10, 2014).

38. Mueller, "ICANN and Internet Governance," 498.

39. Ibid., 499.

40. Ibid., 505.

41. Ibid., 508.

42. Ibid., 507.

43. Ibid., 514.

44. "The imposition of a specific economic model on private sector businesses is a regulatory function. In order to enforce this model upon registrants, ICANN has had to establish a contract-based accreditation system that is highly centralized and regulatory. The U.S. Commerce Dept, likewise, has imposed a cost-plus utility regulation model upon NSI via its cooperative agreement contract. This is not technical coordination but economic regulation." Ibid., 519–20.

45. Ibid., 516.

46. Ibid., 520.

47. "U.S. Principles on the Internet's Domain Name and Addressing System," NTIA, U.S. Department of Commerce, June 30, 2005, available at http://www.ntia.doc.gov/ntiahome/domainname/USDNSprinciples_06302005.htm (accessed July 10, 2014).

48. IANA Functions Contract, Amendment Modification No. 0001, effective October 1, 2012; NTIA, "Commerce Department Awards Contract for Management

of Key Internet Functions to ICANN," Office of Public Affairs, NTIA, U.S. Department of Commerce, July 2, 2012, available at http://www.ntia.doc.gov/print/press-release/2012/commerce-department-awards-contract-management-key-internet-functions-icann (accessed July 10, 2014).For additional details regarding the contractual relationship between IANA/ICANN and the U.S. government, go to http://www.ntia.doc.gov/other-publication/2012/icann-proposal; and http://www.ntia.doc.gov/page/iana-functions-purchase-order (accessed July 10, 2014).

49. Brian Doherty and Marius de Geus, eds., *Democracy and Green Political Thought: Sustainability, Rights, and Citizenship*, European Political Science (New York: Routledge, 1996). Nicolas Rescher, *Pluralism: Against the Demand for Consensus* (Oxford: Oxford University Press, 1993).

50. Recently ICANN has made decisions at odds with the perspective the U.S. government, including .xxx the new gTLD program. However, in both of these cases, ICANN was kowtowing to powerful commercial interests.

51. "Welcome to ICANN," ICANN, available at http://www.icann.org/en/about/welcome (accessed July 10, 2014).

52. Milton Mueller, "ICANN Inc.: Accountability and Participation in the Governance of Critical Internet Resources." Internet Governance Project, November 2009, 18, available at http://www.internetgovernance.org/wordpress/wp-content/uploads/ICANNInc.pdf (accessed July 10, 2014).

53. Mueller, "ICANN Inc.," 3.

54. IGF, "Draft WGIG Issue Paper," 11.

55. Juan Carlos Perez, Tension Envelops U.S. Oversight of ICANN Following Extension," *InfoWorld*, October 4, 2006, available at http://www.infoworld.com/d/security-central/tension-envelops-us-oversight-icann-following-extension-190 (accessed July 1, 2014).

56. "U.S. Report: Government Hands Domain-Name Reins to Private Sector," *ZD-Net*, June 5 1998, available at http://www.zdnet.com/us-report-govt-hands-domain-name-reins-to-private-sector-3002068541 (accessed July 1, 2014).

57. Milton Mueller, *Ruling the Root: Internet Governance and the Taming of Cyberspace* (Cambridge, Mass.: MIT Press, 2002).

58. Mueller, "ICANN and Internet Governance," 506.

59. Lawrence E. Strickling, 11th Transportation, Maritime Affairs and Communications Forum, Ministerial Round Table, Istanbul, Turkey, September 5, 2013.

60. Michael Kende, *Global Internet Report 2014: Open and Sustainable Access for All*, (Reston Va.: Internet Society, June 9, 2014), available at http://www.internetsociety.org/sites/default/files/Global_Internet_Report_2014_0.pdf (accessed July 31, 2014).

61. "How We Work," Internet Society, available at http://www.internetsociety.org/what-we-do/how-we-work (accessed July 1, 2014).

62. "Vision and Operating Model," Internet Society, available at http://www.internetsociety.org/sites/default/files/pdf/2011_Internet_Society_Vision_and_Operating_Model.pdf (accessed July 1, 2014).

63. Edmunds and Wollenberg, "Disadvantaged Groups," 1.

64. The leadership is not elected by the membership; rather, it is nominated through a complex selection process: "ISOC By-Laws and Policies call for the Trustees on its Board of Trustees to be elected or selected by various constituencies, namely Organizational Members, Chapters, the ISOC standards organization embodied by the Internet Architecture Board (IAB) and Individual Members. The Board of Trustees itself is empowered to appoint a limited number of Trustees over and above the constituency-based Trustees," from: http://www.internetsociety.org/who-we-are/board-trustees/policies-and-procedures/selection, (accessed July 1, 2014).

65. "ISOC Successfully Bids for .ORG Registry," Internet Society, June 18, 2002, available at http://www.internetsociety.org/history-timeline/isoc-successfully-bids-org-registry (accessed July 1, 2014).

66. "2014–2016 Business Plan," Internet Society, November 23, 2013, 6, available at http://www.internetsociety.org/sites/default/files/2014-2016-ISOC-Business-Plan-Financial-Outlook-20131123%20FINAL.pdf (accessed July 31, 2014).

67. "List of Members," Internet Society, available at http://www.internetsociety.org/get-involved/join-community/organisations-and-corporations/list-members (accessed July 31, 2014).

68. "Return of Organization Exempt from Income Tax," IRS Form 990, Schedule A, Part IV, 4, filed on behalf of the Internet Society, September 30, 2013. Available at http://www.internetsociety.org/sites/default/files/2012%20ISOC_Form%20990.pdf (accessed July 31, 2014).

69. Ibid., 3, 43, 44, and 47.

70. "Annual Review," Internet Society, January 1 2011, 14, available at http://www.internetsociety.org/sites/default/files/pdf/2011_CompleteReport.pdf (accessed July 1, 2014).

71. Ibid., 28.

72. "2012 Annual Review," Internet Society, July 8, 2012, 31, available at http://www.internetsociety.org/sites/default/files/CompleteReport2012_1.pdf (accessed July 31, 2014).

73. Karen Rose, "AfPIF: Growing Africa's Internet Infrastructure," IEEE Internet Computing 15, no. 6 (November–December 2011): 94–96, quote p. 94.

74. "2012 Annual Review," 1.

75. "Public Interest Registry Releases Report Revealing Continued Growth of the .ORG Domain," Public Interest Registry, February 27, 2013, available at http://pir.org/public-interest-registry-releases-report-revealing-continued-growth-of-the-org-domain (accessed August 1, 2014).

76. "Statement of Capabilities of the Applicant and Contracted Service Providers," Internet Society, available at https://archive.icann.org/en/tlds/org/applications/isoc/section2.html (accessed July 1, 2014).

77. Harald Alvestrand and Håkon Wium Lie, "Development of Core Internet Standards: The Work of IETF and W3C," in *Internet Governance: Infrastructure and In-*

stitutions, edited by Lee A. Bygrave and Jon Bing (Oxford: Oxford University Press, 2009), 126.

78. "Mission Statement," IETF, available at http://www.ietf.org/about/mission.html (accessed July 14, 2014). .

79. Ibid.

80. Ibid.

81. Alvestrand and Lie, "Development," 129.

82. Paulina Borsook, "How Anarchy Works: On Location with the Masters of the Metaverse, the Internet Engineering Task Force," *Wired*, March 2010, available at http://www.wired.com/wired/archive/3.10/ietf_pr.html (accessed July 1, 2014).

83. Castells, Manuel. *Communication Power* (Oxford: Oxford University Press, 2011).

84. Joel R. Reidenberg, "Lex Informatica: The Formulation of Information Policy Rules through Technology," *Texas Law Review* 76 (1998): 582.

85. Peng Hwa Ang, "Self Regulation after WGIG," in *Reforming Internet Governance: Perspectives from the Working Group on Internet Governance*, edited by William J. Drake (New York: United Nations ICT Task Force, 2005), 132, available at http://www.wgig.org/docs/book/toc2.html (accessed July 1, 2014).

86. Richard Hill and Shawn Powers, "Cybersecurity and Spam: WCIT and the Future," submitted to the IEEE 2013 World Cyberspace Cooperation Summit, available at http://cybersummit.info/sites/cybersummit.info/files/EWI%20final%20rev2%20clean.pdf (accessed July 1, 2014); Robert Khan, "The Role of Architecture in Internet Defense," in *America's Cyber Future: Security and Prosperity in the Information Age*, edited by Kristin M. Lord and Travis Sharp (Washington, D.C.: Center for a New American Security, June 2011).

87. Borsook, "How Anarchy Works."

88. Ibid.

89. "Diversity of IETF Leadership," an open letter to the IESG, the IAB, the IAOC and the ISOC Board, March 20, 2013, available at http://ietf.10.n7.nabble.com/Diversity-of-IETF-Leadership-td360175.html (accessed July 1, 2014).

90. Keith Moore, "Re: Diversity of ITEF Leadership," ITEF Mailing List Archive, March 10, 2013 (2:46 P.M.), available at http://ietf.10.n7.nabble.com/Diversity-of-IETF-Leadership-tp360175p360244.html (accessed July 1, 2014).

91. Cullen Jennings, "Re: Diversity of ITEF Leadership," ITEF Mailing List Archive, March 10, 2013 (6:23 P.M.), http://ietf.10.n7.nabble.com/Diversity-of-IETF-Leadership-tp360175p360268.html (accessed July 1, 2014).

92. Dave Cridland, Re: Diversity of ITEF Leadership," ITEF Mailing List Archive, March 11, 2013 (5:53 P.M.).

93. Martin Rex, "Re: Diversity of ITEF Leadership," ITEF Mailing List Archive, March 20, 2013 (7:13 A.M.), available at http://ietf.10.n7.nabble.com/Diversity-of-IETF-Leadership-td360175i80.html (accessed July 1, 2014).

94. Melinda Shore, "Re: Diversity of ITEF Leadership," ITEF Mailing List Archive, March 10, 2013 (5:45 P.M.), available at http://ietf.10.n7.nabble.com/Diversity-of-IETF -Leadership-tp360175p360264.html (accessed July 1, 2014).

95. Eric Burger, "Less Corporate Diversity," ITEF Mailing List Archive, March 20, 2013 (2:18 P.M.), available at http://ietf.10.n7.nabble.com/Less-Corporate-Diversity -td362200.html (accessed July 1, 2014).

96. Keith Moore, "Re: Diversity of ITEF Leadership," ITEF Mailing List Archive, March 20, 2013 (10:08 A.M.), available at http://ietf.10.n7.nabble.com/Diversity-of -IETF-Leadership-td360175i80.html (accessed July 1, 2014).

97. John Klensin, "Re: Less Corporate Diversity" ITEF Mailing List Archive, March 21, 2013 (8:25 A.M.), available at http://ietf.10.n7.nabble.com/Less-Corporate-Diversity -tp362200p362369.html (accessed July 1, 2014).

98. Abdussalam Baryun, "Re: Diversity of IETF Leadership," ITEF Mailing List Archive, March 10, 2013 (7:23 A.M.), available at http://ietf.10.n7.nabble.com/Diversity -of-IETF-Leadership-tp360175p360176.html (accessed July 1, 2014).

99. Alvestrand and Lie "Development," 134.

100. From Borsook, "How Anarchy Works."

101. For example, the ITU's WTPF-13 Opinion 4 invites "Member States, and other stakeholders, according to their roles and responsibilities as defined in paragraph 35 of the Tunis Agenda, to participate in the multistakeholder institutions directly responsible for the development of technical policy and allocation of these resources so that their policy priorities in these matters can be taken into account." The opinion is found in the Report by the Chairman of WTPF-13, available at http://www.itu.int/ md/S13-WTPF13-C-0016/en (accessed July 1, 2014).

102. Edmunds and Wollenberg, "Strategic Approach," 246.

103. Alberto Melucci, *Challenging Codes: Collective Action in the Information Age* (Cambridge: Cambridge University Press, 1996), 183. Randy Wilson, "Community-Based Collaborative Management on the San Juan National

Forest: An Analysis of Participation," presentation at the Association of American Geographers Annual Meeting, Honolulu, March 23–27, 1999.

104. Arne Hintz and Stefania Milan, "At the Margins of Internet Governance: Grassroots Tech Groups and Communication Policy," *International Journal of Media and Culture Policy* 5, nos. 1–2 (2009): 23–38.

105. Richard Kahn and Douglas Kellner. "Oppositional Politics and the Internet: A Critical/Reconstructive Approach." *Cultural Politics* 1, no. 1 (March 1, 2005): 75–100, doi:10.2752/174321905778054926.

106. Edmunds and Wollenberg "Strategic Approach," 242.

107. For example, regarding a resolution (which is not formally part of the ITRs) recommending the ITU "play an active role in the development of broadband and the multistakeholder model of the Internet," AT&T's Eric Loeb wrote to the whole delegation: "I recommend a private discussion with [Hamadoun Touré]. Question to him: do you want the coverage to be about great breakthroughs and progress (list them), or do you want the "impending Internet takeover" coverage to drown out

all the benefits. No doubt, the Res would ensure the latter." GoDaddy's James Bladel added, "The media reaction would be hyperbolic, and exactly what Touré and any wavering allies wanted to avoid." From: James Bladel, "RE: What is the Intervention for Deleting the Resolution," e-mail message to Iren Borissova, Audrey L. Plonk, Marilyn Cade; Vernita D. Harris, and members@uswcitdel.org, December 12, 2012. Correspondence was accessed via Freedom of Information Act request.

108. Terry Kramer, "Beyond WCIT-12," ITU blog, March 28 2013, available at http://itu4u.wordpress.com/2013/03/28/beyond-wcit-12-us-ambassador-pledges-continued-support-for-increased-connectivity-and-access-to-the-internet-around-the-world-2 (accessed July 1, 2014).

109. See "Opinion on the Role of Government in the Multistakeholder Framework for Internet Governance," WTPF-IEG/3/19, submitted to the Fifth World Telecommunication Policy Forum (Geneva, 2013).

110. Daniel B. Cavalcanti, "Operationalizing the Role of Governments in Internet Governance," ITU blog, June 5, 2013, available at http://itu4u.wordpress.com/2013/06/05/operationalizing-the-role-of-governments-in-internet-governance (accessed July 1, 2014).

111. Angelica Mari, "Brazilian Internet Governance Event Disappoints Activists," ZDNet, April 25, 2014, available at http://www.zdnet.com/brazil-internet-governance-event-disappoints-activists-7000028797 (accessed July 31, 2014); Antonella Napolitano, "After NETmundial, Multistakeholder Statement Criticized as 'Weak, Toothless . . . Sterile,'" *TechPresident*, April 29, 2014, available at http://techpresident.com/news/wegov/24969/netmundial-multistakeholder-statement-weak-toothless-sterile (accessed August 1, 2014); Shawn Powers, "WSIS+10: Connected, and Unprotected," CGCS Media Wire, June 20, 2014, available at http://cgcsblog.asc.upenn.edu/2014/06/20/wsis10-connected-and-unprotected (accessed August 1, 2014).

Chapter 6. Toward Information Sovereignty

1. Alec Ross, "How Connective Tech Boosts Political Change," CNN, June 20, 2012, available at http://www.cnn.com/2012/06/20/opinion/opinion-alec-ross-tech-politics/index.html (accessed July 1, 3014).

2. R. H. Weber, "New Sovereignty Concepts in the Age of Internet?" *Journal of Internet Law* 14 (2010): 12–20.

3. Benedict Anderson, *Imagined Communities: Reflections on the Origin and Spread of Nationalism* (New York: Verso, 2006); Karl W. Deutsch, *Nationalism and Social Communication: An Inquiry into the Foundations of Nationality* (Cambridge, Mass.: MIT Press, 1966); Harold A. Innis, *Empire and Communications* (Lanham, Md.: Rowman & Littlefield, 2007).

4. Discussed in greater in detail later in this chapter, an intranet is a collection of private computer networks that include blocking software that restricts access to the internet (or other intranets), and vice versa.

5. Max Weber, *Economy and Society: An Outline of Interpretive Sociology* (Berkeley: University of California Press, 1978), 904.

6. Robert Paul Wolff, *In Defense of Anarchism* (Berkeley: University of California Press, 1998).

7. F. H. Hinsley, *Sovereignty* (Cambridge: Cambridge University Press, 1986), 26.

8. Stephen D. Krasner, *Sovereignty: Organized Hypocrisy* (Princeton, N.J.: Princeton University Press, 1999).

9. James J. Sheehan, "The Problem of Sovereignty in European History," *American Historical Review* 111, no. 1 (February 2006): 3.

10. Thomas J, Biersteker and Cynthia Weber, *State Sovereignty as Social Construct* (Cambridge: Cambridge University Press, 1996).

11. Thomas Hobbes and C. B. MacPherson, *The Leviathan: Reprinted from the Edition of 1651* (Harmondsworth, Eng.: Penguin, 1981).

12. Henryk Samsonowicz, "The City and the Trade Route in the Early Middle Ages," in *Central and Eastern Europe in the Middle Ages: A Cultural History*, International Library of Historical Studies, vol. 51, edited by Piotr Górecki, Nancy Van Deusen, and Paul W. Knoll (London: Tauris, 2009), 20.

13. Ibid., 21.

14. Jan Dumolyn, "The Political and Symbolic Economy of State Feudalism: The Case of Late-Medieval Flanders," *Historical Materialism* 15, no. 2 (June 2007): 105–31; Hendrik Spruyt, *The Sovereign State and Its Competitors: An Analysis of Systems Change* (Princeton, N.J.: Princeton University Press, 1994).

15. Samsonowicz, "Trade Route," 28.

16. Robert Keohane, Stephen Macedo, and Andrew Moravcsik, "Democracy-Enhancing Multilateralism," *International Organization* 63, no. 1 (2009): 1–31.

17. Attributed to: Francis Bacon, *Meditationes Sacrae* (1597). The exact phrase "*scientia potentia est*" was written for the first time by Thomas Hobbes (*Leviathan*, 1651), who was secretary to Bacon as a young man.

18. Michel Foucault, *Power/Knowledge* (New York: Pantheon, 1980).

19. Innis, *Empire and Communications*.

20. Anderson, *Imagined Communities*.

21. Ibid., 38.

22. Innis, *Empire and Communications*, 39.

23. James Wood, *History of International Broadcasting* (London: Peregrinus, 1994), 25.

24. Julian Anthony Stuart Hale, *Radio Power: Propaganda and International Broadcasting* (London: Elek, 1975), 1.

25. Philip M. Taylor, *Munitions of the Mind: A History of Propaganda from the Ancient World to the Present Era* (Manchester: Manchester University Press / New York: Palgrave, 2003).

26. Nicholas J. Cull, *Selling War: The British Propaganda Campaign against American "Neutrality" in World War II* (Oxford: Oxford University Press, 1996).

27. Philip N. Howard, *The Digital Origins of Dictatorship and Democracy: Information Technology and Political Islam* (New York: Oxford University Press, 2010).

28. Ulrich Beck, "The Cosmopolitan Society and Its Enemies," *Theory, Culture and Society* 19, no. 1–2 (2002): 17–44; Ulrich Beck, *What Is Globalization?* (Malden, Mass.: Polity, 2000).

29. Joseph N. Pelton, Robert J. Oslund, and Peter Marshall, *Communications Satellites: Global Change Agents* (London: Taylor and Francis, 2004).

30. See also: Deutsch, *Nationalism and Social Communication.*

31. Thomas L. Friedman, *The Lexus and the Olive Tree: Understanding Globalization* (New York: Macmillan, 1999), 66.

32. Jesse Lichtenstein, "Digital Diplomacy," *New York Times Magazine,* July 16, 2010.

33. Philip M. Taylor, *Global Communications, International Affairs and the Media Since 1945* (London: Routledge, 1997), 3

34. Milton L. Mueller, *Networks and States: The Global Politics of Internet Governance* (Cambridge, Mass.: MIT Press, 2010).

35. Daniel Guerin, Francis Merrill, and Mason Merrill, *Fascism and Big Business,* 2nd ed., (Atlanta: Pathfinder, 2004); Michael Hardt and Antonio Negri, *Empire* (Cambridge, Mass.: Harvard University Press, 2001); Kenichi Ohmae, *The End of the Nation State: The Rise of Regional Economies* (New York: Free Press, 1996); Manuel Castells, *The Rise of the Network Society,* Information Age Series 1 (Malden, Mass.: Blackwell, 1996); Manuel Castells, *The Power of Identity: The Information Age,* Economy, Society, and Culture Volume II, 2nd ed. with new preface (Oxford: Wiley-Blackwell, 2009); Manuel Castells, "A Network Theory of Power," *International Journal of Communication* 5 (2011): 773–87.

36. Immanuel Kant, *Perpetual Peace, and Other Essays on Politics, History, and Morals,* translated by Ted Humphrey (Indianapolis: Hackett, 1983).

37. Ethan Zuckerman, "The Cute Cat Theory Talk at ETech," *My Heart's in Accra,* 2008, available at http://www.ethanzuckerman.com/blog/2008/03/08/the-cute-cat-theory-talk-at-etech (accessed July 1, 2014).

38. Ibid.

39. Asa Briggs and Peter Burke, *Social History of the Media: From Gutenberg to the Internet* (Cambridge: Polity, 2010).

40. Clay Shirky, "The Political Power of Social Media," *Foreign Affairs,* January 1, 2011.

41. Jillian York, "More Than Half a Billion Internet Users Are Being Filtered Worldwide," *OpenNet Initiative,* January 19, 2010, available at https://opennet.net/blog/2010/01/more-half-a-billion-internet-users-are-being-filtered-worldwide (accessed July 1, 2014).

42. Michel Foucault, *Discipline and Punish: The Birth of the Prison,* 2nd ed. (New York: Vintage, 1995).

43. Please note that this chapter is not intended to focus on all the ways states control the internet; rather, its purpose is to explore how states are working toward

better controlling internet-based communications within their territory. We explore some efforts at restricting access to the internet, but by no means is this intended to be a comprehensive review or analysis. For more on restrictions on access to the World Wide Web, see: Ronald Deibert, John Palfrey, Rafal Rohozinski, and Jonathan L. Zittrain, eds. *Access Controlled: The Shaping of Power, Rights, and Rule in Cyberspace* (Cambridge, Mass.: MIT Press, 2010).

44. "Weird but Wired: Online Dating in Pyongyang? Surely Not." *The Economist*, February 1, 2007, available at http://www.economist.com/node/8640881 (accessed July 1, 2014).

45. Robert McMillan, "Egypt Goes Dark as Last Internet Company Pulls the Plug," *Computerworld*, January 31, 2011, available at http://www.computerworld.com/s/article/9207418/Egypt_goes_dark_as_last_Internet_company_pulls_the_plug (accessed July 1, 2014); Sriram Gurunathan, "Egypt Disconnects the Internet and Cellphones, Country Plunges into Chaos," *Tech2*, January 29, 2011, available at http://tech2.in.com/news/web-services/egypt-disconnects-the-internet-and-cellphones-country-plunges-into-chaos/189552 (accessed July 1, 2014).

46. Egyptian ISP Noor remained online until January 31, at which point it was also shut down. See: Earl Zmijewski, "Egypt's Net on Life Support," *Renesys* (blog), January 31, 2011, available at http://www.renesys.com/blog/2011/01/egypts-net-on-life-support.shtml (accessed July 1, 2014).

47. Christopher Rhoads and Geoffrey A. Fowler, "Egypt Shuts Down Internet, Cellphone Services," *Wall Street Journal*, January 29, 2011.

48. ITU World Telecommunication/ICT Indicators Database.

49. Jim Cowie, "Egypt Leaves the Internet," *Renesys* (blog), January 27, 2011, available at http://www.renesys.com/blog/2011/01/egypt-leaves-the-internet.shtml (accessed July 1, 2014).

50. Chloe Albanesius, "OECD: Egyptian Internet Shutdown Could Cost Country $90M," *PCMAG*, February 3, 2011, available at http://www.pcmag.com/article2/0,2817,2379324,00.asp (accessed July 1, 2014).

51. Interview with the author, Atlanta, Georgia, March 2012.

52. Clay Shirky, *Here Comes Everybody: The Power of Organizing without Organizations*, reprint (New York: Penguin, 2009).

53. Iljitsch van Beijnum, "How Egypt Did (and Your Government Could) Shut Down the Internet." *Ars Technica*, January 30, 2011, available at http://arstechnica.com/tech-policy/news/2011/01/how-egypt-or-how-your-government-could-shut-down-the-internet.ars (accessed July 1, 2014).

54. Hal Roberts, "Local Control: About 95% of Chinese Web Traffic is Local," Watching Technology (blog), Berkman Center for Internet and Society, August 15, 2011, available at http://blogs.law.harvard.edu/hroberts/2011/08/15/local-control-about-95-of-chinese-web-traffic-is-local (accessed July 1, 2014).

55. Chengxin Pan, "Westphalia and the Taiwan Conundrum: A Case against the Exclusionist Construction of Sovereignty and Identity," *Journal of Chinese Political*

Science 15, no. 4 (December 2010): 376; Min Jiang, "Authoritarian Informationalism: China's Approach to Internet Sovereignty," *Sais Review* 30 (2010): 71–89.

56. As quoted in Yangyue Liu, "The Rise of China and Global Internet Governance," *China Media Research* 8, no. 2 (April 2012): 52. The current revised version posted on the Information Office of the State Council Web site, http://english.gov.cn/2010-06/08/content_1622956.htm, was changed to read, "To build, utilize and administer the Internet well is an issue that concerns national economic prosperity and development, state security and social harmony, state sovereignty and dignity, and the basic interests of the people."

57. People's Republic of China Information Office of the State Council, "Section IV: Basic Principles and Practices of Internet Administration," Information Office of the State Council, People's Republic of China. June 8, 2010, available at http://english.gov.cn/2010-06/08/content_1622956.html (accessed July 1, 2014).

58. This model of policy analysis is from Monroe Price, *Media and Sovereignty: The Global Information Revolution and Its Challenge to State Power*, (Cambridge, Mass.: MIT Press, 2002).

59. Lyombe Eko, "Many Spiders, One Worldwide Web: Towards a Topology of Internet Regulation," *Communication Law and Policy* 6 (2001): 445–84; Tom Simonite, "Reading the Tea Leaves of Censorship," *MIT Technology Review* 116 (4) (2013): 20.

60. Michael Wines, "China Cracks Down on Web Critics," *New York Times*, May 28, 2012; Michael Wines, "China Expands Microblog Identification Program," *New York Times*, January 18, 2012; Murong Xuecun, "Chinese Internet: 'A New Censorship Campaign Has Commenced,'" *Guardian*, May 15, 2013.

61. "China Employs Two Million Microblog Monitors State Media Say," *BBC*, October 4, 2013, available at http://www.bbc.co.uk/news/world-asia-china-24396957 (accessed July 1, 2014).

62. Edward Wong, "New Restrictions on Social Networking Sites in Beijing, China," *New York Times*, December 16, 2011.

63. "China: Effects of Intellectual Property Infringement and Indigenous Innovation Policies on the U.S. Economy," U.S. International Trade Commission, Investigation Number 332-519, USITC Publication 4226, Washington, D.C.: USITC, May 2011.

64. China Times, "China's Internet Industry Saw Vast Expansion in 2011," *China Times*, January 12, 2012, available at http://www.wantchinatimes.com/news-subclass-cnt.aspx?id=20120112000104&cid=1202 (accessed July 1, 2014).

65. "How Does China Censor the Internet?" *Economist*, April 21, 2013, available at http://www.economist.com/blogs/economist-explains/2013/04/economist-explains-how-china-censors-internet (accessed July 1, 2014).

66. Yuezhi Zhao, *Communication in China: Political Economy, Power, and Conflict* (Lanham, Md.: Rowman and Littlefield, 2008).

67. "A Curse Disguised as a Blessing?" *Economist*, April 6, 2013, available at http://www.economist.com/news/special-report/21574635-internet-may-be-delaying-radical-changes-china-needs-curse-disguised (accessed July 1, 2014).

68. Ibid.

69. "Internet Controls in Other Countries: To Each Their Own," *Economist*, April 6, 2013, available at http://www.economist.com/news/special-report/21574634-chinas -model-controlling-internet-being-adopted-elsewhere-each-their-own (accessed July 1, 2014).

70. Deborah Fallows, "Most Chinese Say They Approve of Government Internet Control," Pew Internet and American Life Project, March 26, 2008, available at http:// www.pewinternet.org/files/old-media/Files/Reports/2008/PIP_China_Internet _2008.pdf.pdf (accessed July 1, 2014).

71. David Kurt Herold, "Captive Artists: Chinese University Students Talk about the Internet," Social Science Research Network, May 1, 2013, available art http:// dx.doi.org/10.2139/ssrn.2259020 (accessed July 1, 2014).

72. "Iranian Internet Infrastructure and Policy Report," Small Media Election Report, April–June 2013, available at http://smallmedia.org.uk/IIIPJune.pdf (accessed July 1, 2014).

73. "Iran Curbs Foreign-Sourced Email Providers," Agence France-Presse (AFP), May 12, 2012.

74. "Survey of Internet Censorship in Iran Results, March 23, 2012," ViewDNS, (updated title: "Current State of Internet Censorship in Iran"), available at http:// viewdns.info/research/current-state-of-internet-censorship-in-iran (accessed July 1, 2014).

75. David Sanger, "Obama Order Sped Up Wave of Cyberattacks against Iran," *New York Times*, June 1, 2012.

76. IT Analysis and News, "Google Earth Is a Spy," *IT Analysis and News*, June 21, 2013, available at http://itanalyze.com/news/2013/06/21/21441.php (accessed July 1, 2014).

77. Cyrus Farivar, "Iran Announces 'Halal Internet,' New Cyberdefense Study Programs," *The Internet of Elsewhere* (blog), April 17, 2011, available at http://internet ofelsewhere.com/2011/04/17/iran-announces-halal-internet-and-new-cyberdefense -study-programs (accessed July 1, 2014).

78. AFP, "Iran Curbs."

79. Small Media, "Iranian Internet."

80. Golnaz Esfandiari, "Iran's National Internet Gets Late Spring Launch Date," Radio Free Europe/Radio Liberty, February 21, 2012, available at http://www.thecutting edgenews.com/index.php?article=72114 (accessed July 1, 2014).

81. Neal Ungerleider, "Iran's 'Second Internet' Rivals Censorship Of China's 'Great Firewall,'" Fast Company, February 23, 2012, available at http://www.fastcompany .com/1819375/irans-second-internet-rivals-censorship-chinas-great-firewall (accessed July 1, 2014).

82. Christopher Rhoads and Farnaz Fassihi, "Iran Vows to Unplug Internet," *Wall Street Journal*, May 28, 2011.

83. Ungerleider, "Iran's 'Second Internet'"

84. Daisy Carrington, "Iran Tightens Grip on Cyberspace with 'Halal Internet,'" *CNN*, June 3, 2013, available at http://www.cnn.com/2013/06/03/world/meast/iran -internet-restrictions-halal-internet/index.html (accessed July 1, 2014).

85. Small Media, "Iranian Internet."

86. "Iran denies has plan to cut Internet access," Agence France-Presse, April 10, 2012.

87. U.S. Presidential Decision Directive 63, May 22, 1998, available at http://fas.org/ irp/offdocs/pdd/pdd-63.htm (accessed July 1, 2014).

88. "CIA Enlists Google's Help for Spy Work," *Times of India*, April 1, 2008, available at http://articles.timesofindia.indiatimes.com/2008–04–01/us/27775135_1 _intelligence-agencies-cia-agents (accessed July 1, 2014).

89. "NSA Site M Expansion Planning Documents and ATFP Study," U.S. Army Corps of Engineers, #W912DR-10-D-0024, May 31, 2011.

90. Jesselyn Radack, "NSA's Cyber Overkill," *Los Angeles Times*, July 14, 2009.

91. Ibid.

92. Siobhan Gorman, "Troubles Plague Cyberspy Defense," *Wall Street Journal*, July 3, 2009.

93. W. J. Lynn, "Remarks at Stratcom Cyber Symposium," U.S. Department of Defense, May 26, 2010, available at http://www.defense.gov/Speeches/Speech.aspx ?SpeechID=1477 (accessed July 1, 2014).

94. Arie Church, "Beyond Government Defending Itself," Air Force Association, *Air Force Magazine*, 2012, available at http://www.airforce-magazine.com/DRArchive/ Pages/2012/March%202012/March%2023%202012/BeyondGovernmentDefending Itself.aspx.

95. Jason Miller, "DHS Buys Software as Part of Einstein 3 Deployment," *FederalNewsRadio.com*, 2011, available at http://www.federalnewsradio.com/?nid =473&sid=2684411 (accessed July 1, 2014).

96. Lisa Daniel, "Cyber Solutions Depend on Partnerships, Official Says," American Forces Press Service, July 8, 2010.

97. Keith Alexander, "Letter to Hon. John McCain, Ranking Member, Committee on Armed Services, United States Senate," 2012, available at http://publicintelligence.net/ u-s-cyber-command-cybersecurity-legislation-position-letter (accessed July 18, 2014).

98. Lynn, "Remarks at Stratcom."

99. "Copyright Infringement and Enforcement in the U.S.," American Assembly, Columbia University, Research Note, November 2011, available at http://piracy.american assembly.org/wp-content/uploads/2011/11/AA-Research-Note-Infringement-and -Enforcement-November-2011.pdf (accessed July 1, 2014).

100. Leaked documents from former NSA contractor Edward Snowden indicate that the NSA, in pursuit of combatting criminal and terrorist behavior, may already monitor and archive data, though it is only capable of analyzing a very small portion of the information collected, and its archival capacity also remains limited.

101. Joel R. Reidenberg, "Lex Informatica: The Formulation of Information Policy Rules through Technology," *Texas Law Review* 76 (1998): 553–94.

102. Leon E. Trakman, "From the Medieval Law Merchant to the E-Merchant Law," *University of Toronto Law Journal* 53, no. 3 (Summer 2003).

103. Pew Internet and American Life Project, 2008.

104. American Assembly, "Copyright Infringement."

105. Ian Katz, "Web Freedom Faces Greatest Threat Ever, Warns Google's Sergey Brin," *Guardian*, April 15, 2012, available at http://www.guardian.co.uk/technology/2012/apr/15/web-freedom-threat-google-brin (accessed July 1, 2014).

Chapter 7. Internet Freedom in a Surveillance Society

1. Sarah Labowitz, telephone interview with the author, April 2013.

2. Hillary Rodham Clinton, "Internet Rights and Wrongs: Choices and Challenges in a Networked World," speech, George Washington University, February 15, 2011, Department of State, available at http://www.state.gov/secretary/20092013clinton/rm/2011/02/156619.htm (accessed July 1, 2014).

3. Ibid.

4. The same applies in many countries to telecommunications in general, with some significant legal consequences. For example, the U.S. Supreme Court has held that users have no expectation of privacy regarding telephone call records because they have voluntarily disclosed their own and the called party's telephone numbers to a private company. See, for example, the Memorandum and Order of December 27, 2013 in *American Civil Liberties Union et al. v. James R. Clapper et al.*, United States District Court, Southern District of New York, 13 Civ. 3994 (WHP). European laws are of course quite different, and privacy does attach to call records in Europe

5. Ibid.

6. Hillary Rodham Clinton, "Remarks on Internet Freedom," Speech delivered at The Newseum, Washington D.C., January 21, 2010, available at http://www.state.gov/secretary/20092013clinton/rm/2010/01/135519.htm (accessed July 1, 2014).

7. Clinton, "Internet Rights and Wrongs," 2011.

8. Ibid.

9. Alan Davidson, "Testimony of Alan Davidson, Director of Public Policy, Google Inc.," before the Congressional-Executive Commission on China Hearing on "Google and Internet Control in China: A Nexus Between Human Rights and Trade?" March 24, 2010.

10. David Drummond, "A New Approach to China," January 12, 2010, *Google: Official Blog*, available at http://googleblog.blogspot.com/2010/01/new-approach-to-china.html (accessed July 1, 2014).

11. Ibid. See also Kim Zetter, "Google Hackers Targeted Source Code of More Than 30 Companies," *Threat Level* (blog), *Wired*, January 13, 2010, available at http://www.wired.com/threatlevel/2010/01/google-hack-attack (accessed July 1, 2014).

12. Christopher H. Smith, "Statement of Honorable Christopher H. Smith," hearing before the Congressional-Executive Commission on China, One-hundred Eleventh

Congress, Second Session, "Google and Internet Control in China: A Nexus Between Human Rights and Trade?" March 24, 2010.

13. Kim Zetter, "Google Asks NSA to Help Secure Its Network," *Threat Level* (blog), *Wired*, February 4, 2010, available at http://www.wired.com/threatlevel/2010/02/google-seeks-nsa-help (accessed July 1, 2014).

14. Siobhan Gorman and Jessica E. Vascellaro, "Google Working With NSA to Investigate Cyber Attack," *Wall Street Journal*, February 4, 2010, available at http://online.wsj.com/article/SB10001424052748704041504575044920905689954.html (accessed July 1, 2014).

15. Zetter, "Google Asks NSA."

16. Dennis Blair, "Hearing of the House Permanent Select Committee on Intelligence: Annual Threat Assessment," *Office of the Director of National Intelligence*, February 25, 2009, available at http://www.dni.gov/files/documents/Newsroom/Testimonies/20090225_transcript.pdf (accessed July 1, 2014).

17. John Huntsman, "Google Update: PRC Role in Attacks and Response Strategy," E.O. 12958, January 26, 2010, available at http://www.wikileaks.org/plusd/cables/10BEIJING207_a.html (accessed July 1, 2014).

18. Bruce Schneier, "U.S. Enables Chinese Hacking of Google," *CNN*, January 23, 2010, available at http://www.cnn.com/2010/OPINION/01/23/schneier.google.hacking/index.html (accessed July 1, 2014).

19. Siobhan Gorman, "U.S. Plans Cyber Shield for Utilities, Companies," *Wall Street Journal*, July 8, 2010, available at http://online.wsj.com/news/articles/SB10001424052748704545004575352983850463108 (accessed July 1, 2014).

20. Ibid.

21. Blair, "Hearing: Annual Threat Assessment."

22. Ibid.

23. Sean Gallagher, "How the NSA's MUSCULAR Tapped Google's and Yahoo's Private Networks," *Ars Technica*, October 31, 2013, available at http://arstechnica.com/information-technology/2013/10/how-the-nsas-muscular-tapped-googles-and-yahoos-private-networks (accessed July 1, 2014).

24. Sean Gallagher, "Googlers Say "F*** You" to NSA, Company Encrypts Internal Network," *Ars Technica*, October 6, 2013, available at http://arstechnica.com/information-technology/2013/11/googlers-say-f-you-to-nsa-company-encrypts-internal-network (accessed July 1, 2014).

25. Sean Gallagher, "NSA 'Touches' more of Internet than Google," *Ars Technica*, August 13, 2013, available at http://arstechnica.com/information-technology/2013/08/the-1-6-percent-of-the-internet-that-nsa-touches-is-bigger-than-it-seems/ (accessed August 1, 2014).

26. Ewen MacAskill, Julian Borger, Nick Hopkins, Nick Davies, and James Ball, "GCHQ Taps Fibre-Optic Cables for Secret Access to World's Communications," *Guardian*, June 21, 2013.

27. Ibid.

28. James Ball, Luke Harding, and Juliette Garside, "BT and Vodafone among Telecoms Companies Passing Details to GCHQ," *Guardian*, August 2, 2013, available at http://www.theguardian.com/business/2013/aug/02/telecoms-bt-vodafone-cables-gchq (accessed July 1, 2014).

29. MacAskill et al., "GCHQ."

30. Ibid.

31. Julian Borger, "GCHQ and European Spy Agencies Worked Together on Mass Surveillance," *Guardian*, November 1, 2013, available at http://www.theguardian.com/uk-news/2013/nov/01/gchq-europe-spy-agencies-mass-surveillance-snowden (accessed July 1, 2014).

32. "BULLRUN CoI—Briefing Sheet," *Pro Publica*, September 5, 2013, available at http://www.propublica.org/documents/item/784284-bullrun-briefing-sheet-from-gchq.html (accessed July 1, 2014).

33. "Computer Network Operations; SIGINT Enabling," 2013 Intelligence Budget Request, Electronic Frontier Foundation, September 5, 2013.

34. Nicole Perlroth, Jeff Larson, and Scott Shane, "N.S.A. Able to Foil Basic Safeguards of Privacy on Web," *New York Times*, September 6, 2013.

35. Jeff Larson, Nicole Perlroth, and Scott Shane, "Revealed: The NSA's Secret Campaign to Crack, Undermine Internet Security," *ProPublica*, September 5, 2013, available at http://www.propublica.org/article/the-nsas-secret-campaign-to-crack-undermine-internet-encryption (accessed July 1, 2014); Joseph Menn, "Exclusive: Secret Contract Tied NSA and Security Industry Pioneer," *Reuters*, December 20, 2013, available at http://www.reuters.com/article/2013/12/20/us-usa-security-rsa-idUSBRE9BJ1C220131220 (accessed July 1, 2014).

36. Nadia Heninger and J. Alex Halderman, "Tales from the Crypto Community: The NSA Hurt Cybersecurity; Now It Should Come Clean," *Foreign Affairs*, October 23, 2013, http://www.foreignaffairs.com/articles/140214/nadia-heninger-and-j-alex-halderman/tales-from-the-crypto-community?cid=soc-twitter-in-snapshots-tales_From_the_crypto_community-102513# (accessed July 1, 2014).

37. Dan Goodin, "NSA Repeatedly Tries to Unpeel Tor Anonymity and Spy on Users, Memos Show," *Ars Technica*, October 4, 2013, available at http://arstechnica.com/security/2013/10/nsa-repeatedly-tries-to-unpeel-tor-anonymity-and-spy-on-users-memos-show (accessed July 1, 2014).

38. 2013 Intelligence Budget Request, "Computer Network Operations."

39. James Ball, Bruce Schneier, and Glenn Greenwald, "NSA and GCHQ Target Tor Network That Protects Anonymity of Web Users," *Guardian*, October 4, 2013, available at http://www.theguardian.com/world/2013/oct/04/nsa-gchq-attack-tor-network-encryption (accessed July 1, 2014).

40. Nathan Gardels. "Vint Cerf of Google on Internet Rights—Interview," *Christian Science Monitor*, March 8, 2012, available at http://www.csmonitor.com/Commentary/

Global-Viewpoint/2012/0308/Vint-Cerf-of-Google-on-Internet-rights-interview (accessed July 1, 2014).

41. 362 U.S. 60 (1960).

42. 525 U.S. 182 (1999)

43. 536 U.S. 150 (2002)

44. *McIntyre v. Ohio Elections Commission*, 514 U.S. 334, 337 (1995).

45. Ibid. (quoting *New York v. Duryea*, 76 Misc. 2d 948, 966–967, 351 N. Y. S. 2d 978, 996 [1974]).

46. Perlroth, Larson, and Shane, "N.S.A. Able to Foil."

47. Kevin Poulsen, "Edward Snowden's E-Mail Provider Defied FBI Demands to Turn Over Crypto Keys, Documents Show," *Threat Level* (blog), *Wired*, October 2, 2013, available at http://www.wired.com/threatlevel/2013/10/lavabit_unsealed (accessed July 1, 2014).

48. Lavabit, accessed December 10, 2013, http://www.lavabit.com.

49. Marshal Kirkpatrick, "Google, Privacy, and the New Explosion of Data," *Techonomy* (blog), August 4, 2010, available at http://techonomy.typepad.com/blog/2010/08/google-privacy-and-the-new-explosion-of-data.html (accessed July 1, 2014).

50. Michael Joseph Gross, "Enter the Cyber-Dragon," *Vanity Fair*, September 2011, available at http://www.vanityfair.com/culture/features/2011/09/chinese-hacking-201109 (accessed July 1, 2014).

51. Perlroth, Larson, and Shane, "N.S.A. Able to Foil."

52. Bruce Schneier, "NSA Surveillance: A Guide to Staying Secure," *Guardian*, September 20, 2013, available at http://www.theguardian.com/world/2013/sep/05/nsa-how-to-remain-secure-surveillance (accessed July 1, 2014).

53. "BRICS Countries Are Building a 'New Internet' Hidden from NSA," Voice of Russia, October 12, 2013, available at http://voiceofrussia.com/2013_10_28/BRICS-countries-are-building-a-new-Internet-hidden-from-NSA-7157 (accessed July 1, 2014).

54. H. E. Dilma Rousseff, "Statement at the Opening of the General Debate of the 68th Session of the United Nations General Assembly," General Assembly of the United Nations, New York, September 24, 2013, available at https://docs.google.com/viewer?url=http%3A%2F%2Fgadebate.un.org%2Fsites%2Fdefault%2Ffiles%2Fgastatements%2F68%2FBR_en.pdf (accessed July 1, 2014).

55. Ibid.

56. Michael Birnbaum, "In Germany, Circling the e-wagons," *Washington Post*, November 2, 2013.

57. Frank Doemen, "Spy-Proofing: Deutsche Telekom Pushes for All-German Internet," *Der Spiegel*, November 12, 2013.

58. Edward Wyatt and Claire C. Miller, "Tech Giants Issue Call for Limits on Government Surveillance of Users," *New York Times*, December 9, 2013, available at http://www.nytimes.com/2013/12/09/technology/tech-giants-issue-call-for-limits-on-government-surveillance-of-users.html?hp&_r=1& (accessed July 1, 2014); John

Gapper, "Silicon Valley Must Keep the Spies Out of Its Honey Trap," *Financial Times*, December 11, 2013.

59. Russ Housley, "IETF88 Technical Plenary Hums," E-Mail, November 6, 2013, available at https://www.ietf.org/mail-archive/web/ietf/current/msg83857.html (accessed July 1, 2014).

60. See, for example, "Global Government Surveillance Reform," available at http://reformgovernmentsurveillance.com (accessed July 1, 2014).

61. Moxie Marlinspike, "We Should All Have Something to Hide," *ThoughtCrime* (blog), June 12, 2013, available at http://www.thoughtcrime.org/blog/we-should-all-have-something-to-hide (accessed July 1, 2014).

62. Arthur Deerin Call, "Our Silent Power for Peace," *Advocate of Peace through Justice* 87, no. 2 (1925): 102–5.

63. Ibid., 105.

64. Private communication with senior ITU staff

65. "The Universal Postal Congress," *Advocate of Peace* 59, no. 6 (1897): 127.

66. Call, "Silent Power for Peace," 1925, 104.

67. Call, "Silent Power for Peace," 1925, 105.

68. Ibid., 105.

69. Ibid., 105.

70. 96 U.S. 727, 735 (1878).

71. 488 F. 2d 193 (9th Cir. 1973).

72. Section 605 of the Communications Act of 1934 originated as Regulation 19 of §4 of the Radio Act of 1912. Pub. L. No. 62-264 §4, reg. 19, 37 Stat. 302.

73. "Constitution of Finland," Finnish Ministry of Justice, 2000.

74. David John Marotta, "Right to Privacy of Correspondence of Other Countries," *Marotta on Money* (blog), June 15, 2013, available at http://www.marottaonmoney.com/right-to-privacy-of-correspondence-of-other-countries (accessed July 1, 2014).

75. Daniel Castro, "How Much Will PRISM Cost the U.S. Cloud Computing Industry?" *Information Technology and Innovation Foundation*, August 2013, available at http://www2.itif.org/2013-cloud-computing-costs.pdf (accessed July 1, 2014).

76. "The Universal Postal Congress," 127.

Conclusion

1. Vincent Mosco, *Political Economy* (2009), 4.

2. For example, the 1897 Universal Postal Congress proclaimed, "The Postal Union is one of the first ripe fruits of the new internationalism of our time, which is ultimately to bring all the nations of the world into a regular and harmonious cooperation in the promotion of the highest interests of each and all. Such a Union established, so far, the peace of the world, and must prove a powerful antidote, in its way, in preventing the periodic outbreak of war with its disturbances and destructions." "The Universal Postal Congress, 1897," *Advocate of Peace* 59, no. 6: 127.

3. John Perry Barlow, "A Cyberspace Independence Declaration," February 9, 1996, available at https://w2.eff.org/Censorship/Internet_censorship_bills/barlow_0296 .declaration (accessed July 1, 2014).

4. Article 19 of The Universal Declaration of Human Rights (1948), available at http://www.un.org/en/documents/udhr/index.shtml#a19 (accessed July 1, 2014).

5. "Freedom on the Net 2013: Despite Pushback, Internet Freedom Deteriorates" (New York: Freedom House), available at http://www.freedomhouse.org/report/ freedom-net/freedom-net-2013#.U1hD_eZdWUk (accessed July 1, 2014); "World Press Freedom Index 2014," Reporters without Borders, available at http://rsf.org/ index2014/en-index2014.php# (accessed July 1, 2014); Jonathan Turley, "Shut Up and Play Nice: How the Western World Is Limiting Free Speech," *Washington Post*, October 12, 2012, available at http://www.washingtonpost.com/opinions/the-four -arguments-the-western-world-uses-to-limit-free-speech/2012/10/12/e0573bd4-116d -11e2-a16b-2c110031514a_story.html (accessed July 1, 2014).

Index

SHAWN POWERS is an Assistant Professor of Communication at Georgia State University.

MICHAEL JABLONSKI is an attorney and presidential fellow in communication at Georgia State University.

THE HISTORY OF COMMUNICATION

The University of Illinois Press
is a founding member of the
Association of American University Presses.

———————————————————————

Composed in 10.5/13 Adobe Minion Pro
by Lisa Connery
at the University of Illinois Press
Manufactured by Sheridan Books, Inc.

University of Illinois Press
1325 South Oak Street
Champaign, IL 61820-6903
www.press.uillinois.edu